GW00514863

Tolley's Tax Data 2015–16

Summer Budget 2015 Edition

Members of the LexisNexis Group worldwide

United Kingdom	Reed Elsevier (UK) Limited trading as LexisNexis, 1-3 Strand, London WC2N 5JR
Australia	LexisNexis Butterworths, Chatswood, New South Wales
Austria	LexisNexis Verlag ARD Orac GmbH & Co KG, Vienna
Benelux	LexisNexis Benelux, Amsterdam
Canada	LexisNexis Canada, Markham, Ontario
China	LexisNexis China, Beijing and Shanghai
France	LexisNexis SA, Paris
Germany	LexisNexis Deutschland GmbH, Munster
Hong Kong	LexisNexis Hong Kong, Hong Kong
India	LexisNexis India, New Delhi
Italy	Giuffrè Editore, Milan
Japan	LexisNexis Japan, Tokyo
Malaysia	Malayan Law Journal Sdn Bhd, Kuala Lumpur
New Zealand	LexisNexis NZ Ltd, Wellington
Singapore	LexisNexis Singapore, Singapore
South Africa	LexisNexis Butterworths, Durban
USA	LexisNexis, Dayton, Ohio

First published in 1981

© Reed Elsevier (UK) Ltd 2015
Published by LexisNexis
This is a Tolley title

All rights reserved. No part of this publication may be reproduced in any material form (including photocopying or storing it in any medium by electronic means and whether or not transiently or incidentally to some other use of this publication) without the written permission of the copyright owner except in accordance with the provisions of the Copyright, Designs and Patents Act 1988 or under the terms of a licence issued by the Copyright Licensing Agency Ltd, Saffron House, 6–10 Kirby Street, London, EC1N 8TS. Applications for the copyright owner's written permission to reproduce any part of this publication should be addressed to the publisher.

Warning: The doing of an unauthorised act in relation to a copyright work may result in both a civil claim for damages and criminal prosecution.

Crown Copyright material is reproduced with the permission of the Controller of HMSO and the Queen's Printer for Scotland. Parliamentary copyright material is reproduced with the permission of the Controller of Her Majesty's Stationery Office on behalf of Parliament. Any European material in this work which has been reproduced from EUR-lex, the official European Communities legislation website, is European Communities copyright.

A CIP Catalogue record for this book is available from the British Library.

ISBN for this volume: 9780754550815

Printed in Great Britain by Hobbs the Printers Ltd, Totton, Hampshire

Visit LexisNexis at www.lexisnexis.co.uk

About this book

Tolley's Tax Data is a compendium of essential factual information for the tax adviser, covering all the main UK taxes and related matters. This edition includes the provisions of the Finance Act 2015 together with further important information up to and including 15 July 2015.

Comparative figures for up to six years are included in many of the tables. Statutory references are also given.

Comments on this annual publication and suggestions for new material and improvements will always be welcome.

Abbreviations

ACT	Advance corporation tax
AIM	Alternative Investment Market
CAA	Capital Allowances Act
CGT	Capital gains tax
Conv	Convertible
CTA	Corporation Tax Act
Cum	Cumulative
EIS	Enterprise Investment Scheme
EU	European Union
ESC	Extra-statutory concession
FA	Finance Act
FB	Finance Bill
FII	Franked investment income
HMRC	Her Majesty's Revenue and Customs
ICTA	Income and Corporation Taxes Act
IHTA	Inheritance Tax Act
IR	Inland Revenue
IRPR	Inland Revenue Press Release
ITA	Income Tax Act
ITEPA	Income Tax (Earnings and Pensions) Act
ITTOIA	Income Tax (Trading and Other Income) Act
NI	Northern Ireland
NIC	National insurance contributions
Ord	Ordinary
PAYE	Pay as you earn
PET	Potentially exempt transfer
PSA	PAYE settlement agreement
Pt	Part
RPI	Retail price index
RTI	Real time information
s	Section
Sch	Schedule
SI	Statutory Instrument
SP	Statement of Practice
SR & O	Statutory Rules and Orders
Stk	Stock
TCGA	Taxation of Chargeable Gains Act
TMA	Taxes Management Act
UK	United Kingdom
VATA	Value Added Tax Act
WDV	Written down value

2015/16 rates and allowances

Income tax

Allowances

	£
Personal allowance	10,600
Income limit (allowance reduced by ½ excess)	100,000
Transferable marriage allowance	1,060
Persons born before 6.4.1938	
Income limit (allowance reduced by ½ excess)	27,700
Personal allowance — person born before 6.4.1938	10,660
Married couple's allowance — either partner born before 6.4.1935	8,355
Married couple's allowance — minimum where income exceeds limit	3,220
Blind person's allowance	2,290

Rates (individuals)

	Taxable income £	Rate	Dividend rate
Basic rate	0–31,785	20%	10%
Higher rate	31,786–150,000	40%	32.5%
Additional rate	Over 150,000	45%	37.5%
Starting rate for savings	0–5,000	0%	0%

Note

(a)   See further pages 59, 60.

National insurance contributions

Class 1

Lower earnings limit	— per week	£112
	— per month	£486
Primary earnings threshold	— per week	£155
	— per month	£672
Secondary earnings threshold	— per week	£156
	— per month	£676
Upper accruals point	— per week	£770
	— per month	£3,337
Upper secondary earnings threshold	— per week	£815
	— per month	£3,532
Upper earnings limit	— per week	£815
	— per month	£3,532
Employees' primary Class 1 rate (primary threshold to upper earnings limit)		12%
Employees' rate above upper earnings limit		2%
Employees' contracted-out rebate (salary-related schemes)		1.4%
Married women's reduced rate (primary threshold to upper earnings limit)		5.85%
Married women's rate above upper earnings limit		2%
Employers' rate above secondary threshold/upper secondary threshold		13.8%
Employers' contracted-out rebate (salary-related schemes)		3.4%

Class 1A rate	13.8%
Class 1B rate	13.8%

Class 2

Weekly rate	£2.80
Weekly rate – share fishermen	£3.45
Weekly rate – volunteer development workers	£5.60
Small profits threshold	£5,965

Class 3 rate	£14.10

Class 4

Lower profits limit	£8,060
Upper profits limit	£42,385
Rate from lower to upper profits limit	9%
Rate above upper profits limit	2%

Note

(a)   See further pages 85–90.

2015/16 rates and allowances

Capital gains tax

Annual exemption	£11,100
Rates	
Individuals	
— up to basic rate limit	18%
— above basic rate limit	28%
Settlements and personal representatives	28%
Gains qualifying for entrepreneurs' relief	10%

Note

(a)　See further pages 20–37.

Inheritance tax

£	Rate
Chargeable lifetime transfers	
0–325,000	Nil
Over 325,000	20%
Transfers on death	
0–325,000	Nil
Over 325,000	40% (36% if 10% or more of net estate is left to charity or community amateur sports club)

Note

(a)　See further pages 70–74.

Corporation tax

Financial year 2015	
Rate	20%

Note

(a)　See further pages 39–41.

Value added tax

Registration threshold	£82,000
Deregistration threshold	£80,000
Standard rate	20%
Reduced rate	5%

Note

(a)　Thresholds apply with effect from 1 April 2015. See further pages 113–121.

Stamp duty land tax

Land transactions and lease premiums

Residential property	Consideration (rates apply to consideration in each slice)	Rate
	Up to £125,000	Nil
	£125,001–£250,000	2%
	£250,001–£925,000	5%
	£925,001–£1,500,000	10%
	£1,500,001 or more	12%

Non-residential or mixed property	Consideration (rates apply to the full consideration)	Rate
	Up to £150,000	Nil
	£150,001–£250,000	1%
	£250,001–£500,000	3%
	£500,001 or more	4%

Lease rentals	On net present value of rent over term of lease (rates apply to the amount of npv in the slice)	Rate
Residential property	Up to £125,000	Nil
	£125,001 or more	1%
Non-residential or mixed property	Up to £150,000	Nil
	£150,001 or more	1%

Notes

(a)　See further page 107.
(b)　SDLT no longer applies to land transactions in Scotland. See page 108 for land and buildings transaction tax.

Bank interest rates

Date	Base Rate %	Date	Base Rate %	Date	Base Rate %
20 March 1985	13.5	14 February 1991	13.5	10 June	5
29 March	13	27 February	13	8 September	5.25
2 April	13.125	22 March	12.5	4 November	5.5
12 April	12.875	12 April	12	13 January 2000	5.75
19 April	12.625	24 May	11.5	10 February	6
12 June	12.5	12 July	11	8 February 2001	5.75
15 July	12	4 September	10.5	5 April	5.5
29 July	11.5	5 May 1992	10	10 May	5.25
9 January 1986	12.5	16 September	12	2 August	5
19 March	11.5	17/18 September	10	18 September	4.75
9 April	11	22 September	9	4 October	4.5
21 April	10.5	16/19 October	8	8 November	4
14 October	11	13 November 1992	7	6 February 2003	3.75
10 March 1987	10.5	26 January 1993	6	10 July	3.5
18 March	10	23 November	5.5	6 November	3.75
29 April	9.5	8 February 1994	5.25	5 February 2004	4
11 May	9	12 September	5.75	6 May	4.25
7 August	10	7 December	6.25	10 June	4.5
26 October 1987	9.5	2 February 1995	6.75	5 August	4.75
5 November	9	13 December	6.5	4 August 2005	4.5
4 December	8.5	19 January 1996	6.25	3 August 2006	4.75
2 February 1988	9	8 March	6	9 November	5
17 March	8.5	6 June	5.75	11 January 2007	5.25
11 April	8	30 October	6	10 May	5.5
1 May	7.5	6 May 1997	6.25	5 July	5.75
3 June	8	6 June	6.5	6 December	5.5
6 June	8.5	10 July	6.75	7 February 2008	5.25
22 June	9	7 August	7	10 April	5
28 June	9.5	6 November	7.25	8 October	4.5
4 July	10	4 June 1998	7.5	6 November	3
18 July	10.5	8 October	7.25	4 December	2
26 August	12	5 November	6.75	8 January 2009	1.5
25 November	13	10 December	6.25	5 February	1
24 May 1989	14	7 January 1999	6	5 March	0.5
5 October	15	4 February	5.5		
8 October 1990	14	8 April	5.25		

Benefits in kind

Benefit provided	Directors and 'P11D' employees (see notes on page 8)	'Lower-paid' employees	Reference
Accommodation, supplies, etc. used in employment duties	Provision of accommodation, supplies or services used by an employee in performing the duties of the employment is not taxable provided that either (i) if the benefit is provided on premises occupied by the employer, any private use by the employee (or his family or household) is not significant; or (ii) in any other case, the sole purpose of providing the benefit is to enable the employee to perform those duties, any private use is not significant, and the benefit is not an 'excluded benefit' (i.e. the provision of a motor vehicle, boat or aircraft, or a benefit which involves the extension, conversion or alteration of any living accommodation or the construction, extension, conversion or alteration of a building or other structure on land adjacent to and enjoyed with living accommodation).	As aside	ITEPA 2003, s 316
Assets given to employees	If new, cost to employer less any part of cost made good by employee If used, greater of (i) market value at time of transfer and (ii) where asset (other than a car or a van) first applied for the provision of a benefit after 5.4.80 and a person has been chargeable to tax on its use, market value when first so applied less amounts charged to tax for use up to and including year of transfer.	Market value	ITEPA 2003, ss 203, 204, 206
Buses to shops	The provision of buses for journeys of 10 miles or less from the workplace to shops, etc. on a working day is not taxable.	As aside	SI 2002 No 205
Cheap loans			
(a) Interest free or beneficial rates	Taxable benefit on employer-related, cheap loans is the difference between interest paid and interest payable at 'official rate' below. Exception applies	Not taxable	ITEPA 2003, ss 174, 175, 181–187
	(i) where all the employer-related loans (or all loans not qualifying for tax relief) do not exceed £10,000 (£5,000 for 2013/14 and earlier years);		ITEPA 2003, s 180
	(ii) where all the interest payable is or would be eligible for tax relief; and		ITEPA 2003, ss 177–179
	(iii) to ordinary commercial loans.		ITEPA 2003, s 176
	The 'official rate' (see notes on page 8) is		
	1.3.09–5.4.10 4.75%		SI 2009 No 199
	6.4.10–5.4.14 4%		SI 2010 No 415
	6.4.14–5.4.15 3.25%		SI 2014 No 496
	6.4.15–5.4.16 3%		SI 2015 No 411
(b) Waiver	Amount written off	Normally taxable	ITEPA 2003, ss 188–190
Christmas parties and annual functions	Not taxable if cost does not exceed £150 per head per tax year and open to staff generally. Otherwise fully taxable. Expenditure may be split between more than one function.	Not taxable	ITEPA 2003, s 264 SI 2003 No 1361
Childcare provision	No liability arises (i) where the premises are not used wholly or mainly as a private dwelling and the provision is made available by the employer; (ii) where the scheme is provided under arrangements with other persons, by one or more of those persons); or (iii) in cases where (i) or (ii) does not apply, on the first £55 per week of registered or approved childcare or, where the employee joins the scheme after 5 April 2011, the first £55 per week for a basic rate taxpayer, the first £28 for a higher rate taxpayer and the first £25 (£22 before 6 April 2013) for an additional rate taxpayer The provisions in (ii) and (iii) are to be replaced for new claimants from 2017. Under the Government's tax-free childcare scheme, top-up payments will be made equal to 25% of the amount paid for childcare of qualifying children. A maximum top-up of £2,000 each year per child (£4,000 for a disabled child) applies. No income tax or NIC liability will arise in respect of the top-up payments.	Not taxable	ITEPA 2003, ss 318–318D SI 2006 No 882
Company cars/car fuel	See pages 82 to 84		

Benefits in kind

Benefit provided	Directors and 'P11D' employees (see notes on page 8)	'Lower-paid' employees	Reference
Company vans/van fuel	No benefit arises where a van is made available mainly for business travel and the terms on which it is made available prohibit private use other than for ordinary commuting; otherwise the benefit is £3,150 (£3,090 for 2014/15; £3,000 for 2013/14 and earlier years). For 2015/16 the benefit is £630 for zero-emission vans (nil for 2010/11 to 2014/15). Where the benefit charge applies and fuel for private travel is provided, there is an additional fuel benefit charge. For 2015/16 the charge is £594 (for 2014/15 it is £581; for 2013/14 it is £564; for 2010/11–2012/13 it is £550; for earlier years it is £500). For 2010/11–2014/15 the charge is reduced to nil for zero-emissions vans.	Not taxable	ITEPA 2003, ss 154–164, 170
Credit tokens	Cost to employer of money, goods or services obtained less any contribution from employee (except where used to obtain certain non-taxable benefits).	As aside	ITEPA 2003, ss 90–96, 268–270, 363
Cyclists' breakfasts	For 2012/13 and earlier years, breakfast provided for consumption of employees on arrival at workplace in recognition of having cycled to work is not taxable.	As aside	SI 2002 No 205; SI 2012 No 1808
Day subsistence	HMRC operate advisory benchmark scale rates for non-taxable day subsistence payments to employees who incur allowable business travel expenses.		HMRC Brief 24/09
Disabled employees	No benefit arises on the provision of or payment for transport for disabled employees for ordinary commuting. No benefit arises on the provision of equipment, services or facilities to disabled employees to help them carry out their duties of employment.	As aside	ITEPA 2003, ss 246, 247 SI 2002 No 1596
Emergency service vehicles	No charge arises where an emergency vehicle is made available to a person employed in an emergency service where private use is prohibited otherwise than when on call.	As aside	ITEPA 2003, s 248A
Employee shareholder agreements	No charge arises where the reasonable costs of independent advice as to the terms and effect of a proposed employee shareholder agreement (see page 21) is met by the company.	As aside	ITEPA 2003, s 326B; FA 2013, Sch 23 paras 37, 38
Employees' liability insurance	Not taxable	As aside	ITEPA 2003, ss 346–350
Expenses generally	Unless covered by specific exemptions elsewhere, all payments to an employee by reason of his employment in respect of expenses, including sums put at the employee's disposal and paid away by him, are taxable. Deduction is allowed for expenses the employee is obliged to incur which are either qualifying travelling expenses (broadly those necessarily incurred other than ordinary commuting or private travel) or other amounts incurred wholly, exclusively and necessarily in the performance of the duties of the employment. For 2016/17 onwards, expenses payments and reimbursements are not taxable if an amount equal to or exceeding the expense would be allowed as a deduction. Also for 2016/17 onwards an exemption applies to reimbursed travel expenses incurred by local authority councillors.	Not taxable	ITEPA 2003, ss 70–72, 289A–289E, 336–340; FA 2015, s 11
Eye tests and corrective appliances	Not taxable provided that provision is required under health and safety legislation and is available as required to employees generally.	As aside	ITEPA 2003, s 320A FA 2006, s 62
Fixed rate expenses	See pages 61 and 62		
Homeworkers	Employer contributions to additional household costs not taxable where employee works at home. Supporting evidence required if contributions exceed £4 per week (or £18 per month for monthly paid employees). For 2011/12 and earlier years the limit was £3 per week.	As aside	ITEPA 2003, s 316A
Incidental overnight expenses	Not taxable where employee stays away from home on business and payment from employer does not exceed £5 per night in the UK or £10 per night overseas.	As aside	ITEPA 2003, ss 240, 241

Benefits in kind

Benefit provided	Directors and 'P11D' employees (see notes on page 8)	'Lower-paid' employees	Reference
Living accommodation (a) Representative	Employees – no liability where (i) necessary for proper performance of duties; (ii) customary to provide employee with accommodation; or (iii) special threat to employee's security Directors – (a) full-time working director whose interest in the company does not exceed 5%, as for employees above; (b) other directors, not taxable when (iii) above applies; otherwise as for beneficial below.	Not taxable	ITEPA 2003, ss 99, 100
(b) Beneficial	Annual rental value (or actual rent if greater) less any sums made good by the employee. For leases of ten years or less commencing or extended after 21 April 2009, a premium is treated as actual rent spread over the lease term. Where the cost of providing accommodation exceeds £75,000 (and the charge under ITEPA 2003, s 105 is not calculated on the full open market rental value), there is an additional charge at an annual rate, equivalent to the excess over £75,000 at the official rate for cheap loans (see above) at the beginning of the year of assessment (less any rent paid in excess of the benefit under s 105).	As aside	ITEPA 2003, ss 102–105B ITEPA 2003, ss 106, 107
	Where there is multiple occupation in a period, the total amount charged cannot exceed that chargeable if the property was available to one person throughout.		ITEPA 2003, s 108
	An exemption applies in respect of occupation of an overseas property owned by a company that is owned by individuals and whose only activities are incidental to its ownership of the property, provided that the property is the company's only or main asset and is not funded by a connected company.		ITEPA 2003, ss 100A, 100B
Living expenses (a) Company's property (i) Representative	Cost to company subject to a maximum of 10% of net earnings	Normally not taxable	ITEPA 2003, ss 313–315
(ii) Beneficial	Normally cost to employer	Normally not taxable	
(b) Own accommodation	Normally cost to employer	Normally as aside	
Long service awards	Not taxable provided at least 20 years' service and cost to employer does not exceed £50 for each year of service. No similar award must have been made in the previous 10 years.	As aside	ITEPA 2003, s 323 SI 2003 No 1361
Medical check-ups	One screening and one check-up each year not taxable.	As aside	ITEPA 2003, s 320B
Medical insurance	Premium paid on behalf of employee taxable unless for treatment outside UK whilst employee performing his duties abroad	Not taxable	ITEPA 2003, s 325
Medical treatment	With effect from 1 January 2015, not taxable up to an annual cap of £500 per employee when an employer meets the cost of recommended medical treatment. Treatment is recommended for this purpose if provided in accordance with a recommendation from an occupational health service to help an employee return to work after absence due to ill-health or injury.		ITEPA 2003, s 320C; FA 2014, s 12; SI 2014 No 3226
Miners' free coal	Miners' free coal and coal allowances in lieu are not taxable.	As aside	ITEPA 2003, s 306
Mobile telephones	Loan of one mobile phone to employee not taxable (and phones first loaned before 6 April 2006 not taxable).	Not taxable	ITEPA 2003, s 319
	Exemption covers making the telephone available (without any transfer of property), line rental, and calls (business and private).		
Parking spaces	Parking spaces at or near place of work for cars, bicycles, motorcycles and vans not taxable.	Not taxable	ITEPA 2003, s 237
Pension advice	Not taxable if available to all employees and benefit does not exceed £150 per tax year.	As aside	SI 2002 No 205
	Payments by employers on or after 6 April 2015 for independent advice to employees on conversion and transfers of pension benefits not taxable.	As aside	ITEPA 2003, s 308B
Public transport strikes	The provision of travel, accommodation and subsistence during public transport disruption caused by industrial action is not taxable.	As aside	ITEPA 2003, s 245

Benefits in kind

Benefit provided	Directors and 'P11D' employees (see notes on page 8)	'Lower-paid' employees	Reference
Relocation expenses	Qualifying removal expenses and benefits up to £8,000 per move in connection with job-related residential moves are not taxable. Included are expenses of disposal, acquisition, abortive acquisition, transporting belongings, travelling and subsistence, bridging loans and duplicate expenses.	As aside	ITEPA 2003, ss 271–289
Scholarships	Cost of any scholarship awarded (i) out of a trust fund etc. not satisfying a 25% distribution test; or (ii) because of employee's employment.	Not taxable	ITEPA 2003, ss 211–215
Sports and recreational facilities	Not taxable	Not taxable	ITEPA 2003, ss 261–263
Subscriptions and fees	Not taxable where paid to professional bodies where employee has a contractual or professional requirement to be a member of the body.	As aside	ITEPA 2003, ss 343–345
Third party entertaining	Not taxable where provided by a party unconnected with the employer and not for services provided in connection with employment.	As aside	ITEPA 2003, s 265
Third party small gifts	Gifts of goods and non-cash vouchers up to £250 during the tax year not taxable where provided by a party unconnected with the employer and not for services provided in connection with employment.	As aside	ITEPA 2003, ss 270, 324 SI 2003 No 1361
Training/counselling	Certain employee training costs, work-related training, and counselling services provided by employers are not taxable.	As aside	ITEPA 2003, ss 250–260, 310–312
Transport to home	Transport and occasional late night journeys from work to home or following a failure of a car-sharing arrangement are not taxable.	As aside	ITEPA 2003, s 248
Trivial benefits	From 6 April 2016, benefits meeting the following conditions are not taxable; the benefit is not cash or a cash voucher; the cost of providing it does not exceed £50; the benefit is not provided under salary sacrifice arrangements, under any other contractual obligation or in recognition of particular services. There is an annual limit of £300 for office holders of close companies and family members of such office holders.	As aside	
Use of employer's assets (other than cars and vans)	Land at annual rental value; other assets at 20% of market value when first lent or rental charge to employer if higher. No benefit arises in respect of	Not taxable	ITEPA 2003, ss 203–205
	(i) use of computer equipment for private home use where equipment first made available before 6 April 2006 (provided use not restricted to directors and senior staff and cash equivalent of benefit does not exceed £500);		ITEPA 2003, s 320 FA 2006, s 61
	(ii) use of works buses with a passenger seating capacity of at least 9 provided for employees (or their children) to travel to and from work;		ITEPA 2003, s 242
	(iii) bicycles and cycling safety equipment made available for employees to get between home and work.		ITEPA 2003, s 244
	No benefit arises on purchase by employee at market value of computer or bicycle previously on loan.		FA 2005, s 17
Vouchers			
(a) Cash vouchers	Amount for which voucher can be exchanged	Cashable value	ITEPA 2003, ss 73–81, 95, 96
(b) Non-cash vouchers	Cost to employer less any contribution from employee (except where used to obtain certain non-taxable benefits)	Cost to employer	ITEPA 2003, ss 82–88, 95, 96, 268–270A, 362
(c) Luncheon vouchers	Taxable (other than 15p per working day before 6 April 2013)	As aside	ITEPA 2003, s 89; FA 2012, Sch 39 para 50
(d) Transport vouchers	Cost to employer less any contribution from employee	As aside (note (c))	ITEPA 2003, ss 82–86

Benefits in kind

Benefit provided	Directors and 'P11D' employees (see notes on page 8)	'Lower-paid' employees	Reference
Vulnerable persons schemes	No charge arises where an employer pays or reimburses an employee's registration fee to the Protection of Vulnerable Groups Scheme or, on or after 10 June 2013, pays or reimburses fees for subscribing to the Disclosure and Barring Service's update service or fees for criminal records certificates applied for when an update service subscription is applied for.	As aside	*ITEPA 2003, s 326A; FA 2011, s 39; SI 2013 No 1133*
Welfare counselling	Not taxable (but excluding medical treatment and advice on finance (other than debt problems), tax, leisure or recreation, and legal advice).	As aside	*SI 2000 No 2080*
Workplace meals	Subsidised meals provided for staff generally at the workplace are not taxable. From 6 April 2011 this exemption does not apply if entitlement arises under salary sacrifice or flexible benefits arrangements.	As aside	*ITEPA 2003, s 317*

Notes

(a) 'P11D' employees are those with earnings, plus benefits etc. to be entered on form P11D (including VAT), at rate of £8,500 p.a. or more. The £8,500 threshold will be abolished for 2016/17 onwards, so that all employees will be taxed on benefits and expenses in the same way. Exemptions will apply for minsters of religion earning less than £8,500 and for board and lodging of certain carers. [*FA 2015, ss 13, 14*].

(b) The official rate is set in advance for the whole of the following tax year, subject to review if the typical mortgage rates *fall* sharply during a tax year. (IRPR 6/00, 25 January 2000).

(c) Transport vouchers provided for 'lower-paid' employees of passenger transport undertakings under arrangements in operation on 25 March 1982 are not taxable. [*ITEPA 2003, s 86*].

Capital allowances

Agricultural buildings

Expenditure after	Allowance	Reference
Initial allowance		
11 April 1978	20%	*CAA 1968, s 68(1)*
		as amended by
		FA 1978, s 39(1)
31 March 1986	Nil	*FA 1986, s 56, Sch 15*
31 October 1992 (note (d))	20%	*CAA 1990, s 124A*
31 October 1993	Nil	
Writing-down allowance (on cost)		
5 April 1946	10%	*CAA 1968, s 68*
31 March 1986 (note (b))	4%	*CAA 2001, s 373*

Notes

(a) Agricultural buildings allowances are **abolished** for income tax purposes for 2011/12 onwards and for corporation tax purposes for the financial year beginning 1 April 2011 onwards. *FA 2008, s 84*

(b) As a transitional measure, writing-down allowances are stepped down over the three financial or tax years prior to abolition. For 2008/09 (for corporation tax, the financial year beginning 1 April 2008) only 75% of the allowance is given. For 2009/10 (or financial year beginning 1 April 2009) only 50% is given and for 2010/11 (or financial year beginning 1 April 2010) only 25%. Where a chargeable period falls in more than one tax or financial year, time apportionment applies to determine the amount of the allowance. *FA 2008, s 85*

(c) Maximum allowance for farmhouse is on one third of expenditure. *CAA 2001, s 369(3)(4)*

(d) The initial allowance of 20% was given on new agricultural buildings where the contract was made between 1 November 1992 and 31 October 1993 inclusive and the building brought into use by 31 December 1994.

Business premises renovation

Expenditure after	Allowance	Reference
Initial allowance		
10 April 2007	100%	*CAA 2001, ss360A–360Z4*
		FA 2005, s 92, Sch 6

Notes

(a) Only for renovation or conversion of business properties that have been vacant for at least a year and are situated in any of the disadvantaged areas of the UK designated as Enterprise Areas. For expenditure incurred on or after 6 April 2014 (1 April 2014 for corporation tax purposes) allowances are not available if another form of EU State aid has been, or will be, received.

(b) Where the initial allowance is not claimed or not claimed in full, a writing-down allowance of 25% on the cost is given.

(c) Allowances are available for expenditure incurred before 6 April 2017 (1 April 2017 for corporation tax).

Dredging

Expenditure after	Allowance	Reference
Initial allowance		
16 January 1966	15%	*CAA 1968, s 67(1)(a)*
31 March 1986	Nil	*FA 1985, s 61*
Writing-down allowance (on cost)		
5 April 1956	2%	*FA 1956, s 17(1)(b)*
5 November 1962	4%	*CAA 2001, s 487*

Dwelling-houses let on assured tenancies

Expenditure after	Allowance	Reference
Initial allowance		
9 March 1982	75%	*FA 1982, Sch 12 paras 1, 2*
13 March 1984	50%	
31 March 1985	25%	
31 March 1986	Nil	*FA 1984, s 58, Sch 12 para 3*
Writing-down allowance (on cost)		
After 9 March 1982 and before 1 April 1992	4%	*CAA 2001, s 508*

Notes

(a) Maximum qualifying expenditure is £60,000 on a construction in Greater London and £40,000 elsewhere. *CAA 2001, s 511(3)*

Flat conversion

Expenditure after	Allowance	Reference
Initial allowance		
10 May 2001	100%	*CAA 2001, ss 393A–393W*

Notes

(a) Flat conversion allowances are **abolished** for expenditure incurred on or after 6 April 2013 (1 April 2013 for corporation tax). The entitlement to writing-down allowances on unrelieved expenditure brought forward ceases with effect from the same dates. [*FA 2012, Sch 39 paras 36–38*].

(b) Allowances were available only for renovation or conversion of certain vacant or storage space above shops and other commercial premises to provide low-value flats for rent.

(c) Where the initial allowance was not claimed or not claimed in full, a writing-down allowance of 25% on the cost was given (but see note (a)).

Capital allowances

Hotels

Expenditure after	Allowance	Reference
Initial allowances (note (c))		
11 April 1978	20%	FA 1978, Sch 6 para 1
31 March 1986	Nil	FA 1985, s 66
31 October 1992 (note (d))	20%	CAA 1990, s 2A
31 October 1993	Nil	
Writing-down allowances (on cost)		
11 April 1978 (note (b))	4%	CAA 2001, ss 271, 279, 310

Notes

(a) Allowances for hotels are **abolished** for income tax purposes for 2011/12 onwards and for corporation tax purposes for the financial year beginning 1 April 2011 onwards. — FA 2008, s 84

(b) As a transitional measure, writing-down allowances are stepped down over the three financial or tax years prior to abolition. For 2008/09 (for corporation tax, the financial year beginning 1 April 2008) only 75% of the allowance is given. For 2009/10 (or financial year beginning 1 April 2009) only 50% is given and for 2010/11 (or financial year beginning 1 April 2010) only 25%. Where a chargeable period falls in more than one tax or financial year, time apportionment applies to determine the amount of the allowance. — FA 2008, s 85

(c) An initial allowance of 100% is given on expenditure incurred or contracted for within ten years of the inclusion of the site in an enterprise zone. — CAA 2001, ss 298, 306

(d) The initial allowance of 20% was given on new hotels where the contract was made between 1 November 1992 and 31 October 1993 inclusive and the hotel was brought into use by 31 December 1994.

Industrial buildings and sports pavilions

Expenditure after	Allowance		Reference
Initial allowance (note (c))			
17 February 1956	10%		FA 1956, s 15
14 April 1958	15%		FA 1958, s 15(1)(5)
7 April 1959	15%		FA 1959, s 21(1)(2), Sch 4
	15%	(where no investment allowance)	
16 January 1966	15%		FA 1966, s 35
5 April 1970	30%		
	40%	(if in development or intermediate area or NI)	FA 1970, s 15(1)
21 March 1972	40%		FA 1972, s 67(2)(d)
12 November 1974	50%		FA 1975, s 13
10 March 1981	75%		FA 1981, s 73
13 March 1984	50%		
31 March 1985	25%		

Expenditure after	Allowance	Reference
31 March 1986	Nil	FA 1984, s 58, Sch 12 para 1
31 October 1992 (note (g))	20%	CAA 1990, s 2A
31 October 1993	Nil	
Writing-down allowance (on cost)		
5 April 1946	2%	ITA 1945, s 2 / ITA 1952, s 266(1) / CAA 1968, s 2(2)
5 November 1962 (note (b))	4%	CAA 2001, s 310

Notes

(a) Industrial buildings allowances and allowances for buildings in enterprise zones are **abolished** for income tax purposes for 2011/12 onwards and for corporation tax purposes for the financial year beginning 1 April 2011 onwards. — FA 2008, s 84

(b) As a transitional measure, writing-down allowances are stepped down over the three financial or tax years prior to abolition. For 2008/09 (for corporation tax, the financial year beginning 1 April 2008) only 75% of the allowance is given. For 2009/10 (or financial year beginning 1 April 2009) only 50% is given and for 2010/11 (or financial year beginning 1 April 2010) only 25%. Where a chargeable period falls in more than one tax or financial year, time apportionment applies to determine the amount of the allowance. — FA 2008, s 85

(c) An initial allowance of 100% is given on expenditure incurred or contracted for within ten years of the inclusion of the site in an enterprise zone. — CAA 2001, ss 298, 306

(d) An initial allowance of 100% was given for expenditure incurred on 'small workshops' (internal floor space 2,500 square feet or less) after 26 March 1980 and before 27 March 1983. — FA 1980, s 75, Sch 13

(e) An initial allowance of 100% was given for expenditure incurred after 26 March 1983 and before 27 March 1985 on 'very small workshops' i.e. units not exceeding 1,250 square feet or which, in a converted building, exceed that area but where the average size of all units in the building does not exceed 1,250 square feet. — FA 1982, s 73 / FA 1983, s 31

(f) Where the allowances in (a) and (c) above are not claimed or not claimed in full, a writing-down allowance of 25% on the cost is given. — FA 1980, ss 74, 75, Sch 13 / CAA 2001, s 310

(g) The initial allowance of 20% was given on new industrial buildings where the contract was made between 1 November 1992 and 31 October 1993 inclusive and the building was brought into use by 31 December 1994.

Know-how

Expenditure after	Allowance	Reference
Writing-down allowance		
31 March 1986	25% (on tax wdv)	CAA 2001, s 458

Capital allowances

Mineral extraction

Expenditure after	Allowance		Reference
Initial allowance			
5 April 1944	10%		*ITA 1945, s 26*
5 April 1952	Nil		*ITA 1952, s 306*
14 April 1953	40%		*FA 1953, s 16(3)*
6 April 1954	Nil		*FA 1954, s 16(4)*
	40%	(where no investment allowance)	
17 February 1956	40%		*FA 1956, s 15(1)*
7 April 1959	20%		*FA 1959, s 21(2)*
	40%	(where no investment allowance)	
16 January 1966	40%		*FA 1966, s 35*
			CAA 1968, s 56(2)
31 March 1986	Nil		*FA 1986, s 55, Schs 13, 14*
Writing-down allowance			
Before 1 April 1986	Residue of expenditure $\times \dfrac{A}{A+B}$ (subject to a minimum of 5% of residue of expenditure) where A = current output B = potential future output		*CAA 1968, s 57*
After 31 March 1986	25% (on tax wdv) 10% on minerals and mineral rights		*CAA 2001, s 418*

Notes

(a) An allowance of 100% was given on expenditure incurred after 26 October 1970 and before 1 April 1986 on the construction of works in a development area or in Northern Ireland. — *FA 1971, s 52*

(b) After 31 March 1986, relief for land was abolished. Allowances are due on the residue of unrelieved expenditure incurred before 1 April 1986. — *FA 1986, s 55, Schs 13, 14*

(c) A 100% first-year allowance is available for certain expenditure incurred after 16 April 2002 wholly for the purposes of a North Sea Oil ring-fence trade or on plant and machinery for use in such a trade. — *CAA 2001, s 416D*

Motor cars suitable for private use

Not normally eligible for annual investment or first-year allowances (but see page 12, note (f))

Expenditure after	Allowance
Writing-down allowance	
5 April 2009 (31 March 2009 for CT)	
—chargeable periods ending after 5.4.12 (31.3.12 for CT)	18% where CO_2 emissions do not exceed the limit in note (b); otherwise 8%
—chargeable periods ending before 6.4.12 (1.4.12 for CT)	20% where CO_2 emissions do not exceed the limit in note (b); otherwise 10%
11 March 1992	maximum £3,000

Notes

(a) Expenditure incurred after 5 April 2009 (31 March 2009 for corporation tax) is allocated either to the main pool, or where the 8% or 10% rate applies, to the special rate pool, unless there is private use of the car. [*CAA 2001, ss 104A, 104AA*]. For chargeable periods beginning before 6 April 2012 and ending on or after that date (or, for corporation tax purposes, beginning before 1 April 2012 and ending on or after that date) a hybrid rate of WDAs applies, calculated by time apportionment of the 20% and 18% rates (or the 10% and 8% rates).

(b) The emissions limit is 130g/km. For expenditure incurred before 6 April 2013 (1 April 2013 for corporation tax purposes) the limit is 160g/km.

(c) Expenditure exceeding £12,000 incurred before 6 April 2009 (1 April 2009 for corporation tax) was allocated to a single asset pool (unless qualifying for first-year allowances). Writing-down allowances were given at the general rate, subject to the above annual maximum limit. Any expenditure remaining in such a single asset pool at the end of the first chargeable period ending on or after 5 April 2014 (31 March 2014 for corporation tax) was transferred to the main pool, the annual maximum ceasing to apply thereafter. [*CAA 2001, ss 74, 75*].

Patent rights

Expenditure after	Allowance	Reference
Writing-down allowance		
31 March 1986	25% (on tax wdv)	*CAA 2001, s 472*

Research and development

Expenditure after	Allowance	Reference
Allowance in year 1		
5 November 1962	100%	*CAA 2001, s 441*

Capital allowances

Plant and machinery

Annual investment allowance [CAA 2001, ss 51A–51N; FA 2010, s 5; FA 2011, s 11; FA 2013, ss 7, 70; FA 2014, s 10, Sch 2]

Qualifying expenditure incurred on or after 6 April 2008 (1 April 2008 for corporation tax purposes) up to the annual maximum incurred in a chargeable period qualifies for the annual investment allowance at **100%**.

	Expenditure after	before	Maximum allowance
Income tax	31 December 2015		£200,000
	5 April 2014	1 January 2016	£500,000
	31 December 2012	6 April 2014	£250,000
	5 April 2012	1 January 2013	£25,000
	5 April 2010	6 April 2012	£100,000
	5 April 2008	6 April 2010	£50,000
Corporation tax	31 December 2015		£200,000
	31 March 2014	1 January 2016	£500,000
	31 December 2012	1 April 2014	£250,000
	31 March 2012	1 January 2013	£25,000
	31 March 2010	1 April 2012	£100,000
	31 March 2008	1 April 2010	£50,000

Notes

(a) Transitional rules apply to all of the changes in the maximum allowance for chargeable periods which straddle the dates of the changes.

(b) The annual maximum is proportionately increased or decreased where the chargeable period is longer or shorter than a year. A group of companies (defined as for company law purposes) can only receive a single maximum amount. This restriction also applies to certain related businesses or companies. Expenditure on cars does not qualify.

First-year allowances

	Expenditure after	before	Rate
(a) General (note (a))			
— for IT purposes	5.4.09	6.4.10	40%
— for CT purposes	31.3.09	1.4.10	40%
(b) Small/medium-sized businesses			
— generally for IT purposes (note (b))	1.7.98	6.4.08	40%
— generally for CT purposes (note (b))	1.7.98	1.4.08	40%
(c) Small businesses			
— generally for IT purposes (note (c))	5.4.04	6.4.05	50%
	5.4.06	6.4.08	50%
— generally for CT purposes (note (c))	31.3.04	1.4.05	50%
	31.3.06	1.4.08	50%
(d) Energy-saving equipment (note (e))	31.3.01		100%
(e) Certain cars/refuelling equipment (note (f))	16.4.02	1.4.18	100%
(f) Environment-friendly equipment (note (g))	31.3.03		100%

	Expenditure after	before	Rate
(g) Zero-emission goods vehicles (note (h))			
— for IT purposes	5.4.10	6.4.18	100%
— for CT purposes	1.4.10	1.4.18	100%
(h) Equipment for use in designated areas of enterprise zones (note (i))	31.3.12	1.4.20	100%

Notes

(a) Qualifying expenditure in the period attracts a FYA of 40%. This does not apply to expenditure on thermal insulation, integral features (see note (d) to writing-down allowances), long-life assets (see note (b) to writing-down allowances), cars, and plant or machinery for leasing.

(b) Qualifying expenditure in the period by small and medium-sized businesses (see (d) below) attracts a FYA of 40% (but see (c) below for enhanced FYAs for small companies only). This does not apply to expenditure on plant and machinery for leasing or letting on hire, cars (but see (f) below), sea-going ships, railway assets or long-life assets (see note (b) to writing-down allowances). [CAA 2001, ss 44, 46–49].

(c) Expenditure incurred by small businesses (see (d) below) in the period attracts a FYA of 50%. The conditions are the same as those outlined under (b) above. Outside of the period, the FYAs revert to 40% as for small and medium-sized businesses. [FA 2004, s 142; FA 2006, s 30; FA 2007, s 37].

(d) A medium-sized business is one satisfying any 2 of the following conditions: turnover £22.8m or less; assets £11.4m or less; employees 250 or less. A small business is one satisfying any 2 of the following conditions: turnover £5.6m or less; assets £2.8m or less; employees 50 or less.

(e) Expenditure on designated energy-saving plant or machinery, in accordance with the Energy Technology Criteria and Product Lists, attracts a FYA of 100%. 100% FYAs are available even if the assets are leased or let on hire. [CAA 2001, ss 45A–45C]. See List E on page 15.

(f) Expenditure in the period attracts a FYA of 100% on:
- new (not second-hand) cars first registered after 16 April 2002 which are either electrically-propelled or emit not more than 75 g/km of carbon dioxide (95 g/km for expenditure before 1 April 2015; 110 g/km for expenditure before 1 April 2013; 120 g/km for expenditure before 1 April 2008), or
- new plant or machinery for use in a refuelling station for the refuelling of vehicles with natural gas, hydrogen fuel or (for expenditure on or after 1 April 2008) biogas.

For expenditure incurred after 31 March 2013 cars provided for leasing do not qualify. [CAA 2001, ss 45D, 45E, 46; SI 2015 No 60].

(g) Expenditure incurred on designated environmentally-friendly plant and machinery attracts a FYA of 100%. Details of the qualifying technologies and products are published in the Water Technology Criteria and Products List. [CAA 2001, s 45H]. See List F on page 15.

(h) Expenditure in the period attracts a FYA of 100% on new (not second-hand) vehicles which cannot produce carbon dioxide emissions when driven and which are of a design primarily suited to the conveyance of goods or burden. This is limited to expenditure of 85 million euros per undertaking (as defined) over the eight years. [CAA 2001, ss 45DA, 212T; F(No 3)A 2010, Sch 7 paras 3, 6; FA 2015, s 45]. For expenditure incurred on or after 6 April 2015 (1 April 2015 for corporation tax), the FYA is limited to businesses that do not claim another State aid in respect of the same expenditure. The FYA also cannot be claimed if such aid is paid on or after that date towards expenditure on a van incurred before that date (and allowances already given are withdrawn).

(i) Expenditure in the period incurred by a trading company attracts a FYA of 100% on new (not second-hand) plant or machinery which represents investment and not replacement expenditure and which is not transport or transport equipment for use in a transport business. This is limited to expenditure of 125 million euros per investment project. The asset must not be held for use in an area outside of the designated assisted area for a period of five years. [CAA 2001, ss 45K–45N; FA 2012, Sch 11 para 3]. The designated assisted areas are listed in SI 2014 No 3183.

(j) For expenditure incurred on or after 1 April 2008, a company can surrender a tax loss attributable to FYAs within categories (e) or (g) above in exchange for a cash payment from the Government. The cash payment is equal to 19% of the loss surrendered, subject to an upper limit of the greater of £250,000 and the company's PAYE and NIC liability for the period concerned. [CAA 2001, s 262A, Sch A1; SI 2013 No 464].

Capital allowances

Writing-down allowances (WDAs)

	Rate
(a) General (expenditure after 26.10.70)	
— chargeable periods ending after 5.4.12 (31.3.12 for CT)	18%
— chargeable periods ending after 5.4.08 (31.3.08 for CT)	20%
— chargeable periods ending before 6.4.08 (1.4.08 for CT)	25%
(b) Long-life assets (expenditure after 26.10.70) (note (b))	
— chargeable periods ending before 6.4.08 (1.4.08 for CT)	6%
(c) Special rate expenditure	
— chargeable periods ending after 5.4.12 (31.3.12 for CT)	8%
— chargeable periods ending before 6.4.12 (1.4.12 for CT)	10%
(d) Foreign leased assets (expenditure after 9.3.82 and before 1.4.06)	10%

Notes

(a) WDAs are calculated on a reducing balance basis. When the rate changes during a chargeable period a hybrid rate of WDAs applies, calculated by time apportionment of the new and old rates. For chargeable periods beginning on or after 6 April 2008 (1 April 2008 for CT purposes), a WDA of up to £1,000 can be claimed in respect of the main pool and/or the special rate pool where the unrelieved expenditure in the pool concerned is £1,000 or less.

(b) The long-life asset rate applied to expenditure of more than £100,000 p.a. on plant and machinery with an expected working life when new of at least 25 years. It did not apply to plant and machinery which is: (i) second-hand where the rate applied to the vendor because the original expenditure pre-dated these rules; (ii) in a building used wholly or mainly as, or for purposes ancillary to, a dwelling-house, retail shop, showroom, hotel or office; (iii) cars; or (iv) sea-going ships and railway assets purchased before 1 January 2011.

For companies, the £100,000 *de minimis* limit is divided by one plus the number of associated companies (if any). [*CAA 2001, ss 90–104, Sch 3 para 20*].

(c) The special rate applies to expenditure on :
- long-life assets;
- integral features of a building and thermal insulation of a building incurred on or after 6 April 2008 (1 April 2008 for CT purposes);
- expenditure on long life assets incurred before 6 April 2008 (1 April 2008 for CT purposes) but not allocated to a pool until a chargeable period beginning on or after that date.
- expenditure on motor cars incurred on or after 6 April 2009 (1 April 2009) (see page 11);
- expenditure on cushion gas incurred on or after 1 April 2010; and
- expenditure on solar panels incurred on or after 6 April 2012 (1 April 2012).

The rate also applies to long-life assets pooled before 6/1 April 2008 for chargeable periods ending on or after 5 April 2008 (31 March 2008), subject to transitional rules. [*CAA 2001, s 104A; FA 2008, s 83*].

(d) Integral features of a building are:
- electrical systems;
- cold water systems;
- space or water heating systems;
- powered ventilation systems;
- air cooling or purification, and any floor or ceiling comprised in such systems;
- lifts;
- escalators and moving walkways; and
- external solar shading.

[*CAA 2001, ss 33A, 33B*].

Capital allowances items qualifying as plant or machinery

Expenditure on
(a) the provision of a building (including assets incorporated, or normally incorporated, in the building),
(b) the provisions of certain structures and assets or works involving the alteration of land, and
(c) the acquisition of any interest in land

does not qualify for plant and machinery allowances. [*CAA 2001, ss 21, 22, 24*].

Subject to certain conditions, these provisions do not apply to
(i) thermal insulation of industrial buildings; fire safety; safety at sports grounds (for expenditure incurred before 6 April 2013 (1 April 2013 for CT)); personal security; integral features; software and rights to software; films; or
(ii) expenditure on assets in List C.

See List A for assets treated as buildings and not qualifying as plant or machinery. [*CAA 2001, ss 21, 23*].

See List B for other assets specifically excluded from being plant or machinery. [*CAA 2001, ss 22, 23*].

See List C for assets not excluded from being plant or machinery. [*CAA 2001, s 23*].

See List D for activities which are qualifying activities for plant and machinery allowances. [*CAA 2001, s 15*].

See List E for classes of plant and machinery specified in the Energy Technology Criteria List.

See List F for classes of plant and machinery specified in the Water Technology Criteria List.

List G, reproduced by kind permission of Edward Magrin FTII, is a list of expenditure which *should*, subject to business use, be regarded as plant or machinery. The list has been compiled from case law (UK and foreign), court, tribunal and Commissioners' decisions and HMRC practice. It is not exhaustive.

See also HMRC Brief 3/10 which includes a list of items specific to the pig industry which may qualify as plant or machinery.

Whether expenditure on items within List C or List D qualifies for capital allowances will depend upon the facts of the case as applied to existing case law.

List A Assets treated as buildings

(1) Walls, floors, ceilings, doors, gates, shutters, windows and stairs.

(2) Mains services, and systems, for water, electricity and gas.
(3) Waste disposal systems.
(4) Sewerage and drainage systems.
(5) Shafts or other structures in which lifts, hoists, escalators and moving walkways are installed.
(6) Fire safety systems.

List B Excluded structures and other assets

(1) A tunnel, bridge, viaduct, aqueduct, embankment or cutting.
(2) A way, hard standing (such as a pavement), road, railway, tramway, a park for vehicles or containers, or an airstrip or runway.
(3) An inland navigation, including a canal or basin or a navigable river.
(4) A dam, reservoir or barrage, including any sluices, gates, generators and other equipment associated with the dam, reservoir or barrage.
(5) A dock, harbour, wharf, pier, marina or jetty or any other structure in or at which vessels may be kept, or merchandise or passengers may be shipped or unshipped.
(6) Any dike, sea wall, weir or drainage ditch.
(7) Any structure not within items 1 to 6 other than
 (a) a structure (but not a building) within the meaning of 'industrial building',
 (b) a structure in use for the purposes of an undertaking for the extraction, production, processing or distribution of gas, and
 (c) a structure in use for the purposes of a trade which consists in the provision of telecommunication, television or radio services.

List C Assets not excluded from being plant or machinery

Note that items 1 to 15 do not include any assets whose principle purpose is to insulate or enclose the interior of a building, or to provide an interior wall, floor or ceiling intended to remain permanently in place.

(1) Machinery (including devices for providing motive power) not within any other item in this list.
(2) Gas and sewerage systems provided mainly
 (a) to meet the particular requirements of the qualifying activity, or
 (b) to serve particular plant or machinery used for the purposes of the qualifying activity.
(3) Manufacturing or processing equipment; storage equipment (including cold rooms); display equipment; and counters, checkouts and similar.
(4) Cookers, washing machines, dishwashers, refrigerators and similar equipment; washbasins, sinks, baths, showers, sanitary ware and similar equipment; and furniture and furnishings.
(5) Lifts, hoists, escalators and moving walkways.
(6) Sound insulation provided mainly to meet the particular requirements of the qualifying activity.
(7) Computer, telecommunication and surveillance systems (including their wiring or other links).
(8) Refrigeration or cooling equipment.
(9) Fire alarm systems; sprinkler and other equipment for extinguishing or containing fires.
(10) Burglar alarm systems.
(11) Strong rooms in bank or building society premises; safes.
(12) Partition walls, where moveable and intended to be moved in the course of the qualifying activity.
(13) Decorative assets provided for the enjoyment of the public in hotel, restaurant or similar trades.
(14) Advertising hoardings; signs, displays and similar.
(15) Swimming pools (including diving boards, slides and structures on which such boards or slides are mounted).
(16) Any glasshouse constructed so that the required environment (namely, air, heat, light, irrigation and temperature) for the growing of plants is provided automatically by means of devices forming an integral part of its structure.
(17) Cold stores.
(18) Caravans provided mainly for holiday lettings.
(19) Buildings provided for testing aircraft engines run within the buildings.
(20) Moveable buildings intended to be moved in the course of the qualifying activity.
(21) The alteration of land for the purpose only of installing plant or machinery.
(22) The provision of dry docks.
(23) The provision of any jetty or similar structure provided mainly to carry plant or machinery.
(24) The provision of pipelines or underground ducts or tunnels with a primary purpose of carrying utility conduits.
(25) The provision of towers to support floodlights.

Capital allowances items qualifying as plant or machinery

(26) The provision of
  (a) any reservoir incorporated into a water treatment works, or
  (b) any service reservoir of treated water for supply within any housing estate or other particular locality.
(27) The provision of
  (a) silos provided for temporary storage, or
  (b) storage tanks.
(28) The provision of slurry pits or silage clamps.
(29) The provision of fish tanks or fish ponds.
(30) The provision of rails, sleepers and ballast for a railway or tramway.
(31) The provision of structures and other assets for providing the setting for any ride at an amusement park or exhibition.
(32) The provision of fixed zoo cages.

List D Qualifying Activities

Each of the following is a qualifying activity for the purposes of plant and machinery allowances but to the extent only that the profits or gains from the activity are, or (if there were any) would be, chargeable to tax.

(a) A trade.
(b) An ordinary property or Schedule A business.
(c) A UK or EEA furnished holiday lettings business.
(d) An ordinary overseas property business.
(e) A profession or vocation.
(f) A concern listed in *ITTOIA, s 12(4), CTA 2009, s 39(4)* (mines, transport undertakings etc).
(g) The management of an investment company.
(h) Special leasing of plant or machinery i.e. the hiring out of plant or machinery otherwise than in the course of another qualifying activity.
(i) An employment or office.

Where a person's qualifying activity falls within (b), (d) or (h) above, plant or machinery for use in a dwelling house is not qualifying expenditure. [*CAA 2001, s 35*].

Where a qualifying activity falls within (i) above, expenditure is qualifying expenditure only if the plant or machinery is necessarily provided for use in the performance of the duties of the employment or office. [*CAA 2001, ss 36, 80*].

List E Energy-saving plant and machinery

The Energy Technology Criteria List specifies the following technology classes as eligible for first-year allowances as energy-saving equipment. See page 12 note (e).

(1) Combined heat and power.
(2) Lighting.
(3) Pipework insulation.
(4) Boilers.
(5) Motors and drives.
(6) Refrigeration
(7) Thermal screens (for expenditure incurred before 7 September 2006).
(8) Heat pumps.
(9) Radiant and warm air heaters.
(10) Compressed air equipment.
(11) Solar thermal systems.
(12) Automatic monitoring and targeting equipment.
(13) Air to air energy recovery equipment.
(14) (For expenditure incurred before 8 October 2010) compact heat exchangers.
(15) Heating, ventilation and air conditioning equipment (for expenditure incurred before 4 August 2009, air conditioning zone controls).
(16) (For expenditure incurred on or after 4 August 2009) uninterruptible power supplies.
(17) High speed hand air dryers.
(18) (For expenditure incurred on or after 2 July 2015) waste heat to electricity conversion equipment.

The equipment must meet the energy-saving criteria set out in that List and, in the case of classes (4) to (17), must be of a type specified in (and not removed from) or which has been accepted for inclusion in, the Energy Technology Product List. [*CAA 2001, s 45A; SI 2001 No 2541*].

For expenditure incurred on or after 6 April 2012 (1 April 2012 for corporation tax purposes) FYAs are not available for expenditure on plant or machinery which generates electricity or heat, or produces biogas or biofuels, that attract tariff payments under the feed-in tariffs scheme or renewable heat incentive scheme introduced by the Department of Energy and Climate Change. This restriction applies to expenditure incurred on or after 6 April 2014 (1 April 2014) for combined heat and power equipment installations.

List F Environmentally-friendly plant and machinery

The Water Technology Criteria List specifies the following technology classes as eligible for first-year allowances as environmentally-friendly equipment. See page 12 note (g).

(1) Meters and monitoring equipment.
(2) Flow controllers.
(3) Leakage detection equipment.
(4) Efficient toilets.
(5) Efficient taps.
(6) Rainwater harvesting equipment.
(7) Water reuse systems (for expenditure before 11 August 2008, efficient membrane filtration systems for the treatment of waste water for recovery and reuse only).
(8) Cleaning in place equipment.
(9) Efficient showers.
(10) (For expenditure incurred on or after 7 September 2006) efficient washing machines.
(11) (For expenditure incurred on or after 7 September 2006) small scale slurry and sludge dewatering equipment.
(12) (For expenditure incurred on or after 16 August 2007) vehicle wash waste reclaim units.
(13) (For expenditure incurred on or after 16 August 2007) water efficient industrial cleaning equipment.
(14) (For expenditure incurred on or after 16 August 2007) water management equipment for mechanical seals (for expenditure before 11 August 2008, waste management for mechanical seals).
(15) (For expenditure incurred on or after 7 August 2013) greywater recovery and reuse equipment.

The equipment must meet the environmental criteria set out in that List and must be of a type specified in (and not removed from) or which has been accepted for inclusion in, the Water Technology Product List. [*CAA 2001, s 45H; SI 2003 No 2076*].

Capital allowances items qualifying as plant or machinery

List G items which can qualify as plant or machinery based on case law, HMRC practice etc.

Acid chambers

Acoustic treatment of e.g. room ducts (specialised installations)

Advertising signs, billboards, hoardings and roller boards

Aerials

Air compressors and services

Air conditioning including ducting and vents

Air lines

Alterations to a building re: plant installation e.g. ventilating ducts

Amusement slides

Annealing ovens

Aquarium tanks

Arc and gas welding plant

Architects and professional fees related to a number of items including plant (part may qualify)

Armco barriers

Art works at a museum etc.

Artificial manure manufacturing plant

Bacon curing plant

Baffles

Baker's plant

Ball feeders and specialist tennis equipment

Banana ripening plant

Baths

Battery chargers

Beehives

Bicycle holders

Biscuit making plant

Bitumen laminating plant

Blast furnace

Blast tunnels

Blinds, curtains, blind boxes and pelmets

Boat shed jetties

Bobbin tamping machines

Boiler plants and auxiliaries

Boilers

Bowling alleys including ball return tracks, gutters, pit signals and terminals

Bowser tanks

Brewing plant including pipes, condenser and expansion

Brick elevators (portable)

Brick kilns

Bullet resistant screens

Burglar alarms

Buzz bars

Cable TV provision and ducting

Cable, both overhead and underground

Cable car systems

Calorifiers

Cameras

Canopy – where certain conditions met e.g. serves purpose of advertising

Canteen fittings and equipment

Capital contribution to a sewerage authority in the UK

Car park illumination

Carpets and other loose floor coverings

Car wash apparatus and housing

Cash dispensers

Casting pit

Cat walks

Catalysts (granuals)

Cathode filling machines

Ceilings – false, but only when performing a function distant from setting e.g. an integral part of a ventilation or air conditioning system

Central dictation systems

Charcoal burning kilns

Checkouts

Chillers

Cleaning cradles (including tracks and anchorages)

Clock installations

Coal carbonising apparatus

Coal hulks

Coffee making machines

Compressed air plant and piping

Computers and associated attachments together with specialised flooring and ceilings

Conduit for security alarm systems

Construction costs of erecting plant on site

Contribution to plant purchased by others (certain conditions must be met)

Conveyor installations and equipment

Cooking baths

Cooking, conveying and servicing equipment

Cooler rooms

Cooling furnaces

Cooling-water systems for (i) drinking and (ii) air-conditioning

Counters and fittings

Court floors – indoor and outdoor (certain cases only)

Cradles and fire balconies (demountable)

Crane gantries and towers

Curing barns e.g. tobacco and peanuts

Cyclic reforming apparatus

Dam (certain situations where not made of earth)

Dark rooms (demountable)

Derricks

Designs and blueprints

Dips for sheep and cattle

Dispensers

Disposal units with all live feeds, wastes and flues

Distillery plant and brewery apparatus including casks

Distribution systems

Documents hoist and other hoists and doors

Door closers

Draglines and buckets

Drilling plant

Drop hammers

Dry dock

Dry riser installation

Dryers

Capital allowances items qualifying as plant or machinery

Dumbwaiters

Dust extraction equipment

Dyehouse – specially designed

Dynamos

Electric dodgems

Electric fences

Electrically operated doors

Electrically operated roller shutters

Electrical sub-stations and generators

Electrical wiring closely related to an accepted piece of plant e.g. to smoke detectors

Electrical wiring and sockets in connection with particular trades e.g. TV shops and departments where the numbers of sockets are more than is normal for the size of the shop or department

Electronic scoring equipment

Electronic timing devices

Emergency lighting

Escalators and travelators

Excavating costs re: plant installation

Exchange losses when linked to capital expenditure

Extinguishers

Fairground and similar amusements

Fans

Fascia lettering

Fermentation chambers

Fire blankets and alarms

Fire protection systems and sprinklers

Fires

Fire safety equipment to comply with the requirements of a fire authority

Fish farming equipment

Fish ponds at garden centres and fish farms

Fitted desks, writing tables and screens

Fixed site caravans in a motor village

Flight simulators and trainers

Floating docks, pontoons and marinas

Floodlighting

Floor covering

Flooring (demountable)

Flooring (raised but only where incorporating special features necessary for trade)

Foreign currency fluctuation relating to expenditure (in certain cases)

Forges

Freezer rooms and chambers

Furnaces

Gamma irradiation apparatus

Gangways

Gantries

Gas bells

Gas installations after incoming main

General control and supervisory systems

Generators

Glasshouse (if of sophisticated design with e.g. a computer system monitoring and controlling such matters as temperature, humidity, ventilation and screens)

Goods and bullion lifts and doors

Grain silos

Gramophones and juke boxes

Grill work (removable)

Gymnasium equipment

Hand dryers

Heating installations, fittings, pipes and radiators

Hoists

Holding bay for oxygen steelmaking installation

Hoses and hose reels

Hot water services and related plumbing

Humidification buildings (specialist)

Hydraulic elevated platforms and hoists e.g. for car parking trade

Hydraulic presses

Ice making apparatus

Immersion and instant water heaters

Incinerators

Installation costs re: plant

Intercom installations

Internal signs

Kennels (moveable)

Kitchen equipment

Knives and lasts

Launches for ships

Laundry equipment and services

Letter-boxes

Lifts and lift shafts

Light fittings and lamps (certain trades e.g. hotels re ambience)

Lighting protection systems

Livestock pens and cages

Loudspeakers

Lockers

Locks (certain situations)

Loose floor coverings and doormats

Loose furniture

LPG cylinders

Mannequin display figures

Mechanical hand dryers

Mechanical gates

Mechanical vehicle barriers

Mechanical ventilation systems

Merry-go-rounds

Mezzanine storage platforms (moveable)

Milking machinery and refrigeration storage facilities

Mining machinery

Mirrors

Model steam trains, permanent way and other equipment for carrying passengers

Moveable partitions (where required by trade)

Murals (certain trades e.g. hotels re ambience)

Museums – items displayed

Name plates

Navigation apparatus (both on and offshore)

Offshore accommodation modules and helidecks

Oil rigs, well linings and platforms

Organic peroxides expansion cell block
Ornaments (certain trades e.g. hotels re ambience)
Outside tennis fencing
Ovens

Paper combining plant
Passenger lifts and doors
Payment for cancellation of options (in certain cases)
PBX
Personnel – location and call systems
Photofinish equipment
Pictures (certain trades e.g. hotels re ambience)
Pig unit (purpose built), automatic feeding etc.
Pipelines
Planetarium and space theatre domes
Plant housing (special circumstances)
Pneumatic tube conveying systems
Poles, cables, conductors and switch boards for the distribution of electricity
Portable toilet
Portakabins, huts of a nomadic type moved from site to site (e.g. the construction industry)
Pottery – works equipment and kiln
Poultry house – specially designed
Power cables
Power installations
Powering barrel mills
Prawn farming ponds
Professional fees specially related to an item of plant acquired
Projecting signs
Protective structures closely related to accepted items of plant
Public address and piped music systems
Pulleys
Pumps
Purifiers

Racking, cupboards and shelving (removable)
Radar installations
Radiators

Radio, television and data receivers
Radio, television and data transmission installations
Railway track including sleepers and ballast
Refinery
Refrigerated fruit juice dispensers
Refrigeration installations and cold stores
Refrigeration plant
Refuse collecting and disposal systems (including chutes and incinerators)
Reinforcing plant
Reticulation services installed in a factory if certain conditions are met
Retorts and associated structures
Revolving mechanical doors
Rock crushing machines
Roller shutter doors
Roofing – cost of strengthening roofs to support plant such as cranes and hoists

Safes, night safes and enclosures
Safety equipment and screens
Salmon farming apparatus
Sanitary installations such as lavatories, urinals and pans together with pipeline fittings
Sauna and jacuzzi
Screens and fire safety curtains – cinemas
Screens in a window display (moveable)
Sculptures (certain trades e.g. hotels re ambience)
Seats
Security assets and devices
Security gates to cash loading area (removable)
Security screens and lobbies
Sewer pipes in relation to e.g. factory or a large hotel
Shafts
Showers and baths
Shutters (mechanical)
Silage storage bunkers
Silos e.g. slurry blending and mixing and cement storage
Skating surface – synthetic

Skidpans and special surface tracks
Sleeping units for workers which are portable and taken from site to site
Slicing and wrapping machines
Smelters
Smoke detectors and heat detectors
Soda water fountains
Soft furnishings
Software purchased at the same time as the hardware re a computer system
Software with a life of more than 2 years
Solar energy systems
Special acoustical or suspended ceilings (in certain cases)
Special buildings which cannot be used as ordinary buildings e.g. boiler house, concrete shells housing plant, wind tunnels and anechoic chambers
Special foundations or reinforced flooring for plant
Special housing around plant
Special lighting related to the trade
Splashbacks (where not part of a wholly-tiled wall or floor)
Sports stadia expenditure re a safety certificate
Spray booth
Sprinkler systems
Squash courts – directly related to certain trading activities e.g. amusement park
Staff lockers
Stage lights and scenery
Stand (racecourse and similar trades (but only if certain conditions are met))
Starting gantries and stalls
Steam and other trains, permanent way and other equipment for carrying passengers or goods
Steam vats
Storage racks
Storage tanks and bins
Stoves
Stream services and condensate return systems
Strong rooms (demountable)
Strong room doors

Capital allowances items qualifying as plant or machinery

Swimming pools directly related to certain trading activities e.g. amusement or caravan park

Switchboards

Switchgear

Tanks (for brine, cream etc.)

Tapestries (certain trades e.g. hotels re ambience)

Tea and coffee dispensers

Telegraph poles

Telephone booths and kiosks

Telephone equipment and conduits

Teleprinters

Telex systems

Tennis courts – directly related to certain trading activities e.g. amusement or caravan park

Testing tanks

Thermal insulation re industrial buildings

Ticket issuing and collecting machines

Toll booths

Totalisator equipment

Towel dispensers

Towel rails

Traffic control apparatus

Tramway rails

Transformers

Transportation costs of plant

Trellis

Trickle irrigation equipment in glasshouses

Trolley parks

Turnstiles

Turntables

Vacuum cleaning installations

Vats e.g. for cyanide

Vaults

Vents

Vibration control

Video equipment

WC partitions (if demountable venestra type)

Wall decor (certain trades e.g. hotels re ambience)

Wash basins including drains

Water slide and associated equipment

Water softening installations

Water tower

Water treatment and filtration

Weighbridge

Welfare facilities

Wells

Wet and dry risers

Wharves – certain situations

Winches

Wind tunnels

Windmills

Window display lighting e.g. shops

Window displays (moveable)

Window panels, lighting and sockets for a shop front

Wiring and trunking to accepted items of plant

X-ray apparatus

Zoo cages (fixed)

Capital gains tax

Annual exemptions

(a) Individuals, personal representatives for the year of death and following two years and trusts for disabled person (as defined) [TCGA 1992, s 3, Sch 1 para 1]

2015/16	£11,100	FA 2014, s 9
2014/15	£11,000	FA 2014, s 8
2013/14	£10,900	SI 2013 No 662
2012/13	£10,600	FA 2012, s 34
2011/12	£10,600	FA 2011, s 8
2010/11	£10,100	SI 2010 No 923
2009/10	£10,100	SI 2009 No 824

In respect of qualifying trusts above, where one person creates more than one settlement, the exemption above is divided by the number of settlements created after 9 March 1981, subject to a minimum of 10% of the annual exemption.

An individual who claims to use the remittance basis for a tax year is not entitled to the capital gains tax annual exemption for that year. This does not apply if the individual's unremitted foreign income and gains for the year are less than £2,000.

(b) Settlements other than trusts covered in (a) above [TCGA 1992, s 3, Sch 1 para 2]

2015/16	£5,550	FA 2014, s 9
2014/15	£5,500	FA 2014, s 8
2013/14	£5,450	SI 2013 No 662
2012/13	£5,300	FA 2012, 34
2011/12	£5,300	FA 2011, s 8
2010/11	£5,050	SI 2010 No 923
2009/10	£5,050	SI 2009 No 824

In respect of settlements made after 6 June 1978, where one person creates more than one settlement, the exemption above is divided by the number of settlements created, subject to a minimum of 10% of the annual exemption for individuals.

Annual rates [TCGA 1992, s 4; F(No 2)A 2010, Sch 1]

Gains are chargeable as follows

2011/12– 2015/16	*Individuals*: treating gains as the top slice of taxable income: 18% up to basic rate limit; 28% above basic rate limit (subject to entrepreneurs' relief (see page 20))
	Settlements and personal representatives: 28% (subject to entrepreneurs' relief (see page 22)
2010/11	*Individuals — gains after 22 June 2010*: treating gains made after that date as the top slice of taxable income: 18% up to basic rate limit; 28% above basic rate limit (subject to entrepreneurs' relief (see page 22))
	Individuals — gains before 23 June 2010: 18%
	Settlements and personal representatives: 18% for gains before 23 June 2010, 28% for gains after 22 June 2010 (subject to entrepreneurs' relief (see page 22))
2009/10	18%

High value disposals of dwellings by companies. The rate of capital gains tax for gains made by companies on or after 6 April 2013 on disposals of dwellings subject to the annual tax on enveloped dwellings is 28%.

Non-resident CGT on UK residential property. The rate of capital gains tax for gains made by non-resident companies on or after 6 April 2015 on disposals of UK residential property interests is 20%. The normal rates apply to individuals subject to the charge.

Business expansion scheme [TCGA 1992, s 150]

In respect of shares issued after 18 March 1986 and before 1 January 1994 a disposal of scheme shares is exempt provided the scheme relief has been given and not withdrawn and other conditions are satisfied.

Charities, etc, gifts to [TCGA 1992, s 257; FA 2012, Sch 14]

Disposals (not at arm's length) to charities, community amateur sports clubs or bodies within *IHTA 1984, Sch 3* by way of gift or at a consideration not exceeding allowable expenditure are deemed to be made for a consideration giving neither a gain nor a loss. See also page 64.

Under the cultural gift scheme, for tax years and accounting periods beginning on or after 1 April 2012, taxpayers who donate pre-eminent objects, or collections of objects, to the nation may qualify for a tax reduction. Individuals qualify for a reduction in capital gains tax (and/or income tax) liability equal to 30% of the value of the objects. For corporation tax purposes the reduction is up to 20% of the value. The cultural gift scheme is administered by the Arts Council and launched on 12 March 2013.

Capital gains tax

Chattels (other than currency) [*TCGA 1992, s 45, s 262*]

Maximum exempt proceeds

1989/90 onwards	£6,000

Marginal relief applies to limit any gain to five-thirds of the excess over the above maximum. For the purposes of loss relief, a disposal for less than the maximum is deemed to be made for that maximum.

Chattels which are wasting assets are exempt whatever the consideration received, but this exemption is restricted or eliminated to the extent that the asset has been or could have been the subject of a capital allowance. For disposals on or after 6 April 2015 (1 April 2015 for corporation tax purposes), the exemption is also eliminated where the asset has become plant as a result of its use for the purposes of a trade, profession or vocation carried on by a person other than the owner and it would not otherwise have been a wasting asset.

Child trust funds [*SI 2004 No 1450*]

No tax is chargeable on the account provider, his nominee or the child on gains on account investments. The child is treated as having sold all the account investments, and as having reacquired them in his personal capacity, for their market value, immediately before attaining the age of 18. See also page 64.

Dwelling houses [*TCGA 1992, ss 222-226B; FA 2015, Schs 7, 9*]

A proportion of the gain accruing to an individual on the disposal of a dwelling house which has been his main residence is exempt given by the fraction

$$\frac{\text{length of the period of ownership after 31.3.82 during which the dwelling-house was the individual's only or main residence (but in any case inclusive of the last 18 months)}}{\text{the length of the period of ownership after 31.3.82}}$$

For disposals before 6 April 2014, the last 36 months of ownership were included in the numerator in the fraction. The 36-month period continues to apply where the property is disposed of by an individual who is, or whose spouse or civil partner is, a disabled person or a long-term resident in a care home, provided that neither holds an interest in any other dwelling house.

Certain periods of absence during which the individual had no other residence available for relief (including any period or periods not exceeding three years) are included in the denominator provided both before and after the period there was a time when the dwelling house was the individual's only or main residence.

For disposals on or after 6 April 2015, a property is treated as not being occupied as a residence for a tax year when it is located in a territory in which neither the person making the disposal nor their spouse or civil partner is tax resident and they do not stay overnight at the property at least 90 times during the year.

Where the dwelling house has been let at any time as residential accommodation, the gain otherwise chargeable by reason of the letting is exempt up to the lower of £40,000 and the amount of the gain otherwise exempt under these provisions.

Non-resident CGT charge on UK residential property. Gains on disposals on or after 6 April 2015 of UK residential property by non-UK residents (including both individuals and certain companies) are chargeable to CGT. Broadly, only the gain accruing from that date is charged. Individuals and trustees may be able to obtain main residence relief. The taxpayer must make a special return to HMRC within 30 days after the date of completion of sale using the online NRCGT return form.

Employee-ownership trusts [*TCGA 1992, ss 236H-236S; FA 2014, s 290, Sch 37*]

A disposal on or after 6 April 2014 by a person other than a company of shares in a trading company or parent company of a trading group to the trustees of a settlement is treated as being made at no gain/no loss if the settlement is for the benefit of all the employees of the company or group and the settlement acquires a controlling interest in the company during the tax year in which the disposal is made.

Employee shareholder shares [*FA 2013, Sch 23*]

A special employment status, known as 'employee shareholder' status, was introduced by *Growth and Infrastructure Act 2013, s 31*. Employee shareholders are issued or allotted at least £2,000 worth of shares in consideration of an employee shareholder agreement. Subject to conditions, a gain on the first disposal of shares worth up to £50,000 on acquisition is exempt from CGT. The exemption applies to shares received through the adoption of employee shareholder status on or after 1 September 2013. The normal share identification rules do not apply to employee shareholder shares. If an employee disposes of part of a holding of shares which includes employee shareholder shares, the employee can determine what proportion of the shares disposed of are employee shareholder shares (subject to the total number of such shares held). See also page 65.

Enterprise investment scheme [*TCGA 1992, ss 150A–150D, Schs 5B, 5BA*]

A disposal of shares on which EIS income tax relief has been given and not withdrawn is exempt. Any loss (net of income tax relief) on a disposal of EIS shares may be relieved against income or capital gains. A chargeable gain arising on disposal of any assets can be deferred by a subscription for shares under the EIS made one year before or three years after the disposal. Deferral is possible regardless of whether or not the EIS investment qualifies for income tax relief or the subscriber is connected with the company, but is restricted to cash subscriptions for new eligible shares in qualifying companies. See also page 66.

Capital gains tax

Entrepreneurs' relief [*TCGA 1992, ss 169H–169S; F(No 2)A 2010, Sch 1; FA 2013, Sch 24; FA 2015, ss 41-44*]

Entrepreneurs' relief applies to disposals by an individual on or after 6 April 2008 of:

- all or part of a trade carried on alone or in partnership;
- assets of such a trade following cessation;
- shares or securities in the individual's 'personal trading company' (as defined).; or
- for disposals on or after 6 April 2013, shares acquired on or after 6 April 2012 on the exercise of an enterprise management incentives option.

Where a disposal of shares or of an interest in the assets of a partnership qualifies for relief, an associated disposal of assets owned by the individual and used by the company or partnership also qualifies for relief. For disposals on or after 18 March 2015, the taxpayer must dispose of at least 5% of the company's shares or a 5% share of the assets of the partnership.

Trustees can claim relief where a qualifying beneficiary has an interest in the business concerned. The relief is available where the relevant conditions are met throughout a period of one year and for gains arising after 22 June 2010 operates by charging the qualifying gains to CGT at 10%. Previously, the relief operated by reducing the amount of qualifying gains by four-ninths (so that the gains were effectively charged to CGT at 10%). Relief is subject to a lifetime limit of gains of £10 million (£5 million for disposals before 6 April 2011; £2 million for disposals before 23 June 2010; £1 million for disposals before 6 April 2010), but disposals before 6 April 2008 do not normally count towards the limit. Relief given to trustees counts towards the limit of the qualifying beneficiary.

A gain on a disposal made on or after 3 December 2014 which qualifies for entrepreneurs' relief can be deferred under the enterprise investment scheme or social investment relief scheme without loss of entitlement to the relief. Entrepreneurs' relief can be claimed when the deferred gain becomes chargeable, There are also transitional rules to allow relief to be claimed in certain circumstances where a gain made before 6 April 2008 is deferred and becomes chargeable on or after that date.

Gifts [*TCGA 1992, ss 165–169G, 260, Sch 7*]

Where an individual makes a disposal not at arm's length (e.g. a gift) of a qualifying business asset, then, on a joint claim by the transferor and transferee, the unrelieved gain of the transferor is held over and the transferee's acquisition cost is reduced by a similar amount. Where any consideration exceeds the allowable expenditure, the held-over gain is the unrelieved gain less the excess. Qualifying business assets are

(a) assets used for the purposes of the trade, profession or vocation carried on by the transferor or his personal company; and

(b) shares or securities of a trading company which is the transferor's personal company or whose shares etc. are not listed. (Transfers of shares or securities *to a company* are excluded.)

Where a transferor makes a disposal not at arm's length of any asset which is a chargeable transfer under *IHTA 1984*, similar hold-over rules apply as above.

Government securities ('gilts') [*TCGA 1992, s 115*]

Disposals by individuals and trustees are exempt.

Indexation [*TCGA 1992, ss 53–57, 109*]

Indexation allowance is available for disposals by companies and is computed by multiplying each item of allowable expenditure by an indexation factor equal to

$$\frac{RD - RI}{RI} \text{ where}$$

RD = the RPI for month of disposal

RI = the RPI for the later of March 1982 or month expenditure incurred (but no later than March 1998 for individuals etc.)

See page 101 for RPI values and pages 26–37 for indexation factors for disposals on or after 1 April 2012.

Indexation allowance is not available for disposals by individuals, trustees and personal representatives.

Losses. Indexation allowance can only be used to reduce or extinguish a gain. It cannot increase or create a capital loss.

Assets acquired before 1 April 1982. Indexation allowance for an asset held on 31 March 1982 is calculated by reference to its market value on that date rather than its cost. The allowance can be claimed on the original cost if this is to the company's advantage.

Individual savings accounts ('ISAs') [*SI 1998 No 1870; SI 2013 No 1743*]

Investors are entitled to exemption from capital gains tax on their investments. There is no lock-in period and withdrawals may be made at any time without loss of tax relief. Where investments are withdrawn *in specie*, the investor is deemed to have made a disposal and reacquisition at market value. See also page 66.

Capital gains tax

Lease depreciation table [TCGA 1992, Sch 8 para 1(3)–(6)]

This table relates to leases of land which have 50 years or less to run (short leases)

Years	Percentage	Years	Percentage	Years	Percentage
50 or more	100	33	90.280	16	64.116
49	99.657	32	89.354	15	61.617
48	99.289	31	88.371	14	58.971
47	98.902	30	87.330	13	56.167
46	98.490	29	86.226	12	53.191
45	98.059	28	85.053	11	50.038
44	97.595	27	83.816	10	46.695
43	97.107	26	82.496	9	43.154
42	96.593	25	81.100	8	39.399
41	96.041	24	79.622	7	35.414
40	95.457	23	78.055	6	31.195
39	94.842	22	76.399	5	26.722
38	94.189	21	74.635	4	21.983
37	93.497	20	72.770	3	16.959
36	92.761	19	70.791	2	11.629
35	91.981	18	68.697	1	5.983
34	91.156	17	66.470	0	0

The fraction of expenditure (original cost and additional expenditure being treated separately) which is not allowed is calculated from the table above as follows

$$\frac{P(1) - P(3)}{P(1)} \text{ or } \frac{P(2) - P(3)}{P(2)}$$

where the percentages for the duration of the lease are

P(1) at acquisition

P(2) at the time of any additional expenditure

P(3) at disposal

If the duration of the lease is not an exact number of years, the percentage is that for the whole number of years plus one-twelfth of the difference between that and the next higher number for each odd month, counting an odd fourteen days or more as one month.

Miscellaneous

The following is a summary of other important exemptions from capital gains tax not covered separately in this section.

(a) **Betting, lottery etc.** Winnings from betting or lotteries of games with prizes are not chargeable gains, and no chargeable gain accrues on the disposal of rights to such winnings obtained by participating [TCGA 1992, s 51(1)].

(b) **Damages and compensation.** Sums received as compensation or damages for any wrong or injury suffered by an individual in his person or in his profession or vocation are not chargeable gains. [TCGA 1992, s 51(2)]. Compensation from foreign governments for assets confiscated, destroyed or expropriated is, subject to conditions, exempt. [HMRC ESC D50].

(c) **Debts.** A debt, other than a debt on a security, disposed of by the original creditor or his personal representative or legatee is exempt. [TCGA 1992, s 251(1)].

(d) **Decorations.** A decoration for valour or gallantry is exempt unless acquired by the vendor for money or money's worth. [TCGA 1992, s 268].

(e) **Foreign currency** acquired for an individual's (or his dependant(s) personal expenditure outside the UK is exempt. [TCGA 1992, s 269]. For disposals on or after 6 April 2012, all gains on withdrawals of money from foreign currency bank accounts by individuals, trustees and personal representatives are exempt.

(f) **Insurance policies.** A gain on the disposal of the rights conferred by a non-life insurance policy is exempt, subject to a restriction in certain cases where the policy is for loss or depreciation of assets which could themselves give rise to a chargeable gain. [TCGA 1992, s 204].

(g) **Motor cars etc.** [TCGA 1992, s 263].

(h) **Qualifying corporate bonds** are exempt. [TCGA 1992, s 115].

(i) **Renewables obligations certificates.** A gain on the disposal by an individual on or after 6 April 2007 of a certificate issued under Electricity Act 1989, s 32B is, subject to conditions, exempt. [TCGA 1992, s 263AZA].

(j) **Right to receive interest on deposit of victim of Nazi persecution.** A gain on the disposal of a right to receive interest eligible for income tax exemption under ITTOIA 2005, s 756A is not a chargeable gain. [TCGA 1992, s 268A].

(k) **Savings certificates, schemes and accounts etc.** No chargeable gain arises on the disposal of savings certificates and non-marketable securities issued under National Loans Acts 1939 and 1968. [TCGA 1992, s 121].

(l) **Settlements.** With certain exceptions, no chargeable gain accrues on the disposal of an interest created by or arising under a settlement by the original beneficiary or any other person. [TCGA 1992, s 76].

(m) **Substantial shareholdings of companies.** A gain on a disposal by a company of shares is exempt if, subject to further conditions, throughout a continuous twelve-month period beginning not more than two years before the disposal, the company held a substantial shareholding (broadly, at least a 10% interest) in the company whose shares are the subject of the disposal. [TCGA 1992, Sch 7AC].

Capital gains tax

Negligible value securities

HMRC have accepted that certain quoted securities have become of negligible value within *TCGA 1992, s 24(2)*. The effect is that, on a claim, the claimant is treated as having sold, and immediately reacquired, the shares for a consideration equal to the amount specified in the claim. The following is a list of securities so accepted in recent years.

Company	Security	Effective date
Albermarle & Bond Holdings Plc	Ord	16/05/14
Alexandra Plc	Ord 10p	29/07/10
Dawson International Plc	Ord	9/12/13
DTZ Holding Plc	Ord 5p	04/12/11
Ennstone Plc	Ord 25p	02/04/09
Entertainment Rights Plc	Ord	01/04/09
Erinaceous Group Plc	Ord 0.5p	23/03/10
Hampson Industries Plc	Ord 25p	04/12/12
Heywood Williams Group Plc	Ord	18/11/09
HMV Media Group Plc	Ord	20/12/13
Jarvis Plc	Ord 5p	26/03/10
Land of Leather Holdings Plc	Ord 10p	12/01/09
Litho Supplies Plc	Ord	21/07/10
London Scottish Bank Plc	10p Ord	08/01/10
Marchpole Holdings Plc	Ord	01/07/09
Mouchel Group Plc	Ord	28/08/12
Premier UK Dual Return Trust Plc	0.1p Capital	16/01/09
Regent Inns Plc	Ord	10/12/10
Waterford Wedgwood UK Plc	Stock units	29/04/10
Warner Estate Holdings Plc	Ord	28/02/14
Woolworths Group Plc	Ord	26/02/09

Payment of tax

Under self-assessment, any CGT liability is taken into account in arriving at the final payment (or repayment) of IT and CGT due on 31 January following the tax year. See page 68.

CGT payable by a non-resident on a disposal of UK residential property is due within 30 days following the completion of the disposal, unless the taxpayer is subject to self-assessment.

Personal representatives (HMRC Statement of Practice SP 2/04)

HMRC have agreed that expenditure based on the following scale (for deaths after 5 April 2004) may be added to the market values of assets at the date of death (as an estimate of the legal and accountancy costs in preparing the inheritance tax account and obtaining probate etc.) in computing chargeable gains on disposal

Gross value of estate	Allowable expenditure
(a) Up to £50,000	1.8% of probate value of assets sold
(b) £50,001–£90,000	£900 — divided among all the assets in the estate in proportion to their probate values
(c) £90,001–£400,000	1% of probate value of assets sold
(d) £400,001–£500,000	£4,000 — divided as in (b) above
(e) £500,001–£1,000,000	0.8% of probate value of assets sold
(f) £1,000,001–£5,000,000	£8,000 — divided as in (b) above
(g) Over £5,000,000	0.16% of probate value of assets sold (maximum £10,000)

Rebasing to 31 March 1982 [*TCGA 1992, ss 35, 36*]

Gains and losses on disposals after 5 April 1988 of assets held on 31 March 1982 are computed by reference to their 31 March 1982 value rather than original cost. However, for disposals by companies, a gain or loss cannot be greater than would have been the case if the rules relating to pre-6 April 1988 disposals had applied, unless a global election is made for 31 March 1982 value to apply irrevocably to all assets held on that date.

Capital gains tax

Rollover relief (replacement of business assets) [TCGA1992, ss 152–160]

A person disposing of a qualifying asset used exclusively for the purposes of a trade who uses the proceeds to purchase other qualifying assets so used may claim to defer the CGT payable by deducting the otherwise chargeable gain from the cost of new assets. Qualifying assets are

(a)   land and buildings occupied and used for the purposes of the trade;
(b)   fixed plant and machinery;
(c)   ships, aircraft and hovercraft;
(d)   satellites, space stations and spacecraft;
(e)   goodwill;
(f)   milk and potato quotas;
(g)   ewe and suckler cow premium quotas;
(h)   fish quotas;
(i)   Lloyd's syndicate capacity;
(j)   payment entitlement under the single payment scheme; and
(k)   (where the disposal of the old asset or the acquisition of the new asset is on or after 20 December 2013) payment entitlement under the basic payment scheme.

Partial relief is available where not all the disposal proceeds are applied in acquiring new qualifying assets. As regards companies only, items (e) to (k) do not apply.

Seed enterprise investment scheme [TCGA 1992, ss 150E-150G, Sch 5BB; FA 2012, Sch 6 paras 2-5; FA 2013, s 57]

A disposal of shares on which SEIS income tax relief has been given and not withdrawn is exempt. Chargeable gains arising on disposals of any assets in 2012/13 can be deferred by a subscription for shares under the SEIS made in 2012/13, up to a maximum relief of £100,000. Deferral is possible only where the SEIS investment qualifies for income tax relief (and such relief is claimed). Deferral relief is also available for 2013/14 onwards but only half of the reinvested amount can be set against chargeable gains. See also page 67.

Share identification rules [TCGA 1992, ss 104–106A; FA 2008, Sch 2]

For disposals by individuals, trustees or personal representatives, shares and securities of the same class in the same company are normally identified with acquisitions in the following order:

- acquisitions on the same day as the disposal;
- acquisitions within 30 days after the day of disposal;
- shares comprised in a single pool incorporating all other shares of the same class, whenever acquired.

The 30-day rule does not apply where the person making the disposal is, or is treated as, neither resident nor ordinarily resident in the UK at the time of acquisition.

Special identification rules apply to shares (or securities) to which enterprise investment scheme relief, seed enterprise investment scheme relief, venture capital trust scheme relief, social investment relief or community investment tax relief is attributable, to shares in respect of which relief has been given (and not withdrawn) under the business expansion scheme, employee shareholder shares, share incentive plan shares and relevant enterprise management incentives shares.

For the purposes of corporation tax on chargeable gains, disposals of shares etc. are identified with acquisitions in the following order:

- same day acquisitions;
- acquisitions within the previous nine days on a first in/first out basis;
- the pool of shares acquired after 31 March 1982;
- any shares held at 31 March 1982;
- any shares acquired on or before 6 April 1965 on a last in/first out basis;
- (if shares disposed of still not fully matched) subsequent acquisitions.

Social investment relief [TCGA 1992, ss 255A-255E, Sch 8B; FA 2014, Sch 12]

A disposal of an asset to which SI income tax relief has been given and not withdrawn is exempt if the asset is held for at least three years. A chargeable gain arising on or after 6 April 2014 and before 6 April 2019 on disposal of any assets can be deferred by an investment which qualifies for SI income tax relief and which is made within the period from one year before to three years after the disposal. See also page 67.

Venture capital trusts [TCGA 1992, ss 151A, 151B, Sch 5C]

An individual's disposals of shares in VCTs are exempt from capital gains tax provided the shares were not *acquired* in excess of the permitted investment limit for any tax year. See page 67.

Capital gains indexation allowances for companies (April 2013 – April 2015)

Month of acquisition	2013 Apr	May	June	July	Aug	Sept	Oct	Nov	Dec	2014 Jan	Feb	Mar	Apr	May	June	July	Aug	Sept	Oct	Nov	Dec	2015 Jan	Feb	Mar	Apr
1982																									
Mar	2.141	2.147	2.143	2.143	2.160	2.171	2.171	2.173	2.190	2.180	2.200	2.207	2.219	2.221	2.226	2.222	2.235	2.243	2.244	2.236	2.241	2.215	2.231	2.236	2.248
Apr	2.079	2.085	2.081	2.081	2.097	2.108	2.108	2.111	2.127	2.117	2.137	2.144	2.155	2.158	2.163	2.159	2.171	2.179	2.180	2.173	2.177	2.152	2.168	2.173	2.184
May	2.057	2.063	2.059	2.059	2.075	2.086	2.086	2.089	2.105	2.095	2.114	2.122	2.133	2.135	2.140	2.136	2.149	2.156	2.157	2.150	2.155	2.129	2.145	2.150	2.161
June	2.048	2.054	2.051	2.051	2.067	2.078	2.078	2.080	2.096	2.086	2.106	2.113	2.124	2.126	2.131	2.128	2.140	2.147	2.148	2.141	2.146	2.120	2.136	2.141	2.152
July	2.047	2.053	2.050	2.050	2.066	2.077	2.077	2.079	2.095	2.085	2.105	2.112	2.123	2.125	2.130	2.127	2.139	2.146	2.147	2.140	2.145	2.119	2.135	2.140	2.151
Aug	2.046	2.052	2.049	2.049	2.065	2.076	2.076	2.078	2.094	2.084	2.104	2.111	2.122	2.124	2.129	2.126	2.138	2.145	2.146	2.139	2.144	2.118	2.134	2.139	2.150
Sept	2.048	2.054	2.051	2.051	2.067	2.078	2.078	2.080	2.096	2.086	2.106	2.113	2.124	2.126	2.131	2.128	2.140	2.147	2.148	2.141	2.146	2.120	2.136	2.141	2.152
Oct	2.033	2.039	2.036	2.036	2.051	2.062	2.062	2.065	2.081	2.071	2.090	2.098	2.109	2.111	2.116	2.112	2.124	2.132	2.133	2.126	2.130	2.105	2.121	2.126	2.137
Nov	2.018	2.024	2.021	2.021	2.036	2.047	2.047	2.050	2.066	2.056	2.075	2.082	2.093	2.096	2.101	2.097	2.109	2.116	2.118	2.110	2.115	2.090	2.105	2.110	2.121
Dec	2.024	2.030	2.026	2.026	2.042	2.053	2.053	2.055	2.071	2.061	2.081	2.088	2.099	2.101	2.106	2.103	2.115	2.122	2.123	2.116	2.121	2.095	2.111	2.116	2.127
1983																									
Jan	2.020	2.026	2.023	2.023	2.038	2.049	2.049	2.052	2.067	2.058	2.077	2.084	2.095	2.098	2.102	2.099	2.111	2.118	2.119	2.112	2.117	2.092	2.107	2.112	2.123
Feb	2.007	2.013	2.010	2.010	2.025	2.036	2.036	2.039	2.054	2.045	2.064	2.071	2.082	2.084	2.089	2.086	2.098	2.105	2.106	2.099	2.104	2.078	2.094	2.099	2.110
Mar	2.002	2.008	2.004	2.004	2.020	2.031	2.031	2.033	2.049	2.039	2.058	2.066	2.076	2.079	2.084	2.080	2.092	2.099	2.100	2.093	2.098	2.073	2.088	2.093	2.104
Apr	1.960	1.966	1.963	1.963	1.978	1.989	1.989	1.991	2.007	1.997	2.016	2.023	2.034	2.036	2.041	2.037	2.049	2.056	2.058	2.050	2.055	2.030	2.046	2.050	2.061
May	1.948	1.954	1.950	1.950	1.966	1.976	1.976	1.979	1.994	1.984	2.003	2.010	2.021	2.023	2.028	2.025	2.036	2.044	2.045	2.038	2.042	2.018	2.033	2.038	2.048
June	1.941	1.947	1.943	1.943	1.958	1.969	1.969	1.971	1.987	1.977	1.996	2.003	2.014	2.016	2.021	2.017	2.029	2.036	2.037	2.030	2.035	2.010	2.026	2.030	2.041
July	1.925	1.931	1.927	1.927	1.943	1.953	1.953	1.956	1.971	1.961	1.980	1.987	1.998	2.000	2.005	2.001	2.013	2.020	2.021	2.014	2.019	1.994	2.009	2.014	2.025
Aug	1.912	1.918	1.914	1.914	1.930	1.940	1.940	1.942	1.958	1.948	1.967	1.974	1.984	1.987	1.991	1.988	2.000	2.007	2.008	2.001	2.005	1.981	1.996	2.001	2.011
Sept	1.899	1.905	1.902	1.902	1.917	1.927	1.927	1.929	1.945	1.935	1.954	1.961	1.971	1.974	1.978	1.975	1.986	1.993	1.994	1.988	1.992	1.968	1.983	1.988	1.998
Oct	1.889	1.895	1.891	1.891	1.906	1.917	1.917	1.919	1.934	1.925	1.943	1.950	1.961	1.963	1.968	1.964	1.976	1.983	1.984	1.977	1.982	1.957	1.972	1.977	1.987
Nov	1.879	1.885	1.881	1.881	1.896	1.907	1.907	1.909	1.924	1.915	1.933	1.940	1.950	1.953	1.957	1.954	1.965	1.972	1.973	1.967	1.971	1.947	1.962	1.967	1.977
Dec	1.871	1.877	1.874	1.874	1.889	1.899	1.899	1.901	1.916	1.907	1.925	1.932	1.943	1.945	1.950	1.946	1.958	1.965	1.966	1.959	1.963	1.939	1.954	1.959	1.969
1984																									
Jan	1.873	1.879	1.875	1.875	1.890	1.901	1.901	1.903	1.918	1.909	1.927	1.934	1.944	1.947	1.951	1.948	1.959	1.966	1.967	1.960	1.965	1.941	1.956	1.960	1.971
Feb	1.861	1.867	1.864	1.864	1.878	1.889	1.889	1.891	1.906	1.897	1.915	1.922	1.932	1.935	1.939	1.936	1.947	1.954	1.955	1.948	1.953	1.929	1.944	1.948	1.959
Mar	1.852	1.858	1.854	1.854	1.869	1.880	1.880	1.882	1.897	1.888	1.906	1.913	1.923	1.925	1.930	1.926	1.938	1.945	1.946	1.939	1.944	1.920	1.934	1.939	1.949
Apr	1.815	1.820	1.817	1.817	1.832	1.842	1.842	1.844	1.859	1.850	1.868	1.874	1.885	1.887	1.891	1.888	1.899	1.906	1.907	1.900	1.905	1.881	1.896	1.900	1.911
May	1.804	1.810	1.806	1.806	1.821	1.831	1.831	1.833	1.848	1.839	1.857	1.864	1.874	1.876	1.881	1.877	1.889	1.895	1.896	1.890	1.894	1.871	1.885	1.890	1.900
June	1.797	1.803	1.799	1.799	1.814	1.824	1.824	1.826	1.841	1.832	1.850	1.856	1.867	1.869	1.873	1.870	1.881	1.888	1.889	1.882	1.887	1.863	1.878	1.882	1.892
July	1.800	1.806	1.802	1.802	1.817	1.827	1.827	1.829	1.844	1.835	1.853	1.860	1.870	1.872	1.877	1.873	1.884	1.891	1.892	1.886	1.890	1.866	1.881	1.886	1.896
Aug	1.774	1.780	1.776	1.776	1.791	1.801	1.801	1.803	1.818	1.809	1.826	1.833	1.843	1.845	1.850	1.846	1.858	1.864	1.865	1.859	1.863	1.840	1.854	1.859	1.869
Sept	1.769	1.774	1.771	1.771	1.785	1.795	1.795	1.798	1.812	1.803	1.821	1.828	1.838	1.840	1.844	1.841	1.852	1.859	1.860	1.853	1.857	1.834	1.849	1.853	1.863
Oct	1.752	1.757	1.754	1.754	1.768	1.778	1.778	1.780	1.795	1.786	1.804	1.810	1.820	1.822	1.827	1.823	1.834	1.841	1.842	1.836	1.840	1.817	1.831	1.836	1.845
Nov	1.743	1.749	1.745	1.745	1.760	1.770	1.770	1.772	1.786	1.777	1.795	1.802	1.811	1.814	1.818	1.815	1.826	1.832	1.833	1.827	1.831	1.808	1.822	1.827	1.837
Dec	1.746	1.751	1.748	1.748	1.762	1.772	1.772	1.774	1.788	1.780	1.797	1.804	1.814	1.816	1.820	1.817	1.828	1.835	1.836	1.829	1.834	1.810	1.825	1.829	1.839

Capital gains indexation allowances for companies (April 2013 – April 2015)

Month of acquisition	2013 Apr	May	June	July	Aug	Sept	Oct	Nov	Dec	2014 Jan	Feb	Mar	Apr	May	June	July	Aug	Sept	Oct	Nov	Dec	2015 Jan	Feb	Mar	Apr
1985																									
Jan	1.736	1.741	1.738	1.738	1.752	1.762	1.762	1.764	1.778	1.770	1.787	1.794	1.804	1.806	1.810	1.807	1.818	1.824	1.826	1.819	1.823	1.800	1.815	1.819	1.829
Feb	1.714	1.719	1.716	1.716	1.730	1.740	1.740	1.742	1.756	1.747	1.765	1.771	1.781	1.783	1.788	1.784	1.795	1.802	1.803	1.796	1.801	1.778	1.792	1.796	1.806
Mar	1.689	1.694	1.691	1.691	1.705	1.714	1.714	1.717	1.731	1.722	1.739	1.746	1.755	1.758	1.762	1.759	1.769	1.776	1.777	1.770	1.775	1.752	1.766	1.770	1.780
Apr	1.632	1.638	1.635	1.635	1.648	1.658	1.658	1.660	1.674	1.665	1.682	1.688	1.698	1.700	1.704	1.701	1.712	1.718	1.719	1.713	1.717	1.695	1.708	1.713	1.722
May	1.621	1.626	1.623	1.623	1.636	1.646	1.646	1.648	1.662	1.653	1.670	1.676	1.686	1.688	1.692	1.689	1.699	1.706	1.707	1.700	1.705	1.683	1.696	1.700	1.710
June	1.615	1.620	1.617	1.617	1.631	1.640	1.640	1.642	1.656	1.647	1.664	1.671	1.680	1.682	1.686	1.683	1.694	1.700	1.701	1.695	1.699	1.677	1.690	1.695	1.704
July	1.620	1.625	1.622	1.622	1.636	1.645	1.645	1.647	1.661	1.652	1.669	1.676	1.685	1.687	1.691	1.688	1.699	1.705	1.706	1.700	1.704	1.682	1.695	1.700	1.709
Aug	1.613	1.618	1.615	1.615	1.629	1.638	1.638	1.640	1.654	1.645	1.662	1.668	1.678	1.680	1.684	1.681	1.691	1.698	1.699	1.692	1.697	1.675	1.688	1.692	1.702
Sept	1.614	1.620	1.616	1.616	1.630	1.639	1.639	1.642	1.655	1.647	1.664	1.670	1.679	1.681	1.686	1.682	1.693	1.699	1.700	1.694	1.698	1.676	1.690	1.694	1.703
Oct	1.610	1.615	1.612	1.612	1.626	1.635	1.635	1.637	1.651	1.643	1.659	1.666	1.675	1.677	1.681	1.678	1.689	1.695	1.696	1.690	1.694	1.672	1.685	1.690	1.699
Nov	1.601	1.606	1.603	1.603	1.617	1.626	1.626	1.628	1.642	1.633	1.650	1.656	1.666	1.668	1.672	1.669	1.679	1.686	1.687	1.680	1.685	1.663	1.676	1.680	1.690
Dec	1.598	1.603	1.600	1.600	1.613	1.623	1.623	1.625	1.638	1.630	1.647	1.653	1.662	1.664	1.669	1.665	1.676	1.682	1.683	1.677	1.681	1.659	1.673	1.677	1.686
1986																									
Jan	1.592	1.597	1.594	1.594	1.608	1.617	1.617	1.619	1.633	1.624	1.641	1.647	1.657	1.659	1.663	1.660	1.670	1.676	1.677	1.671	1.675	1.654	1.667	1.671	1.681
Feb	1.583	1.588	1.585	1.585	1.598	1.608	1.608	1.610	1.623	1.615	1.631	1.638	1.647	1.649	1.653	1.650	1.660	1.667	1.668	1.661	1.666	1.644	1.657	1.661	1.671
Mar	1.579	1.585	1.581	1.581	1.595	1.604	1.604	1.606	1.620	1.611	1.628	1.634	1.643	1.646	1.650	1.647	1.657	1.663	1.664	1.658	1.662	1.640	1.654	1.658	1.667
Apr	1.555	1.560	1.557	1.557	1.570	1.579	1.579	1.581	1.595	1.586	1.603	1.609	1.618	1.620	1.624	1.621	1.631	1.638	1.639	1.632	1.636	1.615	1.628	1.632	1.642
May	1.550	1.555	1.552	1.552	1.565	1.574	1.574	1.577	1.590	1.582	1.598	1.604	1.613	1.615	1.619	1.616	1.627	1.633	1.634	1.628	1.632	1.610	1.624	1.628	1.637
June	1.551	1.556	1.553	1.553	1.567	1.576	1.576	1.578	1.591	1.583	1.599	1.605	1.615	1.617	1.621	1.618	1.628	1.634	1.635	1.629	1.633	1.612	1.625	1.629	1.638
July	1.559	1.564	1.561	1.561	1.574	1.583	1.583	1.585	1.599	1.590	1.607	1.613	1.622	1.624	1.628	1.625	1.635	1.642	1.643	1.636	1.641	1.619	1.632	1.636	1.646
Aug	1.551	1.556	1.553	1.553	1.566	1.575	1.575	1.577	1.590	1.582	1.599	1.605	1.614	1.616	1.620	1.617	1.627	1.633	1.634	1.628	1.632	1.611	1.624	1.628	1.637
Sept	1.538	1.543	1.540	1.540	1.553	1.563	1.563	1.565	1.578	1.570	1.586	1.592	1.601	1.603	1.607	1.604	1.614	1.621	1.622	1.615	1.619	1.598	1.611	1.615	1.625
Oct	1.534	1.539	1.536	1.536	1.549	1.559	1.559	1.561	1.574	1.566	1.582	1.588	1.597	1.599	1.603	1.600	1.610	1.616	1.617	1.611	1.615	1.594	1.607	1.611	1.621
Nov	1.513	1.518	1.515	1.515	1.528	1.537	1.537	1.539	1.552	1.544	1.560	1.566	1.575	1.577	1.581	1.578	1.588	1.594	1.595	1.589	1.593	1.572	1.585	1.589	1.598
Dec	1.505	1.510	1.507	1.507	1.520	1.529	1.529	1.531	1.544	1.536	1.552	1.558	1.567	1.569	1.573	1.570	1.580	1.586	1.587	1.581	1.585	1.564	1.577	1.581	1.590
1987																									
Jan	1.495	1.500	1.497	1.497	1.510	1.519	1.519	1.521	1.534	1.526	1.542	1.548	1.557	1.559	1.563	1.560	1.570	1.576	1.577	1.571	1.575	1.554	1.567	1.571	1.580
Feb	1.485	1.490	1.487	1.487	1.500	1.509	1.509	1.511	1.524	1.516	1.532	1.538	1.547	1.549	1.553	1.550	1.560	1.566	1.567	1.561	1.565	1.544	1.557	1.561	1.570
Mar	1.480	1.485	1.482	1.482	1.495	1.504	1.504	1.506	1.519	1.511	1.527	1.533	1.542	1.544	1.548	1.545	1.555	1.561	1.562	1.556	1.560	1.539	1.552	1.556	1.565
Apr	1.451	1.456	1.453	1.453	1.466	1.474	1.474	1.476	1.489	1.481	1.497	1.503	1.512	1.514	1.518	1.515	1.525	1.530	1.531	1.526	1.529	1.509	1.522	1.526	1.534
May	1.448	1.453	1.450	1.450	1.463	1.472	1.472	1.474	1.487	1.479	1.495	1.500	1.509	1.511	1.515	1.512	1.522	1.528	1.529	1.523	1.527	1.506	1.519	1.523	1.532
June	1.448	1.453	1.450	1.450	1.463	1.472	1.472	1.474	1.487	1.479	1.495	1.500	1.509	1.511	1.515	1.512	1.522	1.528	1.529	1.523	1.527	1.506	1.519	1.523	1.532
July	1.451	1.456	1.453	1.453	1.466	1.474	1.474	1.476	1.489	1.481	1.497	1.503	1.512	1.514	1.518	1.515	1.525	1.530	1.531	1.526	1.529	1.509	1.522	1.526	1.534
Aug	1.444	1.449	1.446	1.446	1.458	1.467	1.467	1.469	1.482	1.474	1.490	1.496	1.504	1.506	1.510	1.507	1.517	1.523	1.524	1.518	1.522	1.501	1.514	1.518	1.527
Sept	1.437	1.441	1.438	1.438	1.451	1.460	1.460	1.462	1.475	1.467	1.482	1.488	1.497	1.499	1.503	1.500	1.510	1.516	1.517	1.511	1.515	1.494	1.507	1.511	1.520
Oct	1.425	1.430	1.427	1.427	1.439	1.448	1.448	1.450	1.463	1.455	1.470	1.476	1.485	1.487	1.491	1.488	1.498	1.503	1.504	1.499	1.502	1.482	1.495	1.499	1.507
Nov	1.413	1.418	1.415	1.415	1.427	1.436	1.436	1.438	1.451	1.443	1.458	1.464	1.473	1.475	1.479	1.476	1.485	1.491	1.492	1.486	1.490	1.470	1.483	1.486	1.495
Dec	1.415	1.420	1.417	1.417	1.430	1.439	1.439	1.440	1.453	1.445	1.461	1.467	1.475	1.477	1.481	1.478	1.488	1.494	1.495	1.489	1.493	1.472	1.485	1.489	1.498

Capital gains indexation allowances for companies (April 2013 – April 2015)

Month of acquisition	2013 Apr	May	June	July	Aug	Sept	Oct	Nov	Dec	2014 Jan	Feb	Mar	Apr	May	June	July	Aug	Sept	Oct	Nov	Dec	2015 Jan	Feb	Mar	Apr
1988																									
Jan	1.415	1.420	1.417	1.417	1.430	1.439	1.439	1.440	1.453	1.445	1.461	1.467	1.475	1.477	1.481	1.478	1.488	1.494	1.495	1.489	1.493	1.472	1.485	1.489	1.498
Feb	1.406	1.411	1.408	1.408	1.420	1.429	1.429	1.431	1.444	1.436	1.451	1.457	1.466	1.468	1.472	1.469	1.478	1.484	1.485	1.479	1.483	1.463	1.475	1.479	1.488
Mar	1.397	1.402	1.399	1.399	1.411	1.420	1.420	1.422	1.434	1.427	1.442	1.448	1.456	1.458	1.462	1.459	1.469	1.475	1.476	1.470	1.474	1.453	1.466	1.470	1.478
Apr	1.358	1.363	1.360	1.360	1.372	1.381	1.381	1.383	1.395	1.388	1.403	1.408	1.417	1.419	1.422	1.420	1.429	1.435	1.436	1.430	1.434	1.414	1.426	1.430	1.439
May	1.349	1.354	1.351	1.351	1.363	1.372	1.372	1.374	1.386	1.379	1.394	1.399	1.408	1.410	1.413	1.411	1.420	1.426	1.427	1.421	1.425	1.405	1.417	1.421	1.429
June	1.341	1.345	1.342	1.342	1.355	1.363	1.363	1.365	1.377	1.370	1.385	1.390	1.399	1.401	1.404	1.402	1.411	1.417	1.417	1.412	1.416	1.396	1.408	1.412	1.420
July	1.338	1.343	1.340	1.340	1.352	1.361	1.361	1.363	1.375	1.367	1.382	1.388	1.396	1.398	1.402	1.399	1.409	1.414	1.415	1.410	1.413	1.394	1.406	1.410	1.418
Aug	1.312	1.317	1.314	1.314	1.326	1.335	1.335	1.336	1.348	1.341	1.356	1.361	1.370	1.372	1.375	1.373	1.382	1.387	1.388	1.383	1.386	1.367	1.379	1.383	1.391
Sept	1.302	1.306	1.304	1.304	1.315	1.324	1.324	1.326	1.338	1.330	1.345	1.351	1.359	1.361	1.364	1.362	1.371	1.376	1.377	1.372	1.375	1.356	1.368	1.372	1.380
Oct	1.279	1.283	1.280	1.280	1.292	1.300	1.300	1.302	1.314	1.307	1.321	1.327	1.335	1.337	1.341	1.338	1.347	1.353	1.353	1.348	1.352	1.332	1.344	1.348	1.356
Nov	1.268	1.273	1.270	1.270	1.282	1.290	1.290	1.292	1.304	1.296	1.311	1.316	1.325	1.326	1.330	1.327	1.336	1.342	1.343	1.337	1.341	1.322	1.334	1.337	1.345
Dec	1.262	1.267	1.264	1.264	1.276	1.284	1.284	1.286	1.297	1.290	1.305	1.310	1.318	1.320	1.324	1.321	1.330	1.335	1.336	1.331	1.335	1.316	1.327	1.331	1.339
1989																									
Jan	1.248	1.252	1.250	1.250	1.261	1.269	1.269	1.271	1.283	1.276	1.290	1.295	1.304	1.305	1.309	1.306	1.315	1.321	1.322	1.316	1.320	1.301	1.313	1.316	1.324
Feb	1.232	1.236	1.233	1.233	1.245	1.253	1.253	1.255	1.267	1.259	1.274	1.279	1.287	1.289	1.292	1.290	1.299	1.304	1.305	1.300	1.303	1.284	1.296	1.300	1.308
Mar	1.222	1.226	1.224	1.224	1.235	1.243	1.243	1.245	1.256	1.249	1.264	1.269	1.277	1.279	1.282	1.280	1.289	1.294	1.295	1.289	1.293	1.274	1.286	1.289	1.297
Apr	1.183	1.187	1.185	1.185	1.196	1.204	1.204	1.206	1.217	1.210	1.224	1.229	1.237	1.239	1.242	1.240	1.248	1.254	1.255	1.249	1.253	1.234	1.246	1.249	1.257
May	1.170	1.174	1.171	1.171	1.183	1.190	1.190	1.192	1.203	1.197	1.210	1.216	1.223	1.225	1.229	1.226	1.235	1.240	1.241	1.236	1.239	1.221	1.232	1.236	1.243
June	1.162	1.166	1.164	1.164	1.175	1.183	1.183	1.185	1.196	1.189	1.203	1.208	1.216	1.218	1.221	1.218	1.227	1.232	1.233	1.228	1.231	1.213	1.224	1.228	1.236
July	1.160	1.165	1.162	1.162	1.173	1.181	1.181	1.183	1.194	1.187	1.201	1.206	1.214	1.216	1.219	1.216	1.225	1.230	1.231	1.226	1.229	1.211	1.223	1.226	1.234
Aug	1.155	1.159	1.156	1.156	1.168	1.175	1.175	1.177	1.188	1.181	1.195	1.200	1.208	1.210	1.213	1.211	1.219	1.225	1.225	1.220	1.224	1.206	1.217	1.220	1.228
Sept	1.140	1.144	1.142	1.142	1.153	1.160	1.160	1.162	1.173	1.166	1.180	1.185	1.193	1.195	1.198	1.196	1.204	1.209	1.210	1.205	1.208	1.190	1.202	1.205	1.213
Oct	1.123	1.128	1.125	1.125	1.136	1.144	1.144	1.146	1.157	1.150	1.163	1.169	1.176	1.178	1.181	1.179	1.187	1.192	1.193	1.188	1.191	1.174	1.185	1.188	1.196
Nov	1.105	1.110	1.107	1.107	1.118	1.126	1.126	1.127	1.138	1.132	1.145	1.150	1.158	1.159	1.163	1.160	1.169	1.174	1.175	1.170	1.173	1.155	1.166	1.170	1.177
Dec	1.100	1.104	1.102	1.102	1.113	1.120	1.120	1.122	1.133	1.126	1.140	1.145	1.152	1.154	1.157	1.155	1.163	1.168	1.169	1.164	1.168	1.150	1.161	1.164	1.172
1990																									
Jan	1.088	1.092	1.090	1.090	1.100	1.108	1.108	1.110	1.121	1.114	1.127	1.132	1.140	1.141	1.145	1.142	1.151	1.156	1.156	1.151	1.155	1.137	1.148	1.151	1.159
Feb	1.076	1.080	1.077	1.077	1.088	1.096	1.096	1.097	1.108	1.101	1.115	1.120	1.127	1.129	1.132	1.130	1.138	1.143	1.144	1.139	1.142	1.125	1.136	1.139	1.146
Mar	1.055	1.059	1.057	1.057	1.068	1.075	1.075	1.077	1.087	1.081	1.094	1.099	1.106	1.108	1.111	1.109	1.117	1.122	1.123	1.118	1.121	1.104	1.114	1.118	1.125
Apr	0.994	0.998	0.996	0.996	1.006	1.014	1.014	1.015	1.026	1.019	1.032	1.037	1.044	1.046	1.049	1.046	1.054	1.059	1.060	1.055	1.058	1.042	1.052	1.055	1.062
May	0.977	0.981	0.979	0.979	0.989	0.996	0.996	0.998	1.008	1.002	1.014	1.019	1.026	1.028	1.031	1.029	1.036	1.041	1.042	1.037	1.040	1.024	1.034	1.037	1.044
June	0.969	0.973	0.971	0.971	0.981	0.988	0.988	0.990	1.000	0.994	1.006	1.011	1.018	1.020	1.023	1.021	1.028	1.033	1.034	1.029	1.032	1.016	1.026	1.029	1.036
July	0.968	0.972	0.969	0.969	0.979	0.987	0.987	0.988	0.998	0.992	1.005	1.009	1.017	1.018	1.021	1.019	1.027	1.032	1.032	1.028	1.031	1.014	1.024	1.028	1.035
Aug	0.948	0.952	0.949	0.949	0.959	0.966	0.966	0.968	0.978	0.972	0.984	0.989	0.996	0.998	1.001	0.998	1.006	1.011	1.012	1.007	1.010	0.994	1.004	1.007	1.014
Sept	0.930	0.933	0.931	0.931	0.941	0.948	0.948	0.950	0.960	0.954	0.966	0.971	0.978	0.979	0.982	0.980	0.988	0.992	0.993	0.988	0.991	0.975	0.985	0.988	0.995
Oct	0.915	0.919	0.916	0.916	0.926	0.933	0.933	0.935	0.945	0.939	0.951	0.955	0.962	0.964	0.967	0.965	0.972	0.977	0.978	0.973	0.976	0.960	0.970	0.973	0.980
Nov	0.919	0.923	0.921	0.921	0.931	0.938	0.938	0.939	0.949	0.943	0.955	0.960	0.967	0.968	0.972	0.969	0.977	0.982	0.982	0.978	0.981	0.965	0.975	0.978	0.985
Dec	0.921	0.925	0.922	0.922	0.932	0.939	0.939	0.941	0.951	0.945	0.957	0.962	0.968	0.970	0.973	0.971	0.978	0.983	0.984	0.979	0.982	0.966	0.976	0.979	0.986

Capital gains indexation allowances for companies (April 2013 – April 2015)

Month of acquisition	2013									2014												2015			
	Apr	May	June	July	Aug	Sept	Oct	Nov	Dec	Jan	Feb	Mar	Apr	May	June	July	Aug	Sept	Oct	Nov	Dec	Jan	Feb	Mar	Apr
1991																									
Jan	0.916	0.920	0.918	0.918	0.928	0.935	0.935	0.936	0.946	0.940	0.952	0.957	0.964	0.965	0.969	0.966	0.974	0.978	0.979	0.975	0.978	0.962	0.972	0.975	0.982
Feb	0.906	0.910	0.908	0.908	0.917	0.924	0.924	0.926	0.936	0.930	0.942	0.947	0.953	0.955	0.958	0.956	0.963	0.968	0.969	0.964	0.967	0.951	0.961	0.964	0.971
Mar	0.899	0.903	0.900	0.900	0.910	0.917	0.917	0.919	0.928	0.922	0.935	0.939	0.946	0.947	0.951	0.948	0.956	0.960	0.961	0.957	0.960	0.944	0.954	0.957	0.963
Apr	0.875	0.878	0.876	0.876	0.886	0.893	0.893	0.894	0.904	0.898	0.910	0.914	0.921	0.923	0.926	0.923	0.931	0.935	0.936	0.932	0.935	0.919	0.929	0.932	0.938
May	0.869	0.873	0.870	0.870	0.880	0.887	0.887	0.888	0.898	0.892	0.904	0.909	0.915	0.917	0.920	0.918	0.925	0.930	0.930	0.926	0.929	0.913	0.923	0.926	0.933
June	0.861	0.864	0.862	0.862	0.872	0.878	0.878	0.880	0.890	0.884	0.896	0.900	0.907	0.908	0.911	0.909	0.916	0.921	0.922	0.917	0.920	0.905	0.914	0.917	0.924
July	0.865	0.868	0.866	0.866	0.876	0.883	0.883	0.884	0.894	0.888	0.900	0.904	0.911	0.913	0.916	0.913	0.921	0.925	0.926	0.922	0.925	0.909	0.919	0.922	0.928
Aug	0.861	0.864	0.862	0.862	0.872	0.878	0.878	0.880	0.890	0.884	0.896	0.900	0.907	0.908	0.911	0.909	0.916	0.921	0.922	0.917	0.920	0.905	0.914	0.917	0.924
Sept	0.854	0.857	0.855	0.855	0.865	0.871	0.871	0.873	0.883	0.877	0.889	0.893	0.900	0.901	0.904	0.902	0.909	0.914	0.915	0.910	0.913	0.897	0.907	0.910	0.917
Oct	0.847	0.850	0.848	0.848	0.858	0.865	0.865	0.866	0.876	0.870	0.882	0.886	0.893	0.894	0.897	0.895	0.902	0.907	0.907	0.903	0.906	0.890	0.900	0.903	0.910
Nov	0.840	0.844	0.841	0.841	0.851	0.858	0.858	0.859	0.869	0.863	0.875	0.879	0.886	0.887	0.890	0.888	0.895	0.900	0.900	0.896	0.899	0.883	0.893	0.896	0.903
Dec	0.839	0.842	0.840	0.840	0.850	0.856	0.856	0.858	0.867	0.861	0.873	0.878	0.884	0.886	0.889	0.887	0.894	0.898	0.899	0.895	0.898	0.882	0.892	0.895	0.901
1992																									
Jan	0.840	0.844	0.841	0.841	0.851	0.858	0.858	0.859	0.869	0.863	0.875	0.879	0.886	0.887	0.890	0.888	0.895	0.900	0.900	0.896	0.899	0.883	0.893	0.896	0.903
Feb	0.831	0.834	0.832	0.832	0.842	0.848	0.848	0.850	0.859	0.853	0.865	0.869	0.876	0.877	0.880	0.878	0.886	0.890	0.891	0.886	0.889	0.874	0.883	0.886	0.893
Mar	0.825	0.829	0.827	0.827	0.836	0.843	0.843	0.844	0.854	0.848	0.860	0.864	0.871	0.872	0.875	0.873	0.880	0.884	0.885	0.881	0.884	0.868	0.878	0.881	0.887
Apr	0.798	0.801	0.799	0.799	0.808	0.815	0.815	0.816	0.826	0.820	0.831	0.836	0.842	0.844	0.847	0.844	0.852	0.856	0.857	0.852	0.855	0.840	0.849	0.852	0.859
May	0.791	0.795	0.793	0.793	0.802	0.808	0.808	0.810	0.819	0.813	0.825	0.829	0.836	0.837	0.840	0.838	0.845	0.849	0.850	0.846	0.849	0.833	0.843	0.846	0.852
June	0.791	0.795	0.793	0.793	0.802	0.808	0.808	0.810	0.819	0.813	0.825	0.829	0.836	0.837	0.840	0.838	0.845	0.849	0.850	0.846	0.849	0.833	0.843	0.846	0.852
July	0.798	0.801	0.799	0.799	0.808	0.815	0.815	0.816	0.826	0.820	0.831	0.836	0.842	0.844	0.847	0.844	0.852	0.856	0.857	0.852	0.855	0.840	0.849	0.852	0.859
Aug	0.796	0.800	0.798	0.798	0.807	0.814	0.814	0.815	0.824	0.819	0.830	0.834	0.841	0.842	0.845	0.843	0.850	0.855	0.855	0.851	0.854	0.839	0.848	0.851	0.857
Sept	0.790	0.793	0.791	0.791	0.801	0.807	0.807	0.808	0.818	0.812	0.824	0.828	0.834	0.836	0.839	0.836	0.844	0.848	0.849	0.844	0.847	0.832	0.841	0.844	0.851
Oct	0.783	0.787	0.785	0.785	0.794	0.801	0.801	0.802	0.811	0.806	0.817	0.821	0.828	0.829	0.832	0.830	0.837	0.841	0.842	0.838	0.841	0.826	0.835	0.838	0.844
Nov	0.786	0.790	0.787	0.787	0.797	0.803	0.803	0.805	0.814	0.808	0.820	0.824	0.830	0.832	0.835	0.832	0.840	0.844	0.845	0.840	0.843	0.828	0.838	0.840	0.847
Dec	0.792	0.796	0.794	0.794	0.803	0.810	0.810	0.811	0.820	0.815	0.826	0.830	0.837	0.838	0.841	0.839	0.846	0.851	0.851	0.847	0.850	0.835	0.844	0.847	0.853
1993																									
Jan	0.809	0.813	0.811	0.811	0.820	0.827	0.827	0.828	0.838	0.832	0.843	0.848	0.854	0.856	0.859	0.856	0.864	0.868	0.869	0.864	0.867	0.852	0.861	0.864	0.871
Feb	0.798	0.801	0.799	0.799	0.808	0.815	0.815	0.816	0.826	0.820	0.831	0.836	0.842	0.844	0.847	0.844	0.852	0.856	0.857	0.852	0.855	0.840	0.849	0.852	0.859
Mar	0.791	0.795	0.793	0.793	0.802	0.808	0.808	0.810	0.819	0.813	0.825	0.829	0.836	0.837	0.840	0.838	0.845	0.849	0.850	0.846	0.849	0.833	0.843	0.846	0.852
Apr	0.775	0.778	0.776	0.776	0.785	0.792	0.792	0.793	0.802	0.797	0.808	0.812	0.819	0.820	0.823	0.821	0.828	0.832	0.833	0.829	0.831	0.817	0.826	0.829	0.835
May	0.768	0.772	0.770	0.770	0.779	0.785	0.785	0.787	0.796	0.790	0.802	0.806	0.812	0.814	0.816	0.814	0.821	0.826	0.826	0.822	0.825	0.810	0.819	0.822	0.828
June	0.770	0.773	0.771	0.771	0.780	0.787	0.787	0.788	0.797	0.791	0.803	0.807	0.813	0.815	0.818	0.816	0.823	0.827	0.828	0.823	0.826	0.811	0.821	0.823	0.830
July	0.773	0.777	0.775	0.775	0.784	0.790	0.790	0.792	0.801	0.795	0.807	0.811	0.817	0.819	0.822	0.819	0.827	0.831	0.832	0.827	0.830	0.815	0.824	0.827	0.834
Aug	0.766	0.769	0.767	0.767	0.776	0.783	0.783	0.784	0.793	0.788	0.799	0.803	0.810	0.811	0.814	0.812	0.819	0.823	0.824	0.820	0.822	0.808	0.817	0.820	0.826
Sept	0.758	0.762	0.760	0.760	0.769	0.775	0.775	0.777	0.786	0.780	0.791	0.796	0.802	0.803	0.806	0.804	0.811	0.815	0.816	0.812	0.815	0.800	0.809	0.812	0.818
Oct	0.760	0.763	0.761	0.761	0.770	0.776	0.776	0.778	0.787	0.781	0.793	0.797	0.803	0.805	0.807	0.805	0.812	0.817	0.817	0.813	0.816	0.801	0.810	0.813	0.819
Nov	0.762	0.766	0.763	0.763	0.773	0.779	0.779	0.780	0.790	0.784	0.795	0.799	0.806	0.807	0.810	0.808	0.815	0.819	0.820	0.816	0.819	0.804	0.813	0.816	0.822
Dec	0.758	0.762	0.760	0.760	0.769	0.775	0.775	0.777	0.786	0.780	0.791	0.796	0.802	0.803	0.806	0.804	0.811	0.815	0.816	0.812	0.815	0.800	0.809	0.812	0.818

Capital gains indexation allowances for companies (April 2013 – April 2015)

Month of acquisition	2013 Apr	May	June	July	Aug	Sept	Oct	Nov	Dec	2014 Jan	Feb	Mar	Apr	May	June	July	Aug	Sept	Oct	Nov	Dec	2015 Jan	Feb	Mar	Apr
1994																									
Jan	0.766	0.769	0.767	0.767	0.776	0.783	0.783	0.784	0.793	0.788	0.799	0.803	0.810	0.811	0.814	0.812	0.819	0.823	0.824	0.820	0.822	0.808	0.817	0.820	0.826
Feb	0.756	0.759	0.757	0.757	0.766	0.773	0.773	0.774	0.783	0.778	0.789	0.793	0.799	0.801	0.804	0.802	0.809	0.813	0.814	0.809	0.812	0.797	0.806	0.809	0.816
Mar	0.751	0.754	0.752	0.752	0.761	0.768	0.768	0.769	0.778	0.773	0.784	0.788	0.794	0.796	0.799	0.796	0.804	0.808	0.808	0.804	0.807	0.792	0.801	0.804	0.811
Apr	0.730	0.734	0.732	0.732	0.741	0.747	0.747	0.748	0.757	0.752	0.763	0.767	0.773	0.775	0.777	0.775	0.782	0.786	0.787	0.783	0.786	0.771	0.780	0.783	0.789
May	0.724	0.728	0.726	0.726	0.735	0.741	0.741	0.742	0.751	0.746	0.757	0.761	0.767	0.768	0.771	0.769	0.776	0.780	0.781	0.777	0.780	0.765	0.774	0.777	0.783
June	0.724	0.728	0.726	0.726	0.735	0.741	0.741	0.742	0.751	0.746	0.757	0.761	0.767	0.768	0.771	0.769	0.776	0.780	0.781	0.777	0.780	0.765	0.774	0.777	0.783
July	0.733	0.736	0.734	0.734	0.743	0.749	0.749	0.751	0.760	0.754	0.765	0.769	0.776	0.777	0.780	0.778	0.785	0.789	0.790	0.785	0.788	0.774	0.783	0.785	0.792
Aug	0.724	0.728	0.726	0.726	0.735	0.741	0.741	0.742	0.751	0.746	0.757	0.761	0.767	0.768	0.771	0.769	0.776	0.780	0.781	0.777	0.780	0.765	0.774	0.777	0.783
Sept	0.721	0.724	0.722	0.722	0.731	0.737	0.737	0.739	0.748	0.742	0.753	0.757	0.763	0.765	0.768	0.766	0.772	0.777	0.777	0.773	0.776	0.761	0.770	0.773	0.779
Oct	0.718	0.722	0.720	0.720	0.729	0.735	0.735	0.736	0.745	0.740	0.751	0.755	0.761	0.762	0.765	0.763	0.770	0.774	0.775	0.771	0.773	0.759	0.768	0.771	0.777
Nov	0.717	0.721	0.719	0.719	0.727	0.734	0.734	0.735	0.744	0.738	0.749	0.754	0.760	0.761	0.764	0.762	0.769	0.773	0.774	0.769	0.772	0.758	0.767	0.769	0.776
Dec	0.709	0.712	0.710	0.710	0.719	0.725	0.725	0.727	0.736	0.730	0.741	0.745	0.751	0.753	0.755	0.753	0.760	0.764	0.765	0.761	0.764	0.749	0.758	0.761	0.767
1995																									
Jan	0.709	0.712	0.710	0.710	0.719	0.725	0.725	0.727	0.736	0.730	0.741	0.745	0.751	0.753	0.755	0.753	0.760	0.764	0.765	0.761	0.764	0.749	0.758	0.761	0.767
Feb	0.698	0.702	0.700	0.700	0.709	0.715	0.715	0.716	0.725	0.720	0.730	0.735	0.741	0.742	0.745	0.743	0.749	0.754	0.754	0.750	0.753	0.739	0.747	0.750	0.756
Mar	0.692	0.695	0.693	0.693	0.702	0.708	0.708	0.709	0.718	0.713	0.723	0.727	0.734	0.735	0.738	0.736	0.742	0.746	0.747	0.743	0.746	0.732	0.740	0.743	0.749
Apr	0.674	0.678	0.676	0.676	0.685	0.691	0.691	0.692	0.701	0.695	0.706	0.710	0.716	0.717	0.720	0.718	0.725	0.729	0.730	0.726	0.728	0.714	0.723	0.726	0.732
May	0.668	0.671	0.669	0.669	0.678	0.684	0.684	0.685	0.694	0.689	0.699	0.703	0.709	0.711	0.713	0.711	0.718	0.722	0.723	0.719	0.721	0.707	0.716	0.719	0.725
June	0.666	0.669	0.667	0.667	0.676	0.682	0.682	0.683	0.692	0.686	0.697	0.701	0.707	0.708	0.711	0.709	0.716	0.720	0.720	0.716	0.719	0.705	0.714	0.716	0.722
July	0.673	0.677	0.675	0.675	0.683	0.689	0.689	0.691	0.700	0.694	0.705	0.709	0.715	0.716	0.719	0.717	0.724	0.728	0.728	0.724	0.727	0.713	0.722	0.724	0.730
Aug	0.664	0.668	0.666	0.666	0.674	0.680	0.680	0.682	0.690	0.685	0.696	0.700	0.706	0.707	0.710	0.708	0.714	0.718	0.719	0.715	0.718	0.704	0.712	0.715	0.721
Sept	0.657	0.660	0.658	0.658	0.667	0.673	0.673	0.674	0.683	0.677	0.688	0.692	0.698	0.699	0.702	0.700	0.707	0.710	0.711	0.707	0.710	0.696	0.705	0.707	0.713
Oct	0.666	0.669	0.667	0.667	0.676	0.682	0.682	0.683	0.692	0.686	0.697	0.701	0.707	0.708	0.711	0.709	0.716	0.720	0.720	0.716	0.719	0.705	0.714	0.716	0.722
Nov	0.666	0.669	0.667	0.667	0.676	0.682	0.682	0.683	0.692	0.686	0.697	0.701	0.707	0.708	0.711	0.709	0.716	0.720	0.720	0.716	0.719	0.705	0.714	0.716	0.722
Dec	0.656	0.659	0.657	0.657	0.666	0.672	0.672	0.673	0.681	0.676	0.687	0.691	0.697	0.698	0.701	0.699	0.705	0.709	0.710	0.706	0.709	0.695	0.703	0.706	0.712
1996																									
Jan	0.661	0.664	0.662	0.662	0.671	0.677	0.677	0.678	0.687	0.682	0.692	0.696	0.702	0.704	0.706	0.704	0.711	0.715	0.716	0.712	0.714	0.700	0.709	0.712	0.718
Feb	0.653	0.657	0.655	0.655	0.663	0.669	0.669	0.671	0.679	0.674	0.685	0.689	0.694	0.696	0.698	0.696	0.703	0.707	0.708	0.704	0.706	0.693	0.701	0.704	0.710
Mar	0.647	0.650	0.648	0.648	0.657	0.663	0.663	0.664	0.673	0.667	0.678	0.682	0.688	0.689	0.692	0.690	0.696	0.700	0.701	0.697	0.700	0.686	0.694	0.697	0.703
Apr	0.635	0.638	0.636	0.636	0.645	0.651	0.651	0.652	0.661	0.655	0.666	0.670	0.676	0.677	0.680	0.678	0.684	0.688	0.689	0.685	0.687	0.674	0.682	0.685	0.691
May	0.632	0.635	0.633	0.633	0.642	0.647	0.647	0.649	0.657	0.652	0.663	0.666	0.672	0.674	0.676	0.674	0.681	0.685	0.685	0.681	0.684	0.670	0.679	0.681	0.687
June	0.631	0.634	0.632	0.632	0.641	0.646	0.646	0.648	0.656	0.651	0.661	0.665	0.671	0.673	0.675	0.673	0.680	0.684	0.684	0.680	0.683	0.669	0.678	0.680	0.686
July	0.637	0.640	0.638	0.638	0.647	0.653	0.653	0.654	0.663	0.657	0.668	0.672	0.678	0.679	0.682	0.680	0.686	0.690	0.691	0.687	0.690	0.676	0.684	0.687	0.693
Aug	0.630	0.633	0.631	0.631	0.639	0.645	0.645	0.647	0.655	0.650	0.660	0.664	0.670	0.671	0.674	0.672	0.679	0.683	0.683	0.679	0.682	0.668	0.677	0.679	0.685
Sept	0.622	0.625	0.624	0.624	0.632	0.638	0.638	0.639	0.648	0.642	0.653	0.657	0.663	0.664	0.666	0.664	0.671	0.675	0.676	0.672	0.674	0.661	0.669	0.672	0.678
Oct	0.622	0.625	0.624	0.624	0.632	0.638	0.638	0.639	0.648	0.642	0.653	0.657	0.663	0.664	0.666	0.664	0.671	0.675	0.676	0.672	0.674	0.661	0.669	0.672	0.678
Nov	0.621	0.624	0.622	0.622	0.631	0.637	0.637	0.638	0.647	0.641	0.652	0.656	0.661	0.663	0.665	0.663	0.670	0.674	0.674	0.671	0.673	0.660	0.668	0.671	0.676
Dec	0.616	0.619	0.617	0.617	0.626	0.631	0.631	0.633	0.641	0.636	0.646	0.650	0.656	0.657	0.660	0.658	0.665	0.668	0.669	0.665	0.668	0.654	0.663	0.665	0.671

Capital gains indexation allowances for companies (April 2013 – April 2015)

Month of acquisition	2013 Apr	May	June	July	Aug	Sept	Oct	Nov	Dec	2014 Jan	Feb	Mar	Apr	May	June	July	Aug	Sept	Oct	Nov	Dec	2015 Jan	Feb	Mar	Apr
1997																									
Jan	0.616	0.619	0.617	0.617	0.626	0.631	0.631	0.633	0.641	0.636	0.646	0.650	0.656	0.657	0.660	0.658	0.665	0.668	0.669	0.665	0.668	0.654	0.663	0.665	0.671
Feb	0.610	0.613	0.611	0.611	0.619	0.625	0.625	0.626	0.635	0.630	0.640	0.644	0.650	0.651	0.654	0.652	0.658	0.662	0.663	0.659	0.661	0.648	0.656	0.659	0.665
Mar	0.606	0.609	0.607	0.607	0.615	0.621	0.621	0.622	0.631	0.625	0.636	0.640	0.645	0.647	0.649	0.647	0.654	0.658	0.658	0.654	0.657	0.644	0.652	0.654	0.660
Apr	0.596	0.599	0.598	0.598	0.606	0.612	0.612	0.613	0.621	0.616	0.626	0.630	0.636	0.637	0.640	0.638	0.644	0.648	0.649	0.645	0.647	0.634	0.642	0.645	0.651
May	0.590	0.593	0.591	0.591	0.600	0.605	0.605	0.607	0.615	0.610	0.620	0.624	0.630	0.631	0.634	0.632	0.638	0.642	0.642	0.639	0.641	0.628	0.636	0.639	0.644
June	0.584	0.587	0.585	0.585	0.594	0.599	0.599	0.601	0.609	0.604	0.614	0.618	0.623	0.625	0.627	0.625	0.632	0.636	0.636	0.632	0.635	0.622	0.630	0.632	0.638
July	0.584	0.587	0.585	0.585	0.594	0.599	0.599	0.601	0.609	0.604	0.614	0.618	0.623	0.625	0.627	0.625	0.632	0.636	0.636	0.632	0.635	0.622	0.630	0.632	0.638
Aug	0.574	0.577	0.575	0.575	0.584	0.589	0.589	0.591	0.599	0.594	0.604	0.608	0.613	0.615	0.617	0.615	0.621	0.625	0.626	0.622	0.625	0.611	0.620	0.622	0.628
Sept	0.566	0.569	0.567	0.567	0.576	0.581	0.581	0.583	0.591	0.586	0.596	0.599	0.605	0.606	0.609	0.607	0.613	0.617	0.618	0.614	0.616	0.603	0.611	0.614	0.620
Oct	0.564	0.567	0.566	0.566	0.574	0.579	0.579	0.581	0.589	0.584	0.594	0.597	0.603	0.604	0.607	0.605	0.611	0.615	0.616	0.612	0.614	0.601	0.609	0.612	0.618
Nov	0.563	0.566	0.565	0.565	0.573	0.578	0.578	0.580	0.588	0.583	0.593	0.596	0.602	0.603	0.606	0.604	0.610	0.614	0.615	0.611	0.613	0.600	0.608	0.611	0.617
Dec	0.559	0.563	0.561	0.561	0.569	0.574	0.574	0.576	0.584	0.579	0.589	0.593	0.598	0.599	0.602	0.600	0.606	0.610	0.611	0.607	0.609	0.596	0.604	0.607	0.613
1998																									
Jan	0.564	0.567	0.566	0.566	0.574	0.579	0.579	0.581	0.589	0.584	0.594	0.597	0.603	0.604	0.607	0.605	0.611	0.615	0.616	0.612	0.614	0.601	0.609	0.612	0.618
Feb	0.556	0.560	0.558	0.558	0.566	0.571	0.571	0.573	0.581	0.576	0.586	0.590	0.595	0.596	0.599	0.597	0.603	0.607	0.608	0.604	0.606	0.593	0.601	0.604	0.609
Mar	0.552	0.555	0.553	0.553	0.561	0.567	0.567	0.568	0.576	0.571	0.581	0.585	0.590	0.591	0.594	0.592	0.598	0.602	0.603	0.599	0.601	0.588	0.596	0.599	0.604
Apr	0.534	0.538	0.536	0.536	0.544	0.549	0.549	0.550	0.558	0.554	0.563	0.567	0.573	0.574	0.576	0.574	0.581	0.584	0.585	0.581	0.584	0.571	0.579	0.581	0.587
May	0.526	0.529	0.527	0.527	0.535	0.541	0.541	0.542	0.550	0.545	0.555	0.558	0.564	0.565	0.568	0.566	0.572	0.576	0.576	0.572	0.575	0.562	0.570	0.572	0.578
June	0.527	0.530	0.528	0.528	0.536	0.542	0.542	0.543	0.551	0.546	0.556	0.559	0.565	0.566	0.569	0.567	0.573	0.576	0.577	0.573	0.576	0.563	0.571	0.573	0.579
July	0.531	0.534	0.532	0.532	0.540	0.545	0.545	0.547	0.555	0.550	0.560	0.563	0.569	0.570	0.572	0.571	0.577	0.580	0.581	0.577	0.580	0.567	0.575	0.577	0.583
Aug	0.524	0.527	0.525	0.525	0.533	0.539	0.539	0.540	0.548	0.543	0.553	0.557	0.562	0.563	0.566	0.564	0.570	0.574	0.574	0.571	0.573	0.560	0.568	0.571	0.576
Sept	0.518	0.521	0.519	0.519	0.527	0.532	0.532	0.533	0.541	0.536	0.546	0.550	0.555	0.557	0.559	0.557	0.563	0.567	0.568	0.564	0.566	0.554	0.561	0.564	0.569
Oct	0.517	0.520	0.518	0.518	0.526	0.531	0.531	0.533	0.540	0.536	0.545	0.549	0.554	0.556	0.558	0.556	0.562	0.566	0.567	0.563	0.565	0.553	0.560	0.563	0.568
Nov	0.518	0.521	0.519	0.519	0.527	0.532	0.532	0.533	0.541	0.536	0.546	0.550	0.555	0.557	0.559	0.557	0.563	0.567	0.568	0.564	0.566	0.554	0.561	0.564	0.569
Dec	0.518	0.521	0.519	0.519	0.527	0.532	0.532	0.533	0.541	0.536	0.546	0.550	0.555	0.557	0.559	0.557	0.563	0.567	0.568	0.564	0.566	0.554	0.561	0.564	0.569
1999																									
Jan	0.527	0.530	0.528	0.528	0.536	0.542	0.542	0.543	0.551	0.546	0.556	0.559	0.565	0.566	0.569	0.567	0.573	0.576	0.577	0.573	0.576	0.563	0.571	0.573	0.579
Feb	0.524	0.527	0.525	0.525	0.533	0.539	0.539	0.540	0.548	0.543	0.553	0.557	0.562	0.563	0.566	0.564	0.570	0.574	0.574	0.571	0.573	0.560	0.568	0.571	0.576
Mar	0.520	0.523	0.522	0.522	0.530	0.535	0.535	0.536	0.544	0.539	0.549	0.553	0.558	0.559	0.562	0.560	0.566	0.570	0.570	0.567	0.569	0.556	0.564	0.567	0.572
Apr	0.510	0.513	0.512	0.512	0.519	0.525	0.525	0.526	0.534	0.529	0.539	0.542	0.548	0.549	0.551	0.550	0.556	0.559	0.560	0.556	0.559	0.546	0.554	0.556	0.562
May	0.507	0.510	0.508	0.508	0.516	0.521	0.521	0.522	0.530	0.525	0.535	0.539	0.544	0.545	0.548	0.546	0.552	0.556	0.556	0.553	0.555	0.542	0.550	0.553	0.558
June	0.507	0.510	0.508	0.508	0.516	0.521	0.521	0.522	0.530	0.525	0.535	0.539	0.544	0.545	0.548	0.546	0.552	0.556	0.556	0.553	0.555	0.542	0.550	0.553	0.558
July	0.511	0.514	0.512	0.512	0.520	0.526	0.526	0.527	0.535	0.530	0.540	0.543	0.549	0.550	0.552	0.551	0.557	0.560	0.561	0.557	0.560	0.547	0.555	0.557	0.563
Aug	0.508	0.511	0.509	0.509	0.517	0.522	0.522	0.523	0.531	0.526	0.536	0.540	0.545	0.546	0.549	0.547	0.553	0.556	0.557	0.553	0.556	0.543	0.551	0.553	0.559
Sept	0.501	0.504	0.502	0.502	0.510	0.516	0.516	0.517	0.525	0.520	0.529	0.533	0.539	0.540	0.542	0.540	0.546	0.550	0.551	0.547	0.549	0.537	0.545	0.547	0.552
Oct	0.498	0.502	0.500	0.500	0.508	0.513	0.513	0.514	0.522	0.517	0.527	0.530	0.536	0.537	0.539	0.538	0.544	0.547	0.548	0.544	0.547	0.534	0.542	0.544	0.550
Nov	0.497	0.500	0.498	0.498	0.506	0.511	0.511	0.512	0.520	0.515	0.525	0.528	0.534	0.535	0.537	0.536	0.542	0.545	0.546	0.542	0.545	0.532	0.540	0.542	0.548
Dec	0.491	0.494	0.493	0.493	0.500	0.506	0.506	0.507	0.515	0.510	0.519	0.523	0.528	0.530	0.532	0.530	0.536	0.540	0.540	0.537	0.539	0.527	0.534	0.537	0.542

Capital gains indexation allowances for companies (April 2013 – April 2015)

Month of acquisition	2013									2014												2015			
	Apr	May	June	July	Aug	Sept	Oct	Nov	Dec	Jan	Feb	Mar	Apr	May	June	July	Aug	Sept	Oct	Nov	Dec	Jan	Feb	Mar	Apr
2000																									
Jan	0.498	0.501	0.499	0.499	0.507	0.512	0.512	0.513	0.521	0.516	0.526	0.529	0.535	0.536	0.538	0.537	0.543	0.546	0.547	0.543	0.546	0.533	0.541	0.543	0.549
Feb	0.490	0.493	0.491	0.491	0.499	0.504	0.504	0.505	0.513	0.508	0.518	0.521	0.527	0.528	0.530	0.528	0.534	0.538	0.539	0.535	0.537	0.525	0.533	0.535	0.540
Mar	0.482	0.485	0.483	0.483	0.490	0.496	0.496	0.497	0.505	0.500	0.510	0.513	0.518	0.520	0.522	0.520	0.526	0.530	0.530	0.527	0.529	0.517	0.524	0.527	0.532
Apr	0.467	0.470	0.468	0.468	0.476	0.481	0.481	0.482	0.490	0.485	0.494	0.498	0.503	0.504	0.507	0.505	0.511	0.514	0.515	0.511	0.514	0.501	0.509	0.511	0.517
May	0.462	0.465	0.463	0.463	0.470	0.476	0.476	0.477	0.484	0.480	0.489	0.493	0.498	0.499	0.501	0.500	0.506	0.509	0.510	0.506	0.508	0.496	0.504	0.506	0.511
June	0.458	0.461	0.459	0.459	0.467	0.472	0.472	0.473	0.481	0.476	0.486	0.489	0.494	0.496	0.498	0.496	0.502	0.506	0.506	0.503	0.505	0.493	0.500	0.503	0.508
July	0.463	0.466	0.465	0.465	0.472	0.477	0.477	0.479	0.486	0.482	0.491	0.494	0.500	0.501	0.503	0.501	0.507	0.511	0.511	0.508	0.510	0.498	0.506	0.508	0.513
Aug	0.463	0.466	0.465	0.465	0.472	0.477	0.477	0.479	0.486	0.482	0.491	0.494	0.500	0.501	0.503	0.501	0.507	0.511	0.511	0.508	0.510	0.498	0.506	0.508	0.513
Sept	0.453	0.456	0.454	0.454	0.462	0.467	0.467	0.468	0.476	0.471	0.480	0.484	0.489	0.490	0.493	0.491	0.497	0.500	0.501	0.497	0.500	0.487	0.495	0.497	0.503
Oct	0.454	0.457	0.455	0.455	0.463	0.468	0.468	0.469	0.477	0.472	0.481	0.485	0.490	0.491	0.494	0.492	0.498	0.501	0.502	0.498	0.501	0.488	0.496	0.498	0.503
Nov	0.450	0.453	0.451	0.451	0.458	0.464	0.464	0.465	0.472	0.468	0.477	0.481	0.486	0.487	0.489	0.488	0.493	0.497	0.497	0.494	0.496	0.484	0.492	0.494	0.499
Dec	0.449	0.452	0.450	0.450	0.458	0.463	0.463	0.464	0.472	0.467	0.476	0.480	0.485	0.486	0.488	0.487	0.492	0.496	0.497	0.493	0.495	0.483	0.491	0.493	0.498
2001																									
Jan	0.458	0.461	0.459	0.459	0.467	0.472	0.472	0.473	0.481	0.476	0.486	0.489	0.494	0.496	0.498	0.496	0.502	0.506	0.506	0.503	0.505	0.493	0.500	0.503	0.508
Feb	0.451	0.453	0.452	0.452	0.459	0.465	0.465	0.466	0.473	0.469	0.478	0.481	0.487	0.488	0.490	0.488	0.494	0.498	0.498	0.495	0.497	0.485	0.492	0.495	0.500
Mar	0.449	0.452	0.450	0.450	0.458	0.463	0.463	0.464	0.472	0.467	0.476	0.480	0.485	0.486	0.488	0.487	0.492	0.496	0.497	0.493	0.495	0.483	0.491	0.493	0.498
Apr	0.441	0.444	0.443	0.443	0.450	0.455	0.455	0.456	0.464	0.459	0.469	0.472	0.477	0.478	0.481	0.479	0.485	0.488	0.489	0.485	0.488	0.475	0.483	0.485	0.490
May	0.432	0.435	0.433	0.433	0.441	0.446	0.446	0.447	0.455	0.450	0.459	0.463	0.468	0.469	0.471	0.470	0.475	0.479	0.479	0.476	0.478	0.466	0.474	0.476	0.481
June	0.431	0.433	0.432	0.432	0.439	0.444	0.444	0.446	0.453	0.448	0.458	0.461	0.466	0.467	0.470	0.468	0.474	0.477	0.478	0.474	0.476	0.464	0.472	0.474	0.479
July	0.440	0.443	0.441	0.441	0.448	0.454	0.454	0.455	0.462	0.458	0.467	0.470	0.475	0.477	0.479	0.477	0.483	0.486	0.487	0.484	0.486	0.474	0.481	0.484	0.489
Aug	0.434	0.437	0.435	0.435	0.443	0.448	0.448	0.449	0.456	0.452	0.461	0.464	0.470	0.471	0.473	0.471	0.477	0.480	0.481	0.478	0.480	0.468	0.475	0.478	0.483
Sept	0.429	0.432	0.430	0.430	0.438	0.443	0.443	0.444	0.451	0.447	0.456	0.459	0.464	0.466	0.468	0.466	0.472	0.475	0.476	0.473	0.475	0.463	0.470	0.473	0.478
Oct	0.431	0.434	0.433	0.433	0.440	0.445	0.445	0.446	0.454	0.449	0.458	0.462	0.467	0.468	0.470	0.469	0.474	0.478	0.478	0.475	0.477	0.465	0.473	0.475	0.480
Nov	0.437	0.440	0.438	0.438	0.446	0.451	0.451	0.452	0.460	0.455	0.464	0.468	0.473	0.474	0.476	0.475	0.480	0.484	0.484	0.481	0.483	0.471	0.479	0.481	0.486
Dec	0.439	0.442	0.440	0.440	0.448	0.453	0.453	0.454	0.461	0.457	0.466	0.469	0.475	0.476	0.478	0.476	0.482	0.486	0.486	0.483	0.485	0.473	0.480	0.483	0.488
2002																									
Jan	0.440	0.443	0.441	0.441	0.448	0.454	0.454	0.455	0.462	0.458	0.467	0.470	0.475	0.477	0.479	0.477	0.483	0.486	0.487	0.484	0.486	0.474	0.481	0.484	0.489
Feb	0.436	0.438	0.437	0.437	0.444	0.449	0.449	0.451	0.458	0.453	0.463	0.466	0.471	0.472	0.475	0.473	0.479	0.482	0.483	0.479	0.482	0.470	0.477	0.479	0.484
Mar	0.430	0.433	0.431	0.431	0.438	0.444	0.444	0.445	0.452	0.448	0.457	0.460	0.465	0.466	0.469	0.467	0.473	0.476	0.477	0.473	0.476	0.464	0.471	0.473	0.479
Apr	0.420	0.423	0.421	0.421	0.429	0.434	0.434	0.435	0.442	0.438	0.447	0.450	0.455	0.456	0.459	0.457	0.463	0.466	0.467	0.463	0.466	0.454	0.461	0.463	0.468
May	0.416	0.419	0.417	0.417	0.425	0.430	0.430	0.431	0.438	0.434	0.443	0.446	0.451	0.452	0.455	0.453	0.459	0.462	0.463	0.459	0.461	0.449	0.457	0.459	0.464
June	0.416	0.419	0.417	0.417	0.425	0.430	0.430	0.431	0.438	0.434	0.443	0.446	0.451	0.452	0.455	0.453	0.459	0.462	0.463	0.459	0.461	0.449	0.457	0.459	0.464
July	0.418	0.421	0.420	0.420	0.427	0.432	0.432	0.433	0.441	0.436	0.445	0.449	0.454	0.455	0.457	0.455	0.461	0.464	0.465	0.462	0.464	0.452	0.459	0.462	0.467
Aug	0.414	0.417	0.416	0.416	0.423	0.428	0.428	0.429	0.437	0.432	0.441	0.444	0.450	0.451	0.453	0.451	0.457	0.460	0.461	0.457	0.460	0.448	0.455	0.457	0.463
Sept	0.405	0.408	0.406	0.406	0.413	0.418	0.418	0.419	0.427	0.422	0.431	0.435	0.440	0.441	0.443	0.441	0.447	0.450	0.451	0.448	0.450	0.438	0.445	0.448	0.453
Oct	0.402	0.405	0.404	0.404	0.411	0.416	0.416	0.417	0.424	0.420	0.429	0.432	0.437	0.438	0.441	0.439	0.445	0.448	0.449	0.445	0.447	0.436	0.443	0.445	0.450
Nov	0.400	0.403	0.401	0.401	0.409	0.414	0.414	0.415	0.422	0.418	0.426	0.430	0.435	0.436	0.438	0.437	0.442	0.446	0.446	0.443	0.445	0.433	0.441	0.443	0.448
Dec	0.398	0.401	0.399	0.399	0.406	0.411	0.411	0.412	0.420	0.415	0.424	0.427	0.432	0.434	0.436	0.434	0.440	0.443	0.444	0.440	0.443	0.431	0.438	0.440	0.445

Capital gains
indexation allowances for companies (April 2013 – April 2015)

Month of acquisition	2013 Apr	May	June	July	Aug	Sept	Oct	Nov	Dec	2014 Jan	Feb	Mar	Apr	May	June	July	Aug	Sept	Oct	Nov	Dec	2015 Jan	Feb	Mar	Apr
2003																									
Jan	0.399	0.401	0.400	0.400	0.407	0.412	0.412	0.413	0.420	0.416	0.425	0.428	0.433	0.434	0.437	0.435	0.441	0.444	0.445	0.441	0.443	0.432	0.439	0.441	0.446
Feb	0.392	0.394	0.393	0.393	0.400	0.405	0.405	0.406	0.413	0.409	0.418	0.421	0.426	0.427	0.429	0.428	0.433	0.437	0.437	0.434	0.436	0.424	0.432	0.434	0.439
Mar	0.387	0390	0.388	0.388	0.395	0.400	0.400	0.401	0.409	0.404	0.413	0.416	0.421	0.422	0.425	0.423	0.429	0.432	0.432	0.429	0.431	0.420	0.427	0.429	0.434
Apr	0.377	0.380	0.378	0.378	0.385	0.390	0.390	0.391	0.398	0.394	0.403	0.406	0.411	0.412	0.414	0.413	0.418	0.422	0.422	0.419	0.421	0.409	0.417	0.419	0.424
May	0.375	0.377	0.376	0.376	0.383	0.388	0.388	0.389	0.396	0.392	0.401	0.404	0.409	0.410	0.412	0.410	0.416	0.419	0.420	0.417	0.419	0.407	0.414	0.417	0.421
June	0.376	0.379	0.377	0.377	0.384	0.389	0.389	0.391	0.398	0.393	0.402	0.405	0.410	0.411	0.414	0.412	0.418	0.421	0.421	0.418	0.420	0.409	0.416	0.418	0.423
July	0.376	0.379	0.377	0.377	0.384	0.389	0.389	0.391	0.398	0.393	0.402	0.405	0.410	0.411	0.414	0.412	0.418	0.421	0.421	0.418	0.420	0.409	0.416	0.418	0.423
Aug	0.374	0.377	0.375	0.375	0.382	0.387	0.387	0.388	0.395	0.391	0.400	0.403	0.408	0.409	0.411	0.410	0.415	0.419	0.419	0.416	0.418	0.406	0.414	0.416	0.421
Sept	0.367	0.370	0.368	0.368	0.375	0.380	0.380	0.381	0.388	0.384	0.393	0.396	0.401	0.402	0.404	0.403	0.408	0.412	0.412	0.409	0.411	0.399	0.407	0.409	0.414
Oct	0.366	0.369	0.367	0.367	0.375	0.380	0.380	0.381	0.388	0.383	0.392	0.395	0.400	0.401	0.404	0.402	0.407	0.411	0.411	0.408	0.410	0.399	0.406	0.408	0.413
Nov	0.366	0.368	0.367	0.367	0.374	0.379	0.379	0.380	0.387	0.383	0.391	0.395	0.400	0.401	0.403	0.401	0.407	0.410	0.411	0.407	0.409	0.398	0.405	0.407	0.412
Dec	0.360	0.362	0.361	0.361	0.368	0.373	0.373	0.374	0.381	0.377	0.385	0.389	0.393	0.395	0.397	0.395	0.401	0.404	0.404	0.401	0.403	0.392	0.399	0.401	0.406
2004																									
Jan	0.363	0.365	0.364	0.364	0.371	0.376	0.376	0.377	0.384	0.380	0.388	0.392	0.397	0.398	0.400	0.398	0.404	0.407	0.407	0.404	0.406	0.395	0.402	0.404	0.409
Feb	0.357	0.360	0.359	0.359	0.366	0.371	0371	0.372	0.379	0.374	0.383	0.386	0.391	0.392	0.394	0.393	0.398	0.402	0.402	0.399	0.401	0.390	0.397	0.399	0.404
Mar	0.352	0.354	0.353	0.353	0.360	0.365	0.365	0.366	0.373	0.368	0.377	0.380	0.385	0.386	0.388	0.387	0.392	0.395	0.396	0.393	0.395	0.384	0.391	0.393	0.398
Apr	0.344	0.346	0.345	0.345	0.352	0.356	0.356	0.358	0.365	0.360	0.369	0.372	0.377	0.378	0.380	0.379	0.384	0.387	0.388	0.384	0.387	0.375	0.382	0.384	0.389
May	0.338	0.340	0.339	0.339	0.346	0.351	0.351	0.352	0.359	0.354	0.363	0.366	0.371	0.372	0.374	0.373	0.378	0.381	0.382	0.379	0.381	0.369	0.376	0.379	0.383
June	0.336	0.338	0.337	0.337	0.344	0.349	0.349	0.350	0.357	0.352	0.361	0.364	0.369	0.370	0.372	0.370	0.376	0.379	0.380	0.376	0.378	0.367	0.374	0.376	0.381
July	0.336	0.338	0.337	0.337	0.344	0.349	0.349	0.350	0.357	0.352	0.361	0.364	0.369	0.370	0.372	0.370	0.376	0.379	0.380	0.376	0.378	0.367	0.374	0.376	0.381
Aug	0.331	0.334	0.332	0.332	0.339	0.344	0.344	0.345	0.352	0.348	0.356	0.360	0.364	0.366	0.368	0.366	0.371	0.375	0.375	0.372	0.374	0.363	0.370	0.372	0.377
Sept	0.326	0.329	0.327	0.327	0.334	0.339	0.339	0.340	0.347	0.343	0.351	0.355	0.359	0.360	0.363	0.361	0.366	0.369	0.370	0.367	0.369	0.358	0.365	0.367	0.372
Oct	0.323	0.326	0.324	0.324	0.331	0.336	0.336	0.337	0.344	0.339	0.348	0.351	0.356	0.357	0.359	0.357	0.363	0.366	0.366	0.363	0.365	0.354	0.361	0.363	0.368
Nov	0.320	0.323	0.321	0.321	0.328	0.333	0.333	0.334	0.341	0.337	0.345	0.348	0.353	0.354	0.356	0.354	0.360	0.363	0.363	0.360	0.362	0.351	0.358	0.360	0.365
Dec	0.314	0.316	0.315	0.315	0.322	0.326	0.326	0.328	0.334	0.330	0.339	0.342	0.346	0.348	0.350	0.348	0.353	0.357	0.357	0.354	0.356	0.345	0.352	0.354	0.359
2005																									
Jan	0.321	0.323	0.322	0.322	0.329	0.334	0.334	0.335	0.341	0.337	0.346	0.349	0.354	0.355	0.357	0.355	0.361	0.364	0.364	0.361	0.363	0.352	0.359	0.361	0.366
Feb	0.316	0.319	0.317	0.317	0.324	0.329	0.329	0.330	0.336	0.332	0.341	0.344	0.349	0.350	0.352	0.350	0.355	0.359	0.359	0.356	0.358	0.347	0.354	0.356	0.361
Mar	0.310	0.312	0.311	0.311	0.318	0.322	0.322	0.323	0.330	0.326	0.334	0.338	0.342	0.343	0.345	0.344	0.349	0.352	0.353	0.350	0.352	0.341	0.348	0.350	0.354
Apr	0.302	0.305	0.303	0.303	0.310	0.315	0.315	0.316	0.323	0.318	0.327	0.330	0.335	0.336	0.338	0.336	0.341	0.344	0.345	0.342	0.344	0.333	0.340	0.342	0.347
May	0.299	0.302	0.301	0.301	0.307	0.312	0.312	0.313	0.320	0.316	0.324	0.327	0.332	0.333	0.335	0.333	0.339	0.342	0.342	0.339	0.341	0.330	0.337	0.339	0.344
June	0.298	0.301	0.299	0.299	0.306	0.311	0.311	0.312	0.318	0.314	0.323	0.326	0.330	0.331	0.334	0.332	0.337	0.340	0.341	0.338	0.340	0.329	0.336	0.338	0.342
July	0.298	0.301	0.299	0.299	0.306	0.311	0.311	0.312	0.318	0.314	0.323	0.326	0.330	0.331	0.334	0.332	0.337	0.340	0.341	0.338	0.340	0.329	0.336	0.338	0.342
Aug	0.295	0.298	0.296	0.296	0.303	0.308	0.308	0.309	0.316	0.312	0.320	0.323	0.328	0.329	0.331	0.329	0.334	0.337	0.338	0.335	0.337	0.326	0.333	0.335	0.340
Sept	0.292	0.295	0.293	0.293	0.300	0.305	0.305	0.306	0.312	0.308	0.316	0.320	0.324	0.325	0.327	0.326	0.331	0.334	0.335	0.331	0.334	0.323	0.329	0.331	0.336
Oct	0.291	0.293	0.292	0.292	0.298	0.303	0.303	0.304	0.311	0.307	0.315	0.318	0.323	0.324	0.326	0.324	0.330	0.333	0.333	0.330	0.332	0.321	0.328	0.330	0.335
Nov	0.289	0.291	0.290	0.290	0.296	0.301	0.301	0.302	0.309	0.305	0.313	0.316	0.321	0.322	0.324	0.322	0.327	0.331	0.331	0.328	0.330	0.319	0.326	0.328	0.333
Dec	0.285	0.288	0.286	0.286	0.293	0.298	0.298	0.299	0.306	0.301	0.310	0.313	0.317	0.318	0.320	0.319	0.324	0.327	0.328	0.325	0.327	0.316	0.323	0.325	0.329

Capital gains indexation allowances for companies (April 2013 – April 2015)

Month of acquisition	2013 Apr	May	June	July	Aug	Sept	Oct	Nov	Dec	2014 Jan	Feb	Mar	Apr	May	June	July	Aug	Sept	Oct	Nov	Dec	2015 Jan	Feb	Mar	Apr
2006																									
Jan	0.290	0.293	0.291	0.291	0.298	0.302	0.302	0.304	0.310	0.306	0.314	0.317	0.322	0.323	0.325	0.324	0.329	0.332	0.332	0.329	0.331	0.321	0.327	0.329	0.334
Feb	0.285	0.287	0.286	0.286	0.292	0.297	0.297	0.298	0.305	0.301	0.309	0.312	0.317	0.318	0.320	0.318	0.323	0.326	0.327	0.324	0.326	0.315	0.322	0.324	0.329
Mar	0.279	0.282	0.281	0.281	0.287	0.292	0.292	0.293	0.299	0.295	0.304	0.307	0.311	0.312	0.314	0.313	0.318	0.321	0.322	0.318	0.321	0.310	0.316	0.318	0.323
Apr	0.270	0.272	0.271	0.271	0.277	0.282	0.282	0.283	0.290	0.285	0.294	0.297	0.301	0.302	0.304	0.303	0.308	0.311	0.311	0.308	0.310	0.300	0.306	0.308	0.313
May	0.262	0.265	0.263	0.263	0.270	0.274	0.274	0.275	0.282	0.278	0.286	0.289	0.293	0.294	0.296	0.295	0.300	0.303	0.303	0.300	0.302	0.292	0.298	0.300	0.305
June	0.257	0.259	0.258	0.258	0.264	0.269	0.269	0.270	0.277	0.273	0.281	0.284	0.288	0.289	0.291	0.290	0.295	0.298	0.298	0.295	0.297	0.287	0.293	0.295	0.300
July	0.257	0.259	0.258	0.258	0.264	0.269	0.269	0.270	0.277	0.273	0.281	0.284	0.288	0.289	0.291	0.290	0.295	0.298	0.298	0.295	0.297	0.287	0.293	0.295	0.300
Aug	0.253	0.255	0.254	0.254	0.260	0.265	0.265	0.266	0.272	0.268	0.276	0.279	0.284	0.285	0.287	0.285	0.290	0.293	0.294	0.291	0.293	0.282	0.289	0.291	0.295
Sept	0.247	0.249	0.248	0.248	0.254	0.259	0.259	0.260	0.266	0.262	0.270	0.273	0.278	0.279	0.281	0.279	0.284	0.287	0.288	0.285	0.287	0.276	0.283	0.285	0.289
Oct	0.245	0.248	0.246	0.246	0.252	0.257	0.257	0.258	0.264	0.260	0.268	0.271	0.276	0.277	0.279	0.277	0.282	0.285	0.286	0.283	0.285	0.274	0.281	0.283	0.287
Nov	0.241	0.243	0.242	0.242	0.248	0.253	0.253	0.254	0.260	0.256	0.264	0.267	0.272	0.273	0.274	0.273	0.278	0.281	0.281	0.278	0.280	0.270	0.276	0.278	0.283
Dec	0.231	0.233	0.232	0.232	0.238	0.243	0.243	0.244	0.250	0.246	0.254	0.257	0.261	0.262	0.264	0.263	0.268	0.271	0.271	0.268	0.270	0.260	0.266	0.268	0.273
2007																									
Jan	0.238	0.240	0.239	0.239	0.245	0.250	0.250	0.250	0.257	0.253	0.261	0.264	0.268	0.269	0.271	0.270	0.275	0.278	0.278	0.275	0.277	0.267	0.273	0.275	0.280
Feb	0.228	0.231	0.229	0.229	0.236	0.240	0.240	0.241	0.248	0.244	0.252	0.255	0.259	0.260	0.262	0.260	0.265	0.268	0.269	0.266	0.268	0.258	0.264	0.266	0.270
Mar	0.221	0.223	0.222	0.222	0.228	0.232	0.232	0.233	0.240	0.236	0.244	0.247	0.251	0.252	0.254	0.252	0.257	0.260	0.261	0.258	0.260	0.250	0.256	0.258	0.262
Apr	0.215	0.217	0.216	0.216	0.222	0.226	0.226	0.227	0.234	0.230	0.238	0.241	0.245	0.246	0.248	0.246	0.251	0.254	0.255	0.252	0.254	0.243	0.250	0.252	0.256
May	0.210	0.212	0.211	0.211	0.217	0.222	0.222	0.223	0.229	0.225	0.233	0.236	0.240	0.241	0.243	0.242	0.246	0.249	0.250	0.247	0.249	0.239	0.245	0.247	0.251
June	0.204	0.206	0.205	0.205	0.211	0.215	0.215	0.216	0.222	0.219	0.226	0.229	0.233	0.234	0.236	0.235	0.240	0.243	0.243	0.240	0.242	0.232	0.238	0.240	0.245
July	0.211	0.213	0.212	0.212	0.218	0.222	0.222	0.223	0.230	0.226	0.233	0.236	0.241	0.242	0.244	0.242	0.247	0.250	0.250	0.247	0.249	0.239	0.246	0.247	0.252
Aug	0.204	0.206	0.205	0.205	0.211	0.215	0.215	0.216	0.222	0.219	0.226	0.229	0.233	0.234	0.236	0.235	0.240	0.243	0.243	0.240	0.242	0.232	0.238	0.240	0.245
Sept	0.200	0.202	0.200	0.200	0.207	0.211	0.211	0.212	0.218	0.214	0.222	0.225	0.229	0.230	0.232	0.231	0.236	0.238	0.239	0.236	0.238	0.228	0.234	0.236	0.240
Oct	0.194	0.197	0.195	0.195	0.202	0.206	0.206	0.207	0.213	0.209	0.217	0.220	0.224	0.225	0.227	0.225	0.230	0.233	0.234	0.231	0.233	0.223	0.229	0.231	0.235
Nov	0.190	0.192	0.191	0.191	0.197	0.201	0.201	0.202	0.208	0.205	0.212	0.215	0.219	0.220	0.222	0.221	0.226	0.228	0.229	0.226	0.228	0.218	0.224	0.226	0.230
Dec	0.183	0.185	0.184	0.184	0.190	0.194	0.194	0.195	0.202	0.198	0.205	0.208	0.212	0.213	0.215	0.214	0.219	0.221	0.222	0.219	0.221	0.211	0.217	0.219	0.223
2008																									
Jan	0.189	0.192	0.190	0.190	0.196	0.201	0.201	0.202	0.208	0.204	0.212	0.214	0.219	0.220	0.222	0.220	0.225	0.228	0.228	0.225	0.227	0.217	0.224	0.225	0.230
Feb	0.180	0.183	0.181	0.181	0.187	0.192	0.192	0.193	0.199	0.195	0.202	0.205	0.210	0.211	0.212	0.211	0.216	0.219	0.219	0.216	0.218	0.208	0.214	0.216	0.220
Mar	0.176	0.179	0.177	0.177	0.183	0.188	0.188	0.189	0.195	0.191	0.198	0.201	0.206	0.207	0.208	0.207	0.212	0.215	0.215	0.212	0.214	0.204	0.210	0.212	0.216
Apr	0.166	0.168	0.167	0.167	0.173	0.177	0.177	0.178	0.184	0.180	0.188	0.191	0.195	0.196	0.198	0.196	0.201	0.204	0.204	0.201	0.203	0.193	0.200	0.201	0.206
May	0.160	0.162	0.161	0.161	0.167	0.171	0.171	0.172	0.178	0.174	0.182	0.185	0.189	0.190	0.192	0.190	0.195	0.198	0.198	0.195	0.197	0.187	0.193	0.195	0.199
June	0.151	0.153	0.152	0.152	0.158	0.162	0.162	0.163	0.169	0.165	0.173	0.175	0.179	0.180	0.182	0.181	0.185	0.188	0.189	0.186	0.188	0.178	0.184	0.186	0.190
July	0.152	0.155	0.153	0.153	0.159	0.164	0.164	0.164	0.170	0.167	0.174	0.177	0.181	0.182	0.184	0.182	0.187	0.190	0.190	0.188	0.189	0.180	0.186	0.188	0.192
Aug	0.149	0.151	0.150	0.150	0.156	0.160	0.160	0.161	0.167	0.163	0.170	0.173	0.177	0.178	0.180	0.179	0.183	0.186	0.186	0.184	0.186	0.176	0.182	0.184	0.188
Sept	0.142	0.145	0.143	0.143	0.149	0.153	0.153	0.154	0.160	0.157	0.164	0.167	0.171	0.172	0.174	0.172	0.177	0.179	0.180	0.177	0.179	0.169	0.175	0.177	0.181
Oct	0.146	0.148	0.147	0.147	0.153	0.157	0.157	0.158	0.164	0.160	0.168	0.170	0.175	0.175	0.177	0.176	0.181	0.183	0.184	0.181	0.183	0.173	0.179	0.181	0.185
Nov	0.155	0.157	0.156	0.156	0.162	0.166	0.166	0.167	0.173	0.169	0.177	0.180	0.184	0.185	0.187	0.185	0.190	0.193	0.193	0.190	0.192	0.182	0.188	0.190	0.194
Dec	0.172	0.174	0.173	0.173	0.179	0.183	0.183	0.184	0.190	0.186	0.194	0.197	0.201	0.202	0.204	0.202	0.207	0.210	0.210	0.208	0.209	0.200	0.206	0.208	0.212

Capital gains
indexation allowances for companies (April 2013 – April 2015)

Month of acquisition	2013 Apr	May	June	July	Aug	Sept	Oct	Nov	Dec	2014 Jan	Feb	Mar	Apr	May	June	July	Aug	Sept	Oct	Nov	Dec	2015 Jan	Feb	Mar	Apr
2009																									
Jan	0.188	0.190	0.188	0.188	0.195	0.199	0.199	0.200	0.206	0.202	0.210	0.213	0.217	0.218	0.220	0.218	0.223	0.226	0.227	0.224	0.226	0.216	0.222	0.224	0.228
Feb	0.180	0.183	0.181	0.181	0.187	0.192	0.192	0.193	0.199	0.195	0.202	0.205	0.210	0.211	0.212	0.211	0.216	0.219	0.219	0.216	0.218	0.208	0.214	0.216	0.220
Mar	0.181	0.183	0.182	0.182	0.188	0.192	0.192	0.193	0.199	0.195	0.203	0.206	0.210	0.211	0.213	0.212	0.216	0.219	0.220	0.217	0.219	0.209	0.215	0.217	0.221
Apr	0.180	0.182	0.181	0.181	0.187	0.191	0.191	0.192	0.198	0.194	0.202	0.205	0.209	0.210	0.212	0.210	0.215	0.218	0.218	0.216	0.217	0.208	0.214	0.216	0.220
May	0.172	0.175	0.173	0.173	0.180	0.184	0.184	0.185	0.191	0.187	0.195	0.197	0.202	0.203	0.204	0.203	0.208	0.211	0.211	0.208	0.210	0.200	0.206	0.208	0.212
June	0.169	0.172	0.170	0.170	0.176	0.180	0.180	0.181	0.187	0.184	0.191	0.194	0.198	0.199	0.201	0.200	0.204	0.207	0.208	0.205	0.207	0.197	0.203	0.205	0.209
July	0.169	0.172	0.170	0.170	0.176	0.180	0.180	0.181	0.187	0.184	0.191	0.194	0.198	0.199	0.201	0.200	0.204	0.207	0.208	0.205	0.207	0.197	0.203	0.205	0.209
Aug	0.164	0.166	0.165	0.165	0.171	0.175	0.175	0.176	0.182	0.178	0.186	0.188	0.193	0.194	0.195	0.194	0.199	0.201	0.202	0.199	0.201	0.191	0.197	0.199	0.203
Sept	0.159	0.161	0.160	0.160	0.166	0.170	0.170	0.171	0.177	0.173	0.181	0.183	0.188	0.189	0.190	0.189	0.194	0.196	0.197	0.194	0.196	0.186	0.192	0.194	0.198
Oct	0.155	0.157	0.156	0.156	0.162	0.166	0.166	0.167	0.173	0.169	0.177	0.180	0.184	0.185	0.187	0.185	0.190	0.193	0.193	0.190	0.192	0.182	0.188	0.190	0.194
Nov	0.152	0.154	0.153	0.153	0.159	0.163	0.163	0.164	0.170	0.166	0.174	0.176	0.181	0.181	0.183	0.182	0.187	0.189	0.190	0.187	0.189	0.179	0.185	0.187	0.191
Dec	0.144	0.147	0.145	0.145	0.151	0.156	0.156	0.156	0.162	0.159	0.166	0.169	0.173	0.174	0.176	0.174	0.179	0.182	0.182	0.179	0.181	0.172	0.178	0.179	0.183
2010																									
Jan	0.145	0.147	0.146	0.146	0.152	0.156	0.156	0.157	0.163	0.159	0.167	0.169	0.173	0.174	0.176	0.175	0.179	0.182	0.183	0.180	0.182	0.172	0.178	0.180	0.184
Feb	0.138	0.141	0.139	0.139	0.145	0.149	0.149	0.150	0.156	0.152	0.160	0.162	0.167	0.167	0.169	0.168	0.172	0.175	0.176	0.173	0.175	0.165	0.171	0.173	0.177
Mar	0.130	0.133	0.131	0.131	0.137	0.141	0.141	0.142	0.148	0.145	0.152	0.155	0.159	0.159	0.161	0.160	0.164	0.167	0.168	0.165	0.167	0.157	0.163	0.165	0.169
Apr	0.120	0.122	0.121	0.121	0.127	0.131	0.131	0.132	0.137	0.134	0.141	0.144	0.148	0.149	0.150	0.149	0.154	0.156	0.157	0.154	0.156	0.146	0.152	0.154	0.158
May	0.116	0.118	0.117	0.117	0.123	0.127	0.127	0.127	0.133	0.130	0.137	0.140	0.144	0.144	0.146	0.145	0.149	0.152	0.153	0.150	0.152	0.142	0.148	0.150	0.154
June	0.113	0.116	0.114	0.114	0.120	0.124	0.124	0.125	0.131	0.127	0.134	0.137	0.141	0.142	0.144	0.142	0.147	0.149	0.150	0.147	0.149	0.140	0.145	0.147	0.151
July	0.116	0.118	0.117	0.117	0.123	0.127	0.127	0.127	0.133	0.130	0.137	0.140	0.144	0.144	0.146	0.145	0.149	0.152	0.153	0.150	0.152	0.142	0.148	0.150	0.154
Aug	0.111	0.114	0.112	0.112	0.118	0.122	0.122	0.123	0.129	0.125	0.132	0.135	0.139	0.140	0.142	0.140	0.145	0.147	0.148	0.145	0.147	0.138	0.143	0.145	0.149
Sept	0.107	0.110	0.108	0.108	0.114	0.118	0.118	0.119	0.125	0.121	0.128	0.131	0.135	0.136	0.138	0.136	0.141	0.143	0.144	0.141	0.143	0.134	0.139	0.141	0.145
Oct	0.105	0.107	0.106	0.106	0.112	0.116	0.116	0.116	0.122	0.119	0.126	0.128	0.132	0.133	0.135	0.134	0.138	0.141	0.141	0.139	0.140	0.131	0.137	0.139	0.143
Nov	0.100	0.102	0.101	0.101	0.107	0.111	0.111	0.112	0.117	0.114	0.121	0.123	0.127	0.128	0.130	0.129	0.133	0.136	0.136	0.134	0.135	0.126	0.132	0.134	0.138
Dec	0.092	0.095	0.093	0.093	0.099	0.103	0.103	0.104	0.109	0.106	0.113	0.116	0.120	0.120	0.122	0.121	0.125	0.128	0.128	0.126	0.127	0.118	0.124	0.126	0.130
2011																									
Jan	0.090	0.092	0.090	0.090	0.096	0.100	0.100	0.101	0.107	0.103	0.110	0.113	0.117	0.117	0.119	0.118	0.122	0.125	0.125	0.123	0.124	0.115	0.121	0.123	0.127
Feb	0.079	0.081	0.080	0.080	0.085	0.089	0.089	0.090	0.096	0.092	0.099	0.102	0.105	0.106	0.108	0.107	0.111	0.114	0.114	0.112	0.113	0.104	0.110	0.112	0.115
Mar	0.073	0.075	0.074	0.074	0.080	0.083	0.083	0.084	0.090	0.086	0.093	0.096	0.100	0.101	0.102	0.101	0.105	0.108	0.108	0.106	0.108	0.098	0.104	0.106	0.110
Apr	0.064	0.067	0.065	0.065	0.071	0.075	0.075	0.076	0.081	0.078	0.084	0.087	0.091	0.092	0.093	0.092	0.096	0.099	0.099	0.097	0.099	0.090	0.095	0.097	0.101
May	0.061	0.063	0.062	0.062	0.067	0.071	0.071	0.072	0.077	0.074	0.081	0.083	0.087	0.088	0.090	0.088	0.093	0.095	0.096	0.093	0.095	0.086	0.091	0.093	0.097
June	0.061	0.063	0.062	0.062	0.067	0.071	0.071	0.072	0.077	0.074	0.081	0.083	0.087	0.088	0.090	0.088	0.093	0.095	0.096	0.093	0.095	0.086	0.091	0.093	0.097
July	0.063	0.065	0.064	0.064	0.069	0.073	0.073	0.074	0.080	0.076	0.083	0.086	0.089	0.090	0.092	0.091	0.095	0.098	0.098	0.095	0.097	0.088	0.094	0.095	0.099
Aug	0.057	0.059	0.058	0.058	0.063	0.067	0.067	0.068	0.073	0.070	0.077	0.079	0.083	0.084	0.086	0.084	0.089	0.091	0.091	0.089	0.091	0.082	0.087	0.089	0.093
Sept	0.049	0.051	0.050	0.050	0.055	0.059	0.059	0.060	0.065	0.062	0.069	0.071	0.075	0.076	0.077	0.076	0.080	0.083	0.083	0.081	0.082	0.074	0.079	0.081	0.084
Oct	0.048	0.050	0.049	0.049	0.055	0.058	0.058	0.059	0.065	0.061	0.068	0.071	0.074	0.075	0.077	0.076	0.080	0.082	0.083	0.080	0.082	0.073	0.079	0.080	0.084
Nov	0.046	0.048	0.047	0.047	0.052	0.056	0.056	0.057	0.062	0.059	0.066	0.068	0.072	0.073	0.075	0.073	0.078	0.080	0.081	0.078	0.080	0.071	0.076	0.078	0.082
Dec	0.042	0.044	0.043	0.043	0.048	0.052	0.052	0.053	0.058	0.055	0.062	0.064	0.068	0.069	0.071	0.069	0.074	0.076	0.076	0.074	0.076	0.067	0.072	0.074	0.078

Capital gains indexation allowances for companies (April 2013 – April 2015)

Month of acquisition	2013									2014												2015			
	Apr	May	June	July	Aug	Sept	Oct	Nov	Dec	Jan	Feb	Mar	Apr	May	June	July	Aug	Sept	Oct	Nov	Dec	Jan	Feb	Mar	Apr
2012																									
Jan	0.048	0.050	0.049	0.049	0.055	0.058	0.058	0.059	0.065	0.061	0.068	0.071	0.074	0.075	0.077	0.076	0.080	0.082	0.083	0.080	0.082	0.073	0.079	0.080	0.084
Feb	0.040	0.042	0.041	0.041	0.046	0.050	0.050	0.051	0.056	0.053	0.060	0.062	0.066	0.067	0.068	0.067	0.071	0.074	0.074	0.072	0.073	0.065	0.070	0.072	0.075
Mar	0.036	0.038	0.037	0.037	0.042	0.046	0.046	0.047	0.052	0.049	0.056	0.058	0.062	0.063	0.064	0.063	0.067	0.070	0.070	0.068	0.069	0.061	0.066	0.068	0.071
Apr	0.029	0.031	0.030	0.030	0.035	0.039	0.039	0.040	0.045	0.042	0.048	0.051	0.054	0.055	0.057	0.056	0.060	0.062	0.063	0.060	0.062	0.053	0.059	0.060	0.064
May	0.029	0.031	0.030	0.030	0.035	0.039	0.039	0.040	0.045	0.042	0.049	0.051	0.055	0.056	0.057	0.056	0.060	0.063	0.063	0.061	0.062	0.054	0.059	0.061	0.064
June	0.032	0.034	0.033	0.033	0.038	0.042	0.042	0.043	0.048	0.045	0.051	0.054	0.057	0.058	0.060	0.059	0.063	0.065	0.066	0.063	0.065	0.056	0.062	0.063	0.067
July	0.031	0.033	0.031	0.031	0.037	0.040	0.040	0.041	0.047	0.043	0.050	0.052	0.056	0.057	0.059	0.057	0.062	0.064	0.064	0.062	0.064	0.055	0.060	0.062	0.066
Aug	0.027	0.029	0.028	0.028	0.033	0.037	0.037	0.037	0.043	0.040	0.046	0.049	0.052	0.053	0.055	0.053	0.058	0.060	0.060	0.058	0.060	0.051	0.056	0.058	0.062
Sept	0.022	0.024	0.023	0.023	0.028	0.032	0.032	0.032	0.038	0.034	0.041	0.043	0.047	0.048	0.050	0.048	0.052	0.055	0.055	0.053	0.054	0.046	0.051	0.053	0.057
Oct	0.016	0.018	0.017	0.017	0.022	0.026	0.026	0.026	0.032	0.029	0.035	0.037	0.041	0.042	0.044	0.042	0.046	0.049	0.049	0.047	0.048	0.040	0.045	0.047	0.050
Nov	0.016	0.018	0.017	0.017	0.022	0.026	0.026	0.026	0.032	0.029	0.035	0.037	0.041	0.042	0.044	0.042	0.046	0.049	0.049	0.047	0.048	0.040	0.045	0.047	0.050
Dec	0.011	0.013	0.012	0.012	0.017	0.021	0.021	0.021	0.027	0.024	0.030	0.032	0.036	0.037	0.038	0.037	0.041	0.044	0.044	0.042	0.043	0.035	0.040	0.042	0.045
2013																									
Jan	0.015	0.017	0.016	0.016	0.021	0.025	0.025	0.026	0.031	0.028	0.034	0.037	0.040	0.041	0.043	0.041	0.046	0.048	0.048	0.046	0.048	0.039	0.044	0.046	0.050
Feb	0.008	0.010	0.008	0.008	0.014	0.017	0.017	0.018	0.023	0.020	0.027	0.029	0.033	0.034	0.035	0.034	0.038	0.040	0.041	0.038	0.040	0.032	0.037	0.038	0.042
Mar	0.003	0.005	0.004	0.004	0.009	0.013	0.013	0.014	0.019	0.016	0.022	0.025	0.028	0.029	0.031	0.029	0.033	0.036	0.036	0.034	0.035	0.027	0.032	0.034	0.037
Apr	—	0.002	0.001	0.001	0.006	0.010	0.010	0.010	0.016	0.012	0.019	0.021	0.025	0.026	0.027	0.026	0.030	0.032	0.033	0.030	0.032	0.024	0.029	0.030	0.034
May	—	—	0.000	0.000	0.004	0.008	0.008	0.008	0.014	0.010	0.017	0.019	0.023	0.024	0.025	0.024	0.028	0.030	0.031	0.028	0.030	0.022	0.027	0.028	0.032
June	—	—	—	0.000	0.005	0.009	0.009	0.010	0.015	0.012	0.018	0.020	0.024	0.025	0.026	0.025	0.029	0.032	0.032	0.030	0.031	0.023	0.028	0.030	0.033
July	—	—	—	—	0.005	0.009	0.009	0.010	0.015	0.012	0.018	0.020	0.024	0.025	0.026	0.025	0.029	0.032	0.032	0.030	0.031	0.023	0.028	0.030	0.033
Aug	—	—	—	—	—	0.004	0.004	0.004	0.010	0.006	0.013	0.015	0.019	0.020	0.021	0.020	0.024	0.026	0.027	0.024	0.026	0.018	0.023	0.024	0.028
Sept	—	—	—	—	—	—	0.000	0.001	0.006	0.003	0.009	0.012	0.015	0.016	0.017	0.016	0.020	0.023	0.023	0.021	0.022	0.014	0.019	0.021	0.024
Oct	—	—	—	—	—	—	—	0.001	0.006	0.003	0.009	0.012	0.015	0.016	0.017	0.016	0.020	0.023	0.023	0.021	0.022	0.014	0.019	0.021	0.024
Nov	—	—	—	—	—	—	—	—	0.005	0.002	0.008	0.011	0.014	0.015	0.017	0.015	0.019	0.022	0.022	0.020	0.021	0.013	0.018	0.020	0.023
Dec	—	—	—	—	—	—	—	—	—	0.000	0.006	0.009	0.012	0.013	0.015	0.013	0.017	0.020	0.020	0.018	0.019	0.011	0.016	0.018	0.021
2014																									
Jan	—	—	—	—	—	—	—	—	—	—	0.006	0.009	0.012	0.013	0.015	0.013	0.017	0.020	0.020	0.018	0.019	0.011	0.016	0.018	0.021
Feb	—	—	—	—	—	—	—	—	—	—	—	0.002	0.006	0.007	0.008	0.007	0.011	0.013	0.014	0.011	0.013	0.005	0.010	0.011	0.015
Mar	—	—	—	—	—	—	—	—	—	—	—	—	0.004	0.004	0.006	0.005	0.009	0.011	0.011	0.009	0.011	0.002	0.007	0.009	0.013
Apr	—	—	—	—	—	—	—	—	—	—	—	—	—	0.001	0.002	0.001	0.005	0.007	0.008	0.005	0.007	0.000	0.004	0.005	0.009
May	—	—	—	—	—	—	—	—	—	—	—	—	—	—	0.002	0.000	0.004	0.007	0.007	0.005	0.006	0.000	0.003	0.005	0.008
June	—	—	—	—	—	—	—	—	—	—	—	—	—	—	—	0.000	0.003	0.005	0.005	0.003	0.005	0.000	0.002	0.003	0.007
July	—	—	—	—	—	—	—	—	—	—	—	—	—	—	—	—	0.004	0.006	0.007	0.004	0.006	0.000	0.003	0.004	0.008
Aug	—	—	—	—	—	—	—	—	—	—	—	—	—	—	—	—	—	0.002	0.003	0.000	0.002	0.000	0.000	0.000	0.004
Sept	—	—	—	—	—	—	—	—	—	—	—	—	—	—	—	—	—	—	0.000	0.000	0.000	0.000	0.000	0.000	0.002
Oct	—	—	—	—	—	—	—	—	—	—	—	—	—	—	—	—	—	—	—	0.000	0.000	0.000	0.000	0.000	0.001
Nov	—	—	—	—	—	—	—	—	—	—	—	—	—	—	—	—	—	—	—	—	0.002	0.000	0.000	0.000	0.004
Dec	—	—	—	—	—	—	—	—	—	—	—	—	—	—	—	—	—	—	—	—	—	0.000	0.000	0.000	0.002

Capital gains indexation allowances for companies (April 2013 – April 2015)

Month of acquisition 2015	2013 April	May	June	July	Aug	Sept	Oct	Nov	Dec	2014 Jan	Feb	Mar	Apr	May	June	July	Aug	Sept	Oct	Nov	Dec	2015 Jan	Feb	Mar	Apr
Jan	—	—	—	—	—	—	—	—	—	—	—	—	—	—	—	—	—	—	—	—	—	—	0.005	0.007	0.010
Feb	—	—	—	—	—	—	—	—	—	—	—	—	—	—	—	—	—	—	—	—	—	—	—	0.002	0.005
Mar	—	—	—	—	—	—	—	—	—	—	—	—	—	—	—	—	—	—	—	—	—	—	—	—	0.004
Apr	—	—	—	—	—	—	—	—	—	—	—	—	—	—	—	—	—	—	—	—	—	—	—	—	—

Certificates of tax deposit

Rates of interest

Deposits of less than £100,000

Date	A	B
9 February — 5 April 2001	2¼%	1¼%
6 April — 2 August	2%	1%
3 August — 18 September	1½%	¾%
19 September — 4 October	1¼%	¾%
5 October — 8 November	1%	½%
9 November — 6 February 2003	½%	¼%
7 February — 10 July	¼%	Nil
11 July — 6 November	Nil	Nil
7 November — 5 February 2004	¼%	Nil
6 February — 6 May	½%	¼%
7 May — 10 June	¾%	¼%
11 June — 5 August	1%	½%
6 August — 4 August 2005	1¼%	½%
5 August — 3 August 2006	1%	½%
4 August — 9 November	1¾%	¾%
10 November — 10 May 2007	1½%	¾%
11 May — 5 July	2%	1%
6 July — 6 December	2¼%	1 1/10%
7 December — 7 February 2008	3%	1½%
8 February — 10 April	2%	1%
11 April — 8 October	2%	1%
9 October — 6 November	2½%	1¼%
7 November — 4 December	1¾%	¾%
5 December —	0%	0%

Deposits of £100,000 or more

Date	A and held for					B and held for				
	Under 1 mth	1–3 mths	3–6 mths	6–9 mths	9–12 mths	under 1 mth	1–3 mths	3–6 mths	6–9 mths	9–12 mths
9 February — 5 April 2001	2¼%	4¾%	4¼%	4¼%	4%	1¼%	2½%	2¼%	2¼%	2%
6 April — 10 May	2%	4¼%	4%	3¾%	3½%	1%	2¼%	2%	2%	1¾%
11 May — 2 August	2%	4%	4%	3¾%	3¾%	1%	2%	2%	2%	2%
3 August — 18 September	1½%	4%	3¾%	3¾%	3¾%	¾%	2%	1⅞%	1⅞%	1⅞%
19 September — 4 October	1¼%	3½%	3¼%	3¼%	3%	¾%	1¾%	1¾%	1¾%	1½%
5 October — 8 November	1%	3¼%	3%	3%	3%	½%	1¾%	1½%	1½%	1½%
9 November — 6 February 2003	½%	2¾%	2½%	2¼%	2¼%	¼%	1½%	1¼%	1¼%	1¼%
7 February — 10 July	¼%	2¾%	2¼%	2¼%	2%	Nil	1¼%	1%	1%	1%
11 July — 6 November	Nil	2½%	2¼%	2%	2%	Nil	1¼%	1%	1%	1%
7 November — 5 February 2004	¼%	3%	3%	3%	3%	Nil	1½%	1½%	1½%	1½%
6 February — 6 May	½%	3%	3%	3%	3%	¼%	1½%	1½%	1½%	1½%
7 May — 10 June	¾%	3¼%	3¼%	3¼%	3¼%	¼%	1½%	1½%	1½%	1½%
11 June — 5 August	1%	3¾%	3½%	3¾%	3¾%	½%	1¾%	1¾%	1¾%	1¾%
6 August — 4 August 2005	1¼%	3¾%	3¾%	3¾%	3¾%	½%	1¾%	1¾%	1¾%	1¾%
5 August — 3 August 2006	1%	3½%	3¼%	3%	3%	½%	1¾%	1½%	1½%	1½%
4 August — 9 November	1¾%	4¼%	4¼%	4%	4%	¾%	2%	2%	2%	2%
10 November — 11 January 2007	1½%	4%	4%	3¾%	3¾%	¾%	2%	2%	2%	2%
12 January — 10 May	1½%	4¼%	4%	4%	4%	¾%	2%	2%	2%	2%
11 May — 5 July	2%	4¾%	4½%	4½%	4½%	1%	2¼%	2¼%	2¼%	2¼%
6 July — 6 December	2¼%	5%	4¾%	4¾%	4¾%	1 1/10%	2½%	2¼%	2¼%	2¼%
7 December — 7 February 2008	3%	5½%	5%	4¾%	4½%	1½%	2¾%	2½%	2¼%	2¼%
8 February — 10 April	2%	4½%	4¼%	4%	3¾%	1%	2¼%	2%	2%	1½%
11 April — 8 October	2%	4¾%	4½%	4¼%	4¼%	1%	2¼%	2¼%	2%	2%
9 October — 6 November	2½%	5¼%	5%	5%	4¾%	1¼%	2½%	2½%	2½%	2¼%
7 November — 4 December	1¾%	4½%	4¼%	4¼%	4%	¾%	2¼%	2%	2%	2%
5 December — 8 January 2009	0%	2½%	2½%	2½%	2¼%	0%	1¼%	1¼%	1¼%	1%
9 January — 5 February	0%	1½%	1¼%	1¼%	1¼%	0%	¾%	½	½%	½%
6 February — 5 March	0%	1%	1%	1%	¾%	0%	½%	½%	½%	¼%
6 March —	0%	¾%	¾%	¾%	¾%	0%	¼%	¼%	¼%	¼%

A = used to pay tax
B = withdrawn for cash

Notes

(a) Certificates may be used by taxpayers generally — that is to say companies, individuals, partnerships, personal representatives, trustees etc. for payment of tax and petroleum royalties but not PAYE, tax deducted from payments to construction subcontractors, capital gains tax payable by companies on disposals of high value dwellings (see page 20) or VAT. Certificates are no longer available for purchase for use against corporation tax liabilities.

(b) The first deposit must be for a minimum of £500. Further deposits must be either at least £250 or enough to bring total deposits up to £500 (i.e. where total deposits have fallen below that amount).

(c) Interest accrues daily (without compounding) for a maximum of six years from the date of deposit to (i) the deemed due date for tax paid with deposits; or (ii) the day on which the deposit is withdrawn for cash. It is payable gross but taxable.

(d) Rates of interest on certificates are, for the first year, those applying on the date of deposit, and thereafter rates are realigned with current rates on each anniversary.

Corporation tax

Rates

Financial year	2015	2014	2013	2012	2011	2010	2009	2008
Full rate	20%	21%	23%	24%	26%	28%	28%	28%
Small profits rate	—	20%	20%	20%	20%	21%	21%	21%
Upper profit limit	—	£300,000	£300,000	£300,000	£300,000	£300,000	£300,000	£300,000
Marginal relief — upper profit limit	—	£1.5m	£1.5m	£1.5m	£1.5m	£1.5m	£1.5m	£1.5m
Marginal relief fraction	—	1/400	3/400	1/100	3/200	7/400	7/400	7/400
Effective marginal rate	—	21.25%	23.75%	25%	27.5%	29.75%	29.75%	29.75%

Chargeable gains

(a) The whole of the chargeable gains (less allowable losses) is included in the taxable total profits. The rate of corporation tax applicable will be either the full rate, or the small profits rate (with marginal relief as appropriate). Gains and losses within the charge to capital gains tax in respect of high value disposals of dwellings (see page 20) and of non-resident disposals of residential property interests (see page 20) are excluded from the taxable total profits.

(b) For authorised unit and investment trusts, gains are not chargeable. Gains on disposals of investment properties by UK real estate investment trusts are not chargeable.

Notes

(a) The small profits rate is abolished for the financial year 2015 and subsequent years. This does not apply to North Sea oil and gas ring fence activities — see note (f) below.

(b) For the financial year 2014 and earlier years, where 'profits' of an accounting period exceed the upper profit limit for the small profits rate, but are less than the appropriate marginal relief upper profit limit, corporation tax is reduced by:

$$F(U - \text{augmented profits}) \times \frac{\text{taxable total profits}}{\text{augmented profits}}$$

where F is the marginal relief fraction and U is the marginal relief upper profit limit.

(c) 'Augmented profits' are total taxable profits plus franked investment income (other than from UK companies within the same group or owned by a consortium of which the recipient is a member). Where a company has chargeable gains or losses within the charge to capital gains tax on high value disposals of dwellings subject to the annual tax on enveloped dwellings (see pages 20 and 80), the taxable total profits are adjusted for the purpose of computing the augmented profits to what would have been the taxable total profits in the absence of the capital gains tax charge.

(d) The upper profit limits and the marginal relief upper profit limits for the small profits rate are proportionately reduced for accounting periods of less than 12 months.

(e) Where a company has associated companies, the upper profit limits and the marginal relief upper profit limits for the small profits rate are divided by one plus the number of associated companies in the accounting period, including those associated for part only of the period but ignoring companies which have not traded at any time in the period.

(f) For all years, the corporation tax rates applicable to North Sea oil and gas ring fence activities are as follows: main rate 30%; small profits rate 19%; upper profit limit £300,000; marginal relief upper profit limit £1,500,000; marginal relief fraction 11/400. For the financial year 2015 and subsequent years, rules similar to those at notes (b) to (e) above continue to apply.

(g) For financial year 2016 the full rate of corporation tax will be 20%. For financial years 2017 to 2019 it will be 19%. For financial year 2020 the rate will be 18%.

(h) A corporation tax surcharge of 8% will be chargeable on the taxable profits of banks and building societies with effect from 1 January 2016.

Corporation tax

Payment of tax

Corporation tax	Without assessment, no later than nine months and one day after the end of the accounting period (the 'due date').	*CTA 2009, s 8*

Instalments. Subject to the exceptions below, a 'large company' (i.e. one whose taxable profits exceed £1.5m a year, divided by one plus the number of active related 51% group companies (for accounting periods beginning before 1 April 2015, active associated companies), if any, must pay its CT in four quarterly instalments on the basis of anticipated liabilities for the accounting period. For a company with a 12 month accounting period, the first two instalments are due on the 14th day of months 7 and 10 in the accounting period, the third is due 14 days after the end of the accounting period and the final instalment is due 3 months and 14 days after the end of the accounting period.

TMA 1970, s 59
SI 1998 No 3175
SI 2014 No 2409

For accounting periods beginning on or after 1 April 2017, companies with profits exceeding £20 million will have to pay instalments in the third, sixth, ninth and twelfth months of the accounting periods. The £20 million threshold will be divided between members of a group.

Exceptions. (i) A company which would otherwise be large is not treated as such for an accounting period if its CT liability for that period does not exceed £10,000. (ii) A company is not large for an accounting period if it was not large in the 12 months preceding the accounting period and its profits for the accounting period do not exceed £10m, divided by one plus the number of related 51% group companies (or active associated companies) as at the end of the preceding accounting period.

The limits of £1.5m, £10,000 and £10m are proportionately reduced for accounting periods of less than 12 months.

Groups can enter into group payment arrangements provided the paying company enters into a standard contract at least two months prior to the first instalment payment due date.

Income tax	Within 14 days of end of return period during which the income tax was deducted. Return periods end on 31 March, 30 June, 30 September, 31 December, at the end of each of the company's accounting periods.	*ITA 2007, ss 947–950*
Tax returns	Filing date is normally the later of (i) twelve months after the end of the return period; and (ii) three months after the receipt of Notice. Special rules apply where accounts are prepared for periods exceeding twelve months. Returns may not be amended more than twelve months after the filing date unless otherwise provided. Non-resident companies subject to the capital gains tax charge on disposals of residential property must deliver a special return within 30 days following the disposal.	*TMA 1970, s 12ZB; FA 1998, Sch 18 paras 14, 15*
Interest on tax	See pages 75 and 76.	

Research and development	*Deduction scheme*. An 'SME' incurring R & D expenditure can claim to deduct 230% of the expenditure (225% for expenditure incurred before 1 April 2015; 200% before 1 April 2012; 175% before 1 April 2011) when computing its trading profit or loss. A company not yet in profit, or which has not started to trade, can claim relief up front as a cash payment (an 'R & D tax credit'). These reliefs (together with vaccine research relief) are limited to €7.5m per project. For accounting periods ending before 1 April 2012 the SME had to incur R & D expenditure of at least £10,000 in a 12-month accounting period to qualify.	*CTA 2009, ss 104A–104Y, 1039–1142*

An SME can also claim relief for expenditure on R & D contracted out to it by a large company or by any other person not carrying on a trade etc. and for R & D expenditure which is subsidised or to which the project limit above applies. The relief provides for a deduction equal to 130% of the expenditure. For accounting periods ending before 1 April 2012 the relief is subject to the same minimum expenditure rules as above.

FA 2011, s 43
FA 2012, s 20, Sch 3
FA 2013, Sch 15
FA 2014, s 31
FA 2015, s 27

An 'SME' is a company with fewer than 500 employees and either or both of annual turnover not exceeding €100m and annual balance sheet total not exceeding €86m.

Large companies (i.e. companies which are not SMEs) incurring R & D expenditure (for accounting periods ending before 1 April 2012, of at least £10,000) can generally claim to deduct 130% of the expenditure from trading profits.

Large companies can also claim a relief similar to that for SMEs above, including tax credits, for expenditure incurred on certain vaccine research. The relief is also available to SMEs for expenditure incurred before 1 April 2012. The rate of relief is 140% for large companies and 120% (140% for expenditure incurred before 1 April 2011) for SMEs. See also page 11.

Above the line scheme. For R& D expenditure incurred on or after 1 April 2013, large companies (and certain SMEs with subcontracted or subsidised R & D, or R & D subject to the project limit) can claim an above the line (ATL) credit to the value of 11% of the qualifying expenditure (10% for expenditure incurred before 1 April 2015; 49% for ring fence trades). The ATL credit is a taxable receipt and is paid net of tax to companies with no corporation tax liability. The scheme is initially optional but will become mandatory for large companies on 1 April 2016. Higher education institutions and charities are excluded for expenditure incurred on or after 1 August 2015.

Corporation tax

Corporate venturing scheme	In respect of shares issued after 31 March 2000 and before 1 April 2010, an investing company can obtain 20% CT relief on amounts subscribed for ordinary shares in small higher-risk unquoted trading companies which are held for at least 3 years. Any chargeable gains on disposal of the shares can be deferred by reinvestment in another shareholding under the scheme; any allowable losses (net of the 20% relief) can be set against income if not deducted from chargeable gains. The investing company must not control the investee company or own or be entitled to acquire more than 30% of its ordinary shares. At least 20% of the investee company's ordinary shares must be owned by independent individuals.	*FA 2000, s 63, Sch 15* *FA 2001, s 64, Sch 16*
Community investment tax credit	Tax relief worth up to 25% of qualifying investments. See page 64.	*CTA 2010, ss 218–269* *FA 2002, s 57, Sch 16*
Charitable giving		
Gift aid scheme	Relief is available for qualifying donations to charity or to a community amateur sports club. Relief is given by deducting the amount of the donation from the company's total profits for the accounting period in which the payment is made. The donation is not taxable in the hands of the charity or club if applied to charitable purposes only.	*CTA 2010, ss 189–202* *ICTA 1988, ss 338–339*
Gifts in kind	Relief is available for gifts by companies to charities, community amateur sports clubs or educational establishments of goods produced or sold or of plant and machinery used in the donor's trade, etc.	*CTA 2009, ss 105–108* *ICTA 1988, ss 83A, 84* *CAA 2001, s 63(2)*
Gifts of land, shares and securities etc.	Relief is available where a company disposes of a freehold or leasehold interest in land, listed shares or securities, units in an authorised unit trust, etc. to a charity by way of gift or sale at an undervalue. The market value of the land, shares etc. on the date of disposal (plus, in the case of a gift, incidental disposal costs) less any consideration or value of benefits received by the donor or a connected person is deducted from the total profits of the company for the accounting period in which the disposal is made.	*CTA 2010, ss 189, 190, 203–216* *ICTA 1988, s 587B*
Gifts of pre-eminent objects to the nation	Under the cultural gift scheme from 1 April 2012, companies which donate pre-eminent objects, or collections of objects, to the nation may qualify for a tax reduction of 20% of the value of the objects.	*FA 2012, s 49*
Groups of companies		
Group relief	A company which is a member of a group of companies can surrender certain losses, etc. to be claimed by another member of the group against its own corporation tax liability. Companies are members of a group of companies for this purpose broadly if one is the 75% subsidiary of the other or both are 75% subsidiaries of a third company. The following are eligible for surrender as group relief: trading losses, non-trading loan relationship deficits, certain excess capital allowances on plant or machinery used for special leasing, management expenses, qualifying charitable donations, property business losses, non-trading losses on intangible fixed assets and qualifying overseas losses of non-resident companies.	*CTA 2010, ss 97–188* *ICTA 1988, ss 402–413* *FA 2013, s 30*
Chargeable gains	Disposals of capital assets by one member of a group to another member are treated as if made at a 'no gain/no loss' disposal value. A 'group' for this purpose consists of a principal company, its 75% subsidiaries and those subsidiaries' 75% subsidiaries (and so on), but excluding any subsidiary which is not an effective 51% subsidiary of the principal company. Two members of a group can elect to transfer a gain or loss between them. A de-grouping charge will apply where a company leaves a group and owns a capital asset which has been transferred to it by another group member within the preceding six years.	*TCGA 1992, ss 170–171B, 179*
Patent box	For profits arising on or after 1 April 2013, a company can make an election under which its trading profits from patents and certain other intellectual property are effectively charged to corporation tax at 10%. The lower rate is given effect by way of a deduction in computing the trading profits of the company. The relief is being phased in, so that for financial year 2013 only 60% of the relevant profits qualify. The percentage is increased by 10 percentage points in each subsequent financial year until 100% of the profits qualify in financial year 2017. For financial year 2015 the percentage is 80%.	*CTA 2010, ss 357A–357GE; FA 2012, s 19, Sch 2*

Agreements covering taxes on income and capital gains

Country	SI or SR & O Number	Country	SI or SR & O Number	Country	SI or SR & O Number
Albania	2013 No 3145	Cyprus	1975 No 425		1998 No 3151
Antigua and Barbuda	1947 No 2865		1980 No 1529	Isle of Man	1955 No 1205
	1968 No 1096	Czech Republic (see note (c))	1991 No 2876		1991 No 2880
Argentina	1997 No 1777	Denmark	1980 No 1960		1994 No 3208
Armenia	2011 No 2722		1991 No 2877		2009 No 228
Australia	2003 No 3199		1996 No 3165		2013 No 3148
Austria	1970 No 1947	Egypt	1980 No 1091	Israel	1963 No 616
	1979 No 117	Estonia	1994 No 3207		1971 No 391
	1994 No 768	Ethiopia	2011 No 2725	Italy	1990 No 2590
	2010 No 2688	Falkland Islands	1997 No 2985	Ivory Coast	1987 No 169
Azerbaijan	1995 No 762	Faroes	2007 No 3469	Jamaica	1973 No 1329
Bahrain	2012 No 3075	Fiji	1976 No 1342	Japan	2006 No 1924
Bangladesh	1980 No 708	Finland	1970 No 153		2014 No 1881
Barbados	2012 No 3076		1980 No 710	Jersey	1952 No 1216
Belarus (see note (b))	1986 No 224		1985 No 1997		1994 No 3210
Belgium	1987 No 2053		1991 No 2878		2009 No 3012
	2010 No 2979		1996 No 3166	Jordan	2001 No 3924
	2014 No 1875	France	2009 No 226	Kazakhstan	1994 No 3211
Belize	1947 No 2866	Gambia	1980 No 1963		1998 No 2567
	1968 No 573	Georgia	2004 No 3325	Kenya	1977 No 1299
	1973 No 2097		2010 No 2972	Kiribati (and Tuvalu)	1950 No 750
Bolivia	1995 No 2707	Germany	2010 No 2975		1968 No 309
Bosnia-Herzegovina (see note (d))	1981 No 1815		2014 No 1874		1974 No 1271
Botswana	2006 No 1925	Ghana	1993 No 1800	Korea (South)	1996 No 3168
British Virgin Islands	2009 No 3013	Greece	1954 No 142	Kuwait	1999 No 2036
Brunei	1950 No 1977	Grenada	1949 No 361	Kyrgyzstan (see note (b))	
	1968 No 306		1968 No 1867	Latvia	1996 No 3167
	1973 No 2098	Guernsey	1952 No 1215	Lesotho	1997 No 2986
	2013 No 3146		1994 No 3209	Libya	2010 No 243
Bulgaria	1987 No 2054		2009 No 3011	Liechtenstein	2012 No 3077
Burma (see Myanmar)		Guyana	1992 No 3207	Lithuania	2001 No 3925
Canada	1980 No 709	Hong Kong	2010 No 2974		2002 No 2847
	1980 No 1528	Hungary	2011 No 2726	Luxembourg	1968 No 1100
	1985 No 1996	Iceland	1991 No 2879		1980 No 567
	2003 No 2619		2014 No 1879		1984 No 364
	2014 No 3274	India	1993 No 1801		2010 No 237
Cayman Islands	2010 No 2973		2013 No 3147	Macedonia	2007 No 2127
Chile	2003 No 3200	Indonesia	1994 No 769	Malawi	1956 No 619
China	2011 No 2724	Irish Republic	1976 No 2151		1964 No 1401
	2013 No 3142		1976 No 2152		1968 No 1101
Croatia (see note (d))	1981 No 1815		1995 No 764		1979 No 302

Double taxation treaties

Country	SI or SR & O Number	Country	SI or SR & O Number	Country	SI or SR & O Number
Malaysia	**1997 No 2987**		2010 No 2687	Sudan	**1977 No 1719**
	2010 No 2971	Pakistan	**1987 No 2058**	Swaziland	**1969 No 380**
Malta	**1995 No 763**	Panama	**2013 No 3149**	Sweden	**1984 No 366**
Mauritius	**1981 No 1121**	Papua New Guinea	**1991 No 2882**	Switzerland	**1978 No 1408**
	1987 No 467	Philippines	**1978 No 184**		1982 No 714
	2003 No 2620	Poland	**2006 No 3323**		1994 No 3215
	2011 No 2442	Portugal	**1969 No 599**		2007 No 3465
Mexico	**1994 No 3212**	Qatar	**2010 No 241**		2010 No 2689
	2010 No 2686		2011 No 1684		**2012 No 3079**
Moldova	**2008 No 1795**	Romania	**1977 No 57**	Taiwan	**2002 No 3137**
Mongolia	**1996 No 2598**	Russian Federation	**1994 No 3213**	Tajikistan (see note (b))	
Montenegro (see note (d))	**1981 No 1815**	St. Kitts and Nevis	**1947 No 2872**	Thailand	**1981 No 1546**
Montserrat	**1947 No 2869**	Saudi Arabia	**2008 No 1770**	Trinidad & Tobago	**1983 No 1903**
	1968 No 576	Serbia (see note (d))	**1981 No 1815**	Tunisia	**1984 No 133**
	2011 No 1083	Sierra Leone	**1947 No 2873**	Turkey	**1988 No 932**
Morocco	**1991 No 2881**		1968 No 1104	Turkmenistan (see note (b))	**1986 No 224**
Myanmar (Burma)	**1952 No 751**	Singapore	**1997 No 2988**	Tuvalu (and Kiribati)	**1950 No 750**
Namibia	**1962 No 2352**		2010 No 2685		1968 No 309
	1962 No 2788		2012 No 3078		1974 No 1271
	1967 No 1490	Slovak Republic (see note (c))	**1991 No 2876**	Uganda	**1993 No 1802**
Netherlands	**2009 No 227**	Slovenia	**2008 No 1796**	Ukraine	**1993 No 1803**
	2013 No 3143	Solomon Islands	**1950 No 748**	USA	**2002 No 2848**
New Zealand	**1984 No 365**		1968 No 574	Uzbekistan	**1994 No 770**
	2004 No 1274		1974 No 1270	Venezuela	**1996 No 2599**
	2008 No 1793	South Africa	**2002 No 3138**	Vietnam	**1994 No 3216**
Nigeria	**1987 No 2057**		2011 No 2441	Yugoslavia (see note (d))	**1981 No 1815**
Norway	**2013 No 3144**	Spain	**2013 No 3152**	Zambia	**2014 No 1876**
Oman	**1998 No 2568**	Sri Lanka	**1980 No 713**	Zimbabwe	**1982 No 1842**

Notes

(a) Entries in bold are for main agreements. Entries in Roman are for amending protocols.

(b) The Agreement published as *SI 1986 No 224* (which also continued in force the Air Transport agreement published as *SI 1974 No 1269*) between the UK and the former Soviet Union was to be applied by the UK as if it were still in force between the UK and the former Soviet Republics until such time as new agreements took effect with particular countries. It later came to light that Armenia, Georgia, Kyrgyzstan, Lithuania and Moldova did not consider themselves bound by the UK/USSR convention and were not operating it in relation to UK residents. Accordingly, the UK ceased to apply it to residents of those countries from 1 April 2002 for corporation tax and from 6 April 2002 for income tax and capital gains tax (although new treaties are in force with Armenia, Lithuania, Georgia and Moldova). A similar discovery has subsequently been made in relation to Tajikistan and the agreement ceased to be applied by the UK from 1 April 2014 for corporation tax and from 6 April 2014 for income tax and capital gains tax. A new agreement with Tajikistan was, however, signed on 1 July 2014. *SI 1986 No 224* is regarded as continuing in force between the UK and Turkmenistan and also between the UK and Belarus until the coming into force of *SI 1995 No 2706* (HMRC SP 4/01).

(c) The convention published as *SI 1991 No 2876* is treated as remaining in force between the UK and, respectively, the Czech Republic and the Slovak Republic. (HMRC SP 5/93).

(d) The Agreement published as *SI 1981 No 1815* between the UK and Yugoslavia is regarded as in force between the UK and Bosnia-Herzegovina, Croatia and Serbia and Montenegro. (HMRC SP 3/07). A new agreement with Croatia was signed on 15 January 2015.

Double taxation treaties

Tax information exchange agreements

Country	SI Number
Agreements in force	
Anguilla (note (a))	2010 No 2677
	2014 No 1357
Antigua and Barbuda	2011 No 1075
Aruba	2011 No 2435
Bahamas	2010 No 2684
Belize	2011 No 1685
Bermuda	2008 No 1789
British Virgin Islands (note (a))	2009 No 3013
	2014 No 1359
Curaçao, Sint Maarten and BES Islands	2011 No 2433
Dominica	2011 No 1686
Gibraltar (note (a))	2010 No 2680
	2014 No 1356
Grenada	2011 No 1687
Guernsey (note (a))	2009 No 3011
	2013 No 3154
Isle of Man	2009 No 228
Jersey	2009 No 3012
	2013 No 3151
Liberia	2011 No 2434
Liechtenstein	2010 No 2678
San Marino	2011 No 1688
St Christopher and Nevis	2011 No 1077
St Lucia	2011 No 1076
St Vincent and the Grenadines	2011 No 1078
Turks and Caicos Islands (note (a))	2010 No 2679
	2014 No 1360
Agreements signed but not in force	
Brazil	
Macao	2015 No 801
Marshall Islands	2013 No 3153
Monaco	2015 No 804
Uruguay	2014 No 1358

EU savings directive agreements

Aruba	2005 No 1458
British Virgin Islands	2005 No 1457
Gibraltar	2006 No 1453
Guernsey	2005 No 1262
Isle of Man	2005 No 1263
Jersey	2005 No 1261
Montserrat	2005 No 1459
Netherlands Antilles	2005 No 1460
Tax compliance agreements	
Isle of Man, Guernsey, Jersey, Gibraltar	2014 No 520
USA	2015 No 878

Agreements covering taxes on capital

Country	SI/ SR& O Number
Estate duty agreements	
France	1963 No 1319
India	1956 No 998
Italy	1968 No 304
Pakistan	1957 No 1522
Capital transfer and inheritance tax agreements	
Irish Republic	1978 No 1107
Netherlands	1980 No 706
	1996 No 730
South Africa	1979 No 576
Sweden	1981 No 840
	1989 No 986
Switzerland	1994 No 3214
USA	1979 No 1454

Shipping and air transport only

Country	SI or SR & O Number
Algeria (air transport only)	1984 No 362
Brazil	1968 No 572
—aircraft crew only	2011 No 2723
Cameroon (air transport only)	1982 No 1841
China (air transport only)	1981 No 1119
Congo Democratic Republic (formerly Zaire)	1977 No 1298
Ethiopia (air travel only)	1977 No 1297
Hong Kong SAR	
(air transport only)	1998 No 2566
(shipping only)	2000 No 3248
Iran (air transport only)	1960 No 2419
Lebanon	1964 No 278
Saudi Arabia	1994 No 767
USSR (see note (b))	1974 No 1269

Reciprocal agreements on social security

(see notes (c) and (d))

Country	SI Number
Barbados	1992 No 812
Bermuda	1969 No 1686
Bosnia-Herzegovinia	1958 No 1263
Canada	1995 No 2699
	1998 No 263
Croatia	1958 No 1698
Iceland (note (d))	1985 No 1202
	1992 No 3211
Isle of Man	1977 No 2150
	1989 No 483
	1989 No 2001
Israel	1957 No 1879
	1984 No 354
Jamaica	1997 No 871
Japan	2000 No 3063
Jersey and Guernsey	1994 No 2802
Korea (Republic of)	2000 No 1823
Macedonia	1958 No 1698
Mauritius	1981 No 1542
Montenegro	1958 No 1698
New Zealand	1964 No 495
	1983 No 1894
Norway (note (d))	1991 No 767
	1992 No 3212
Philippines	1989 No 2002
Serbia	1958 No 1698
Switzerland (note (d))	1969 No 384
Turkey	1961 No 584
USA	1984 No 1817
	1997 No 1778

Notes

(a) The 2013 and 2014 exchanges of letters amending the agreements are not yet in force.

(b) See note (b) on page 43.

(c) Agreements with countries containing articles specifically relating to contribution (as distinct from benefit) matters are listed.

(d) Agreements with other EC member states have been superseded for most purposes by *EC Council Regulations 883/2004* and *987/2009* and are not listed. The *Regulations* are applied also to Switzerland and, from 1 June 2012, to Iceland, Liechtenstein and Norway. For social security purposes, the UK includes Gibraltar but excludes the Isle of Man and the Channel Islands.

Foreign exchange rates averages for tax year

Country	Method of quoting	Currency per £1			
		2014/15	2013/14	2012/13	2011/12
Afghanistan	Afghani	Not quoted	87.572436	78.818194	69.855065
Albania	Lek	177.562875	166.511211	170.706903	162.359977
Algeria	Dinar	135.184926	126.062557	124.193788	117.306367
Angola	Readj Kwanza	161.431601	150.756438	151.064442	150.405122
Antigua	E Caribbean Dollar	4.368359	4.281115	4.268432	4.314367
Argentina	Peso	13.518555	9.580773	7.430757	6.707446
Armenia	Dram	680.756376	649.094961	641.398038	602.531816
Aruba	Florin	2.895548	2.838246	2.829834	2.860271
Australia	Dollar	1.844671	1.698716	1.555564	1.527388
Azerbaijan	New Manat	1.290865	1.24235	1.240105	1.257910
Bahamas	Dollar	1.598652	1.584390	1.580925	1.595813
Bahrain	Dinar	0.609907	0.597748	0.596023	0.623104
Bangladesh	Taka	125.427223	123.287538	128.040884	122.097979
Barbados	Dollar	3.2358	3.174632	3.161775	3.1958
Belarus	Rouble	18,178.92469	14,485.594230	13,366.751923	10,098.713469
Belize	Dollar	3.232967	3.171282	3.076021	3.153559
Benin	CFA Franc	832.173132	777.458673	804.848596	758.896061
Bermuda	Dollar (US)	1.598652	1.584390	1.580925	1.595813
Bhutan	Ngultrum	98.809869	95.733332	85.898432	76.204480
Bolivia	Boliviano	11.179465	10.95566	10.923555	11.0613551
Bosnia-Herzegovina	Marka	2.482128	2.318132	2.399796	2.262785
Botswana	Pula	14.75493	13.623530	12.532628	11.116155
Brazil	Real	3.949423	3.551688	3.177780	2.7055
Brunei	Dollar	2.076375	1.994973	1.965832	1.999428
Bulgaria	Lev	2.481734	2.318082	2.399794	2.262806
Burma (Myanmar)	Kyat	1,602.103403	1,516.657115	1,301.357123	10.242542
Burkina Faso	CFA Franc	832.173132	777.458673	804.848596	758.896061
Burundi	Franc	2,513.09824	2,463.063076	2,356.293269	2,065.460816

Foreign exchange rates averages for tax year

Country	Method of quoting	Currency per £1			
		2014/15	2013/14	2012/13	2011/12
Cambodia	Riel	6,531.265625	6,355.799423	6,364.800192	6,475.170204
Cameroon Republic	CFA Franc	832.173132	777.458673	804.848596	758.896061
Canada	Dollar	1.831271	1.667123	1.582757	1.582388
Cape Verde Islands	Escudo	138.240394	129.296134	134.738980	125.241448
Cayman Islands	Dollar	1.326696	1.300207	1.296357	16.875577
Central African Republic	CFA Franc	832.173132	777.458673	804.848596	758.896061
Chad	CFA Franc	832.173132	777.458673	804.848596	758.896061
Chile	Peso	946.055778	812.637711	763.586596	771.868046
China	Renminbi Yuan	9.926634	9.697792	9.943490	10.233969
Colombia	Peso	3,371.950846	3,041.423846	2,838.02	2,918.789591
Comoros	Franc	611.577542	583.267134	603.636576	569.173571
Congo (Brazzaville)	CFA Franc	832.173132	777.458673	804.848596	758.896061
Congo Dem Rep (Zaire)	Cong Franc	1,491.183525	1,447.820423	1,428.350653	1,452.243163
Costa Rica	Colon	876.715363	800.230134	791.741903	810.611653
Cote d'Ivoire	CFA Franc	832.173132	777.458673	804.848596	758.896061
Croatia	Kuna	9.697926	8.997532	9.225951	8.641553
Cuba	Peso	1.617905	1.585617	1.580919	1.597918
Czech Republic	Koruna	35.00173	31.288415	30.986419	28.608051
Denmark	Krone	9.463411	8.841261	9.150131	8.623805
Djibouti	Franc	287.467869	277.324653	277.583038	279.288836
Dominica	E Caribbean Dollar	4.368359	4.281115	4.268432	4.314367
Dominican Republic	Peso	70.785615	66.857996	62.601088	61.140210
Ecuador	Dollar	1.598652	1.584390	1.580925	1.595813
Egypt	Egyptian pound	11.62905	10.998159	9.825932	9.556418
El Salvador	Colon	14.144994	13.8699	13.828840	13.977663
Equatorial Guinea	CFA Franc	832.173132	777.458673	804.848596	758.896061
Eritrea	Nakfa	24.205738	22.413994	23.712465	23.968518
Ethiopia	Birr	32.199032	29.991955	28.487605	27.373510
European Community	Euro	1.270009	1.185417	1.228351	1.158234
Fiji	Dollar	3.08985	3.302976	2.835903	2.838495
French Polynesia	CFP franc	151.415111	141.435269	146.418076	138.058836

Foreign exchange rates averages for tax year

Country	Method of quoting	Currency per £1			
		2014/15	2013/14	2012/13	2011/12
Gabon	CFA Franc	832.173132	777.458673	804.848596	758.896061
Gambia	Dalasi	66.209526	56.026905	50.614803	46.145063
Georgia	Lari	2.94908	22.412782	49.249373	47.147438
Ghana	Cedi	5.235273	3.476582	3.004503	2.534230
Grenada/Windward Isles	E. Caribbean dollar	4.368359	4.2811153	4.268432	4.314367
Guatemala	Quetzal	12.468307	12.446438	12.421161	12.427604
Guinea Bissau	CFA Franc	832.173132	777.458673	804.848596	758.896061
Guinea Republic	Franc	11,212.55817	11,127.276923	10,969.924396	11,045.720408
Guyana	Dollar	331.443521	320.772346	317.966134	323.391816
Haiti	Gourde	73.930236	68.409605	66.498282	64.538159
Honduras	Lempira	33.571838	31.841978	30.858517	30.241383
Hong Kong	Dollar	12.547017	12.297534	12.263534	12.412126
Hungary	Forint	392.366607	355.054096	354.579403	328.864489
Iceland	Krona	194.715648	188.893884	183.822076	187.988285
India	Rupee	98.809869	95.7333320	85.898432	76.204480
Indonesia	Rupiah	19,449.2437	17,358.536538	15,031.823076	14,013.842857
Iran	Rial	Not quoted	22,404.017307	19,423.219230	17,459.891836
Iraq	Dinar	1,876.876603	1,841.446346	1,836.929423	1,863.107346
Israel	Shekel	5.932238	5.650203	6.074167	5.769878
Jamaica	Dollar	182.027048	162.911096	142.587557	137.063469
Japan	Yen	176.516505	158.325192	130.738615	126.098730
Jordan	Dinar	1.145896	1.122151	1.119798	1.132322
Kazakhstan	Tenge	295.638825	247.49325	236.7405961	234.887938
Kenya	Kenyan shilling	143.896907	136.329173	134.697884	142.959510
Korea (North)	Won	Not quoted	2.061119	2.055076	2.077273
Korea (South)	Won	1,712.111742	1,729.588269	1,762.881346	1,769.754230
Kuwait	Dinar	0.464909	0.469126	0.617563	0.441012
Kyrgyz Republic	Som	89.656744	66.114298	49.249373	47.147438
Laos	Kip	13,016.24603	12,452.840384	12,565.259615	12,758.136734
Latvia (note (b))	Lats	n/a	0.908507	0.856659	0.815826
Lebanon	Lebanese pound	2,443.96398	2,390.3125	2,378.453461	2,407.453061
Lesotho	Loti	18.3761	15.973736	13.418936	11.804930
Liberia	Dollar	1.598652	1.584390	1.580925	1.595813
Libya	Libyan dinar	1.997203	1.986651	1.985165	1.939242
Lithuania	Litas	3.685982	4.092365	4.236559	3.994697

Foreign exchange rates averages for tax year

Country	Method of quoting	Currency per £1 2014/15	2013/14	2012/13	2011/12
Macao	Pataca	12.920921	12.669376	12.628963	12.802108
Macedonia	Denar	77.971421	73.037817	75.882167	71.130687
Madagascar	Malagasy Ariary	4,165.12949	3,546.859615	3,489.240576	3,282.515102
Malawi	Kwacha	686.484492	604.846	468.932769	255.308673
Malaysia	Ringgit	5.399236	5.066923	4.888323	4.881986
Maldive Islands	Rufiyaa	24.855546	24.366065	24.29945	24.037028
Mali Republic	CFA Franc	832.173132	777.458673	804.848596	758.896061
Mauritania	Ouguiya	473.63995	468.377980	471.309192	452.906224
Mauritius	Rupee	50.568207	48.5412192	48.207744	45.684714
Mexico	Peso	22.087078	20.439413	20.697690	20.160430
Moldova	Leu	24.06798	20.384972	19.256219	18.644859
Mongolia	Tugrik	3,003.960344	2,534.994230	2,162.609038	2,054.568163
Montserrat	E Caribbean Dollar	4.368359	4.281115	4.268432	4.314367
Morocco	Dirham	14.039213	13.249678	13.614140	12.764963
Mozambique	Metical	51.399896	47.967882	45.840640	44.630057
Nepal	Rupee	158.123055	152.856480	137.469769	121.368040
New Caledonia	CFP Franc	151.415111	141.435269	146.418076	138.058836
New Zealand	Dollar	1.993251	1.932296	1.946634	1.981894
Nicaragua	Gold Cordoba	42.398398	39.627757	37.646307	36.206320
Niger Republic	CFA Franc	832.173132	777.458673	804.848596	758.896061
Nigeria	Naira	277.120103	254.236692	250.418019	250.632612
Norway	Krone	10.747198	9.485832	9.137515	8.964901
Oman (Sultanate of)	Rial	0.622811	0.610471	0.608694	0.615242
Pakistan	Rupee	162.236948	163.388115	150.345730	139.665653
Panama	Balboa	1.617934	1.585617	1.580919	1.597918
Papua New Guinea	Kina	4.172923	3.844990	3.266240	3.575102
Paraguay	Guarani	7,289.729365	6,995.278653	6,870.789038	6,668.881020
Peru	New sol	4.666884	4.367671	4.130073	4.366532
Philippines	Peso	71.664084	68.755323	65.911836	68.79605
Poland	Zloty	5.316865	4.981088	5.113782	4.834936
Qatar	Riyal	5.890167	5.773226	5.755930	5.818567
Romania	Leu	5.625182	5.270330	5.485075	4.937955
Russia	Rouble	71.37214	51.232159	49.249373	47.147438
Rwanda	Rwanda franc	1,110.898894	1,046.674134	981.322019	961.236734

Foreign exchange rates averages for tax year

Country	Method of quoting	Currency per £1 2014/15	2013/14	2012/13	2011/12
São Tomé & Principe	Dobra	29,958.59048	28,147.853846	29,487.034615	28,351.277551
Saudi Arabia	Riyal	6.070709	5.945146	5.929651	5.984640
Senegal	CFA Franc	832.173132	777.458673	804.848596	758.896061
Serbia	Dinar	150.396971	135.015480	139.836903	118.896142
Seychelles	Seychelles rupee	21.147042	19.004840	21.195038	20.373306
Sierra Leone	Leone	7,017.841884	6,861.479807	6,846.487307	6,990.352448
Singapore	Dollar	2.078003	1.994125	1.965540	2.000944
Solomon Islands	Dollar	11.983561	11.395278	11.209030	11.822644
Somali Republic	Shilling	1,321.721605	1,970.632884	2,479.860576	2,511.687346
South Africa	Rand	17.834982	15.977884	13.413334	11.852196
Sri Lanka	Rupee	211.766992	206.1235	205.027153	178.794204
St Christopher & Nevis	E Caribbean Dollar	4.368359	4.281115	4.268432	4.314367
St Lucia	E Caribbean Dollar	4.368359	4.281115	4.268432	4.314367
St Vincent	E Caribbean Dollar	4.368359	4.281115	4.268432	4.314367
Sudan Republic	Pound	9.163836	7.730271	6.246534	4.285691
Surinam	Dollar	5.329569	5.232471	5.216963	5.273114
Swaziland	Lilangeni	17.807253	15.974261	13.418936	11.8049306
Sweden	Krona	11.712365	10.334775	10.595496	10.448853
Switzerland	Franc	1.501175	1.457903	1.48565	1.407255
Syria	Syrian pound	Not quoted	188.354192	105.433448	80.319404
Taiwan	New Taiwan Dollar	49.464353	47.330036	46.662044	47.0277576
Tajikistan	Somoni	Not quoted	25.186496	49.249373	47.147438
Tanzania	Tanzanian shilling	2,750.949825	2,566.585576	2,515.534038	2,565.878367
Thailand	Baht	52.555153	49.676876	48.714236	48.795525
Togo Republic	CFA Franc	832.173132	777.458673	804.848596	758.896061
Tonga Islands	Pa anga	1.844671	1.698716	1.555564	1.527388
Trinidad &Tobago	Dollar	10.316169	10.169007	10.130469	10.232887
Tunisia	Dinar	2.852901	2.593001	2.490180	2.276393
Turkey	Turkish Lira	3.60965	3.175461	2.840913	2.752214
Turkmenistan	New Manat	4.788902	4.512580	4.498830	4.543610
Uganda	New shilling	4,327.1103	4,041.717307	4,059.66442	4,055.644693
Ukraine	Hryvnia	23.276661	13.177934	12.813223	12.784306
United Arab Emirates	Dirham	5.941769	5.823459	6.767975	5.869067
Uruguay	Peso uruguayo	38.430992	33.429732	31.873157	30.635430
USA	Dollar	1.598652	1.584390	1.580925	1.5958134
Uzbekistan	Sum	3,809.483059	3,390.213269	3,056.430769	2,792.517959

Foreign exchange rates averages for tax year

Country	Method of quoting	Currency per £1			
		2014/15	2013/14	2012/13	2011/12
Vanuatu	Vatu	160.865048	154.663769	149.114173	148.545367
Venezuela	Bolivar Fuerte	15.849496	9.975996	7.080534	6.862446
Vietnam	Dong	34,369.76326	33,421.130769	32,986.353846	33,256.906122
Wallis & Futuna Islands	CFP Franc	151.415111	141.435269	146.418076	138.058836
Western Samoa	Tala	3.823928	3.687730	3.623753	3.666714
Yemen (Rep of)	Rial	347.80949	340.972288	339.741673	345.455408
Zambia	Kwacha	10.324705	8.674986	6,262.30405	7,907.839387
Zimbabwe	Dollar	605.873298	600.03614	597.903784	604.135510

Notes

(a)   The material on pp 45–50 is reproduced from information provided by HMRC and is Crown copyright. The averages for the tax year 2012/13 have been updated and are correct as at 24 October 2013.
(b)   Latvia joined the Euro on 1 January 2014.

Foreign exchange rates averages for calendar year

For general use

Country	Method of quoting	Currency per £1			
		2014	2013	2012	2011
Afghanistan	Afghani	Not quoted	84.465203	76.767648	69.078780
Albania	Lek	173.436528	165.328264	171.529816	161.708470
Algeria	Dinar	132.463735	124.489188	123.093387	117.053862
Angola	Readj Kwanza	161.931792	147.997901	150.805061	150.193725
Antigua	E Caribbean Dollar	4.451947	4.222122	4.271626	4.328835
Argentina	Peso	13.341358	8.5036377	7.181784	6.611286
Armenia	Dram	680.630415	638.991547	635.239489	595.023235
Aruba	Florin	2.951509	2.799132	2.831951	2.869862
Australia	Dollar	1.825207	1.633679	1.530380	1.553232
Azerbaijan	New Manat	1.291618	1.225513	1.241604	1.266621
Bahamas	Dollar	1.650730	1.562598	1.582875	1.603844
Bahrain	Dinar	0.621643	0.589507	0.596475	0.624317
Bangladesh	Taka	127.864377	122.257660	129.561714	118.157254
Barbados	Dollar	3.301111	3.127469	3.164138	3.206519
Belarus	Rouble	16,815.24717	13,870.637735	13,228.889795	8,126.321960
Belize	Dollar	3.292843	3.132690	3.050991	3.165149
Benin	CFA Franc	812.555075	773.000641	809.512836	755.748666
Bermuda	Dollar	1.65073	1.562598	1.582875	1.603844
Bhutan	Ngultrum	100.645467	91.217953	84.532805	74.557648
Bolivia	Boliviano	11.393639	10.804692	10.931695	11.126
Bosnia-Herzegovina	Marka	2.422771	2.304841	2.413702	2.2534
Botswana	Pula	14.76213	13.061015	12.296653	10.915992
Brazil	Real	3.86497	3.361409	3.091557	2.67755
Brunei	Dollar	2.086947	1.953496	1.978051	2.013958
Bulgaria	Lev	2.42269	2.304803	2.413708	2.253421
Burma (Myanmar)	Kyat	1,615.16849	1,446.222830	998.850914	10.276898
Burkina Faso	CFA Franc	812.555075	773.000641	809.512836	755.748666
Burundi	Franc	2,560.384528	2,445.396037	2,278.453877	2,015.156274

Foreign exchange rates averages for calendar year

For general use

Country	Method of quoting	Currency per £1			
		2014	2013	2012	2011
Cambodia	Riel	6,622.176603	6,271.774150	6,389.105714	6,475.575490
Cameroon Republic	CFA Franc	812.555075	773.000641	809.512836	755.748666
Canada	Dollar	1.819945	1.607662	1.583601	1.584378
Cape Verde Islands	Escudo	134.578792	128.738622	135.763795	124.081607
Cayman Islands	Dollar	1.352092	1.282288	1.297328	16.269574
Central African Republic	CFA Franc	812.555075	773.000641	809.512836	755.748666
Chad	CFA Franc	812.555075	773.000641	809.512836	755.748666
Chile	Peso	935.85715	771.172075	770.0784489	771.550411
China	Renminbi/Yuan	10.153441	9.623090	9.988053	10.374478
Colombia	Peso	3,276.59283	2,912.133018	2,846.81	2,959.414509
Comoros	Franc	597.791415	579.920377	607.134714	566.812980
Congo (Brazzaville)	CFA Franc	812.555075	773.000641	809.512836	755.748666
Congo Dem Rep (Zaire)	Cong Franc	1,521.934716	1,401.709924	1,454.9075510204	1,458.637352
Costa Rica	Colon	885.970396	781.661754	795.48502040816	810.964078
Cote d'Ivoire	CFA Franc	812.555075	773.000641	809.512836	755.748666
Croatia	Kuna	9.455503	8.921675	9.276048	8.560872
Cuba	Peso	1.648888	1.563767	1.582097	1.603278
Czech Republic	Koruna	34.108347	30.507841	31.050883	28.314162
Denmark	Krone	9.240611	8.788083	9.181059	8.576243
Djibouti	Franc	290.802226	273.375075	277.746816	280.387372
Dominica	E Caribbean Dollar	4.451947	4.222122	4.271626	4.328835
Dominican Republic	Peso	71.510156	64.986096	61.943573	60.816127
Ecuador	Dollar	1.65073	1.562598	1.582875	1.603844
Egypt	Egyptian pound	11.668037	10.699456	9.598010	9.519580
El Salvador	Colon	14.422643	13.678796	13.839181	14.024547
Equatorial Guinea	CFA Franc	812.555075	773.000641	809.512836	755.748666
Eritrea	Nakfa	24.580169	22.180984	23.730136	24.048915
Ethiopia	Birr	32.383033	29.216401	28.144177	27.1943392
European Community	Euro	1.239501	1.178398	1.233473	1.151701
Fiji	Dollar	3.107326	3.210179	2.834738	2.874145
French Polynesia	CFP franc	147.820075	140.624264	147.266612	137.471117

Foreign exchange rates averages for calendar year

For general use

Country	Method of quoting	Currency per £1			
		2014	2013	2012	2011
Gabon	CFA Franc	812.555075	773.000641	809.512836	755.748666
Gambia	Dalasi	65.453343	53.476052	49.346304	45.487305
Georgia	Lari	2.9018	33.842681	49.320938	47.057882
Ghana	Cedi	4.971169	3.208164	2.9353	2.471605
Grenada/Windward Isles	E. Caribbean dollar	4.451947	4.222122	4.271626	4.328835
Guatemala	Quetzal	12.772226	12.298324	12.402746	12.498837
Guinea Bissau	CFA Franc	812.555075	773.000641	809.512836	755.748666
Guinea Republic	Franc	11,390.26564	10,966.441509	11,031.342216	11,127.678431
Guyana	Dollar	337.651132	315.198792	318.159979	325.0505294
Haiti	Gourde	74.33492	66.817347	65.880948	64.599154
Honduras	Lempira	33.751245	31.413249	30.551165	30.287207
Hong Kong	Dollar	12.801635	12.125373	12.279098	12.484348
Hungary	Forint	381.704584	349.450622	356.920591	321.140764
Iceland	Krona	191.904113	191.535207	181.907653	185.767450
India	Rupee	100.645467	91.217953	84.532805	74.557648
Indonesia	Rupiah	19,544.89811	16,184.624528	14,803.457142	14,037.286274
Iran	Rial	Not quoted	19,284.292452	19,282.640816	16,977.892156
Iraq	Dinar	1,915.916981	1,815.725283	1,838.802040	1,872.536274
Israel	Shekel	5.881066	5.653766	6.108028	5.724734
Jamaica	Dollar	182.43383	155.152849	139.787857	137.1204117
Japan	Yen	173.790568	151.646301	126.15025	128.003692
Jordan	Dinar	1.167201	1.107303	1.120644	1.135860
Kazakhstan	Tenge	293.937603	237.796226	235.948204	235.107098
Kenya	Kenyan shilling	144.741188	134.673415	133.743897	142.140686
Korea (North)	Won	Not quoted	2.032716	2.056610	6.119613
Korea (South)	Won	1,733.923529	1,710.245094	1,785.194230	1,774.787692
Kuwait	Dinar	0.46899	0.462549	0.627044	0.443325
Kyrgyz Republic	Som	87.892811	56.700590	49.320938	47.057882
Laos	Kip	13,228.63774	12,237.392452	12,601.877551	12,823.652941
Latvia	Lats (note (b))	n/a	0.827262	0.860487	0.814049
Lebanon	Pound	2,488.848679	2,357.406603	2,380.240816	2,413.901568
Lesotho	Loti	17.821445	14.953369	13.0064102	11.560037
Liberia	Dollar	1.65073	1.562598	1.582875	1.603844
Libya	Libyan Dinar	2.011416	1.968643	1.977814	1.946633
Lithuania	Litas	4.277101	4.068907	4.261118	3.978150

Foreign exchange rates averages for calendar year

For general use

Country	Method of quoting	Currency per £1			
		2014	2013	2012	2011
Macao	Pataca	13.169922	12.493056	12.640185	12.854964
Macedonia	Denar	76.234615	72.915816	76.009671	70.877366
Madagascar	Malagasy Ariary	4,071.393207	3,467.388867	3,479.529183	3,246.625294
Malawi	Kwacha	693.281811	567.309264	395.980142	250.396784
Malaysia	Ringgit	5.389764	4.913211	4.889942	4.899313
Maldive Islands	Rufiyaa	25.3498528	24.031879	24.315871	23.093664
Mali Republic	CFA Franc	812.555075	773.000641	809.512836	755.748666
Mauritania	Ouguiya	483.262094	464.934811	469.061795	451.256274
Mauritius	Rupee	50.449962	48.083773	47.713481	46.046884
Mexico	Peso	21.887945	19.946430	20.875711	19.867946
Moldova	Leu	23.018781	19.610196	19.169014	18.811905
Mongolia	Tugrik	2,976.821509	2,366.378679	2,149.365918	2,021.839215
Montserrat	E Caribbean Dollar	4.451947	4.222122	4.271626	4.328835
Morocco	Dirham	13.829083	13.151809	13.681197	12.740574
Mozambique	Metical	51.521915	46.942524	44.731187	46.630631
Nepal	Rupee	160.896358	145.634113	135.203061	119.028039
New Caledonia	CFP Franc	147.820075	140.624264	147.266612	137.471117
New Zealand	Dollar	1.985364	1.905811	1.959825	2.029523
Nicaragua	Gold Cordoba	42.728809	38.584190	37.239314	35.904198
Niger Republic	CFA Franc	812.555075	773.000641	809.512836	755.748666
Nigeria	Naira	271.102471	248.796037	251.436428	249.169352
Norway	Krone	10.337056	9.165418	9.233155	8.977276
Oman (Sultanate of)	Rial	0.634818	0.602060	0.609144	0.617333
Pakistan	Rupee	166.792811	158.273566	147.702285	138.291588
Panama	Balboa	1.648888	1.563767	1.582097	1.603278
Papua New Guinea	Kina	4.234735	3.6015	3.260636	3.792364
Paraguay	Guarani	7,361.936792	6,724.010943	7,021.556938	6,744.826274
Peru	New sol	4.669281	4.210445	4.177540	4.416507
Philippines	Peso	73.274819	66.235656	66.912084	69.410809
Poland	Zloty	5.179733	4.939332	5.169414	4.731154
Qatar	Riyal	6.003833	5.693373	5.760416	5.837937
Romania	Leu	5.505837	5.205075	5.512736	4.887498
Russia	Rouble	62.438177	48.785824	49.320938	47.0578823
Rwanda	Rwanda franc	1,127.871509	1,013.289	971.315836	961.775333

Foreign exchange rates averages for calendar year

For general use

Country	Method of quoting	Currency per £1			
		2014	2013	2012	2011
Saotome & Principe	Dobra	29,438.28868	27,972.626415	29,877.959183	28,235.141176
Saudi Arabia	Riyal	6.192084	5.862673	5.936051	6.014736
Senegal	CFA Franc	812.555075	773.000641	809.512836	755.748666
Serbia	Dinar	145.042773	133.136490	139.699734	117.515235
Seychelles	Seychelles rupee	20.896807	18.988941	21.708744	19.832025
Sierra Leone	Leone	7,163.135094	6,758.089056	6,872.885714	6,965.582156
Singapore	Dollar	2.0881	1.953333	1.980832	2.015259
Solomon Islands	Dollar	12.040309	11.177784	11.224248	12.114521
Somali Republic	Shilling	1,483.809433	2,146.782452	2,491.090204	2,510.116862
South Africa	Rand	17.860896	15.011341	13.006967	11.578746
Sri Lanka	Rupee	215.284849	201.652396	202.164448	177.075039
St Chrisopher & Nevis	E Caribbean Dollar	4.451947	4.222122	4.271626	4.328835
St Lucia	E Caribbean Dollar	4.451947	4.222122	4.271626	4.328835
St Vincent	E Caribbean Dollar	4.451947	4.222122	4.271626	4.328835
Sudan Republic	Pound	9.393952	7.098594	5.594983	4.230813
Surinam	Dollar	5.441267	5.160362	5.220865	5.205325
Swaziland	Lilangeni	17.821445	14.953884	13.006410	11.560037
Sweden	Krona	11.283692	10.176862	10.741259	10.395490
Switzerland	Franc	1.506213	1.449658	1.486984	1.421359
Syria	Syrian pound	Not quoted	156.194264	100.277797	76.863907
Taiwan	New Taiwan Dollar	49.940276	46.346854	46.858536	47.0815961
Tajikistan	Somoni	Not quoted	35.339220	49.320938	47.0578823
Tanzania	Tanzanian shilling	2,737.118679	2,528.795094	2,509.602040	2,535.730980
Thailand	Baht	53.594978	47.940149	49.223330	48.820230
Togo Republic	CFA Franc	812.555075	773.000641	809.512836	755.748666
Tonga Islands	Pa anga	1.825207	1.633679	1.530380	1.553232
Trinidad &Tobago	Dollar	10.533339	10.030886	10.137330	10.261809
Tunisia	Dinar	2.790675	2.534460	2.476826	2.253631
Turkey	Turkish Lira	3.596256	2.959177	2.850042	2.677966
Turkmenistan	New Manat	4.691332	4.450096	4.500820	4.560825
Uganda	New shilling	4,271.98849	4,055.188301	3,956.551836	4,042.469215
Ukraine	Hryvnia	19.41222	12.739381	12.792736	12.797878
United Arab Emirates	Dirham	6.056283	5.743216	6.831167	5.888749
Uruguay	Peso uruguayo	38.155898	31.813079	32.104220	30.822629
USA	Dollar	1.65073	1.562598	1.582875	1.603844
Uzbekistan	Sum	3,792.296981	3,257.227358	2,986.947755	2,741.073725

Foreign exchange rates averages for calendar year

For general use

Country	Method of quoting	Currency per £1			
		2014	2013	2012	2011
Vanuatu	Vatu	162.196641	150.247377	149.246306	149.979921
Venezuela	Bolivar Fuerte	15.771784	9.297733	6.794202	6.885468
Vietnam	Dong	34,938.75245	32,865.616981	33,021.285714	33,063.927450
Wallis & Futuna Islands	CFP Franc	147.820075	140.624264	147.266612	137.471117
Western Samoa	Tala	3.841328	3.607826	3.631644	3.720178
Yemen (Rep of)	Rial	354.570207	336.214943	341.023040	345.071235
Zambia	Kwacha	10.101411	322.908109	8,132.805510	7,779.138823
Zimbabwe	Dollar	623.263884	591.439254	598.385187	606.220352

Notes

(a) The material on p 43–55 is reproduced from information provided by HMRC and is Crown copyright.
(b) Latvia joined the Euro on 1 January 2014.

Foreign exchange rates at specified dates

For general use

Country	Method of quoting	Currency per £1							
		31.3.15	31.12.14	31.3.14	31.12.13	31.3.13	31.12.12	31.3.12	31.12.11
Australia	Dollar	1.9432	1.9054	1.7988	1.8513	1.4626	1.5657	1.5423	1.5159
Canada	Dollar	1.8801	1.806	1.8401	1.7598	1.5489	1.6185	1.5969	1.5825
Denmark	Krone	10.3261	9.5953	9.031	8.9671	8.8392	9.1989	8.9259	8.8978
European Community	Euro	1.3822	1.2886	1.2096	1.202	1.1857	1.233	1.1998	1.1972
Hong Kong	Dollar	11.5094	12.0918	12.9322	12.8422	11.826	12.5991	12.405	12.0701
Japan	Yen	178.02	186.946	171.691	174.08	142.058	140.549	131.487	119.572
Norway	Krone	11.9637	11.6906	9.9813	10.0483	8.8618	9.0463	9.1137	9.2748
South Africa	Rand	17.9865	18.0386	17.535	17.3472	13.9881	13.7914	12.262	12.5469
Sweden	Krona	12.8024	12.2062	10.8091	10.6374	9.9125	10.5746	10.6016	10.6539
Switzerland	Franc	1.4419	1.5494	1.4727	1.473	1.4439	1.4879	1.4442	1.4532
USA	Dollar	1.4845	1.5593	1.6672	1.6563	1.5233	1.6255	1.5978	1.5541

Note

(a)   The material on p 43–55 is reproduced from information provided by HMRC and is Crown copyright.

Government securities

Security		Interest dates	Security		Interest dates	Security		Interest dates
Treasury Stock Index Linked			Treasury Loan/Stock			4¼%	2049	7 Jun/Dec
0⅛%	2019	22 May/Nov	1%	2017	7 Mar/Sept	4¼%	2055	7 Jun/Dec
0⅛%	2024	22 Mar/Sept	1¼%	2018	22 Jan/Jul	4½%	2019	7 Mar/Sept
0⅛%	2026	22 Mar/Sept	1¾%	2017	22 Jan/Jul	4½%	2034	7 Mar/Sept
0⅛%	2029	22 Mar/Sept	1¾%	2019	22 Jan/Jul	4½%	2042	7 Jun/Dec
0⅛%	2044	22 Mar/Sept	1¾%	2022	7 Mar/Sept	4¾%	2015	7 Mar/Sept
0⅛%	2046	22 Mar/Sept	2%	2016	22 Jan/Jul	4¾%	2020	7 Mar/Sept
0⅛%	2058	22 Mar/Sept	2%	2020	22 Jan/Jul	4¾%	2030	7 Jun/Dec
0⅛%	2068	22 Mar/Sept	2%	2025	7 Mar/Sept	4¾%	2038	7 Jun/Dec
0¼%	2052	22 Mar/Sept	2¼%	2023	7 Mar/Sept	5%	2018	7 Mar/Sep
0⅜%	2062	22 Mar/Sept	2¾%	2024	7 Mar/Sept	5%	2025	7 Mar/Sept
0½%	2050	22 Mar/Sept	3¼%	2044	22 Jan/Jul	6%	2028	7 Jun/Dec
0⅝%	2040	22 Mar/Sept	3½%	2045	22 Jan/Jul	8%	2015	7 Jun/Dec
0⅝%	2042	22 May/Nov	3½%	2068	22 Jan/Jul	8%	2021	7 Jun/Dec
0¾%	2034	22 Mar/Sept	3¾%	2019	7 Mar/Sept	8¾%	2017	25 Feb/Aug
0¾%	2047	22 May/Nov	3¾%	2020	7 Mar/Sept			
1⅛%	2037	22 May/Nov	3¾%	2021	7 Mar/Sept			
1¼%	2017	22 May/Nov	3¾%	2052	22 Jan/Jul			
1¼%	2027	22 May/Nov	4%	2016	7 Mar/Sept			
1¼%	2032	22 May/Nov	4%	2022	7 Mar Sept			
1¼%	2055	22 May/Nov	4%	2060	22 Jan/Jul			
1⅞%	2022	22 May/Nov	4¼%	2027	7 Jun/Dec			
2%	2035	26 Jan/Jul	4¼%	2032	7 Jun/Dec			
2½%	2016	26 Jan/Jul	4¼%	2036	7 Mar/Sept			
2½%	2020	16 Apr/Oct	4¼%	2039	7 Mar/Sept			
2½%	2024	17 Jan/Jul	4¼%	2040	7 Jun/Dec			
4⅛%	2030	22 Jan/Jul	4¼%	2046	7 Jun/Dec			

Notes

(a) The government securities listed above are those in issue on 28 July 2015.

(b) Interest on all government securities is exempt from income tax if beneficially owned by persons who are not resident (for securities issued before 6 April 2013, not ordinarily resident) in the UK. [*FA 1998, s 161*; *ITTOIA 2005, ss 713, 714*].

The securities are also excluded property for inheritance tax purposes if beneficially owned by persons who are not resident (ordinarily resident) in the UK. [*IHTA 1984, s 6(2)*].

Income tax rates

Starting, basic, higher and additional rates

2015/16	Taxable income £	Rate	Tax £	Cumulative tax £
Basic rate	0–31,785	20%	6,357	6,357
Higher rate	31,786–150,000	40%	47,286	53,643
Additional rate	Over 150,000	45%		
2014/15	£		£	£
Basic rate	0–31,865	20%	6,373	6,373
Higher rate	31,866–150,000	40%	47,254	53,627
Additional rate	Over 150,000	45%		
2013/14	£		£	£
Basic rate	0–32,010	20%	6,402	6,402
Higher rate	32,011–150,000	40%	47,196	53,598
Additional rate	Over 150,000	45%		
2012/13	£		£	£
Basic rate	0–34,370	20%	6,874	6,874
Higher rate	34,371–150,000	40%	46,252	53,126
Additional rate	Over 150,000	50%		
2011/12	£		£	£
Basic rate	0–35,000	20%	7,000	7,000
Higher rate	35,001–150,000	40%	46,000	53,000
Additional rate	Over 150,000	50%		

2010/11	Taxable income £	Rate	Tax £	Cumulative tax £
Basic rate	0–37,400	20%	7,480	7,480
Higher rate	37,401–150,000	40%	45,040	52,520
Additional rate	Over 150,000	50%		
2009/10	£		£	£
Basic rate	0–37,400	20%	7,480	7,480
Higher rate	Over 37,400	40%		

Trust rate (note (d))

	Rate
2013/14–2015/16	45%
2010/11–2012/13	50%
2009/10	40%

Construction industry sub-contractors' rates

	Rate
Registered rate	20%
Unregistered rate	30%

Notes

(a) There is also a starting rate for savings band. For 2015/16 the band is £5,000; for 2014/15 it is £2,880; for 2013/14 it is £2,790; for 2012/13 it is £2,710; for 2011/12 it is £2,560; for 2009/10 and 2010/11 it is £2,440. Where an individual's non-savings income is less than the starting rate limit for savings, the savings income is taxable at the 0% starting rate for savings up to the limit (10% for 2014/15 and earlier years). Where non-savings income exceeds the limit, the starting rate for savings does not apply.

(b) **Dividend income.** Where dividend income falls within the starting rate or the basic rate band (treating dividend income as the top slice of taxable income), the rate is set at 10% so that the liability is met by the 10% tax credit, where applicable. To the extent that taxable income exceeds the basic rate limit but not, for 2010/11 onwards, the higher rate limit, the rate is set at 32.5% (with a tax credit at 10%). Dividend income within the additional rate band is taxable at the rate of 37.5% for 2013/14 to 2015/16, and at the rate of 42.5% for 2010/11 to 2012/13 (in both cases with a tax credit at 10%). The tax credit cannot be repaid where allowances are set against dividends, and tax credits may only be set against liability in respect of dividends brought into charge.

Discretionary and accumulation trusts pay tax on dividends at the rate of 37.5% (42.5% for 2010/11 to 2012/13; 32.5% for 2009/10). The non-repayable tax credit attaching to the dividend does not form part of the trustees' tax pool.

(c) **Interest income.** Interest income (i.e. bank and building society interest, interest distributions from authorised unit trusts, interest on gilts and other securities including qualifying corporate bonds and purchased life annuities) is treated as the second top slice of taxable income behind dividends. Where the income falls within the basic rate band, it is chargeable at 20% and to the extent that if falls within the higher rate band it is taxed at 40%. For 2010/11 onwards, interest income within the additional rate band is taxed at the rate of 45% for 2013/14 to 2015/16, and at the rate of 50% for 2010/11 to 2012/13. See note (a) above where the income falls within the starting rate for savings band.

Tax deducted at source (at 20%) from interest income is repayable to the extent (if any) that it exceeds the liability on that income, computed as above.

(d) Trusts for vulnerable beneficiaries can be taxed (on election) as if the income arising were that of the beneficiary, taking into account personal allowances and the starting, basic, higher and additional rate bands.

Where any trust income consists of or includes income otherwise chargeable at the dividend trust rate or the trust rate ('special trust tax rate income'), so much of that income as does not exceed £1,000 is chargeable to income tax at the basic rate, savings rate or the ordinary dividend rate, depending on the nature of the income.

(e) **Personal representatives etc.** The starting, higher and additional rates do not apply to persons other than individuals (e.g. personal representatives). Tax is chargeable at the ordinary dividend rate for dividends (covered by the tax credit where applicable) and at the basic rate for other income.

(f) **Scottish rate of income tax.** The *Scotland Act 2012* introduced the Scottish rate of income tax which is expected to be implemented in April 2016. Further powers to set non-savings income tax rates and bands are included in the Scotland Bill currently before Parliament.

(g) **Future developments.** For 2016/17 the basic rate band will be £32,000 and for 2017/18 it will be £32,400. For 2016/17 onwards, the starting rate for savings band will be replaced by a tax-free personal savings allowance of £1,000 for basic rate taxpayers and £500 for higher rate taxpayers. The dividend tax credit will be abolished and replaced by a tax-free personal dividend allowance of £5,000. The dividend ordinary rate will be 7.5%, the dividend higher rate 32.5% and the dividend additional rate 38.1%.

Income tax allowances

	2015/16	2014/15	2013/14	2012/13	2011/12	2010/11	2009/10
	£	£	£	£	£	£	£
Personal allowance	10,600	10,000	9,440	8,105	7,475	6,475	6,475
Transferable marriage allowance (note (a))	1,060	—	—	—	—	—	—
Income limit (allowance reduced by ½ excess)	100,000	100,000	100,000	100,000	100,000	100,000	—
Persons born before 6.4.1948 and over 65 (note (b))							
Income limit (allowance reduced by ½ excess)	27,700	27,000	26,100	25,400	24,000	22,900	22,900
Personal allowance — person born before 6.4.1948 and after 5.4.1938	—	10,500	10,500	—	—	—	—
— effective maximum income for claim	—	28,000	28,220	—	—	—	—
Personal allowance age 65 to 74	—	—	—	10,500	9,940	9,490	9,490
— effective maximum income for claim	—	—	—	30,190	28,930	28,930	28,930
Personal allowance — person born before 6.4.1938	10,660	10,660	10,660	—	—	—	—
— effective maximum income for claim	27,820	28,320	28,540	—	—	—	—
Personal allowance age over 75	—	—	—	10,660	10,090	9,640	9,640
— effective maximum income for claim	—	—	—	30,510	29,230	29,230	29,230
Married couple's allowance — either partner born before 6.4.1935 and over 75 (note (b))	8,355	8,165	7,915	7,705	7,295	6,965	6,965
— reduced to minimum if income exceeds							
relevant partner born after 5.4.1948/under 65	37,970	37,050	35,850	34,890	32,990	31,490	31,490
relevant partner born after 5.4.1938 and before 6.4.1948/65–74	37,970	38,050	37,970	39,680	37,920	37,520	37,520
relevant partner born before 6.4.1938/over 75	38,090	38,370	38,290	40,000	38,220	37,820	37,820
Married couple's allowance — minimum where income exceeds limit	3,220	3,140	3,040	2,960	2,800	2,670	2,670
Blind person's allowance	2,290	2,230	2,160	2,100	1,980	1,890	1,890

Notes

(a) For 2015/16 onwards, a spouse or civil partner may elect to transfer part of their personal allowance to their spouse or civil partner. The relief is only available where neither spouse or civil partner is a higher or additional rate taxpayer. It is not available if either spouse or partner makes a claim to the married couple's allowance. For 2015/16 the transferable amount is £1,060. For 2016/17 onwards the transferable amount will be 10% of the personal allowance for the year in question (rounded up to the nearest £10).

(b) For 2015/16, age-related allowances apply only to individuals born before 6 April 1938. For 2013/14 and 2014/15, age-related allowances apply only to individuals born before 6 April 1948, and the higher level allowance applies only to those born before 6 April 1938. Previously, such allowances operated by reference to age thresholds; the allowances applying in the first tax year in which the relevant threshold was reached. The allowance is reduced by £1 for every £2 by which the adjusted net income (i.e. after deductions for allowable reliefs and pension contributions) exceeds the income limit.

The age-related personal allowance is first reduced to the basic personal allowance and then any married couple's allowance is reduced (but not below the minimum amount).

(c) The married couple's allowance is available only where at least one of the spouses or civil partners reached the age of 65 before 6 April 2000. For 2009/10 at least one of the spouses or partners must reach the age of at least 75 during the year and so qualify for the over 75 allowance.

For marriages entered into before 5 December 2005, the allowance is given initially to the husband and the amount is determined by the level of his income. For marriages and civil partnerships entered into on or after that date, the allowance is initially given to whichever of the two individuals has the higher total income for the tax year and the amount is determined by the level of that individual's income. (If their total incomes are exactly the same, the partners may make a joint election to determine which of them receives the allowance.) A couple who married before 5 December 2005 may make a joint election for the rules for marriages on or after that date to apply.

The partner not initially entitled can elect in advance to be entitled to claim one-half of the minimum allowance. A couple may jointly elect for the full amount of the minimum allowance to be transferred between them (although the partner initially entitled can subsequently elect to be able to transfer back one-half of the basic allowance).

The allowance is given as a reduction in income tax liability restricted to the lower of 10% of the amount of the allowance and the claimant's total income tax liability.

(d) For 2016/17 the personal allowance will be £11,000 and for 2017/18 it will be £11,200.

Income tax fixed rate employee expense allowances

	2008/09 onwards £		2008/09 onwards £
Agriculture — all workers	100	All other workers	120
Aluminium (Note (b))		**Fire service**	
Continual casting and process operators, de-dimplers, driers, drill punchers, dross unloaders, firemen, furnace operators and their helpers, leaders, mouldmen, pourers, remelt department labourers, roll flatteners	140	Uniformed fire fighters and fire officers	80
		Food — all workers	60
		Forestry — all workers	100
Cable hands, case-makers, labourers, mates, truck drivers and measurers, storekeepers	80	**Glass** — all workers	80
		Healthcare (staff in the NHS, private hospitals and nursing homes)	
Apprentices	60	Ambulance staff on active service	140
All other workers	120	Nurses, midwives, chiropodists, dental nurses, occupation, speech and other therapists, orthoptists, phlebotomists, physiotherapists, radiographers	100
Banks and building societies — uniformed doormen and messengers	60		
Brass and copper — all workers	120	Plaster room orderlies, hospital porters, ward clerks, sterile supply workers, hospital domestics, hospital catering staff	100
Building			
Joiners and carpenters	140	Laboratory staff, pharmacists, pharmacy assistants	60
Cement workers and roofing felt and asphalt labourers	80	Uniformed ancillary staff, maintenance workers, ground staff, drivers, parking attendants and security guards, receptionists and other uniformed staff	60
Labourers and navvies	60		
All other workers	120		
Building materials		**Heating**	
Stone masons	120	Pipe fitters and plumbers	120
Tile makers and labourers	60	Coverers, laggers, domestic glaziers, heating engineers and their mates	120
All other workers	80		
Clothing		All gas workers and all other workers	100
Lacemakers, hosiery bleachers, dyers, scourers and knitters, and knitwear bleachers and dyers	60	**Iron and steel**	
		Day labourers, general labourers, stockmen, timekeepers, warehouse staff and weighmen	80
All other workers	60		
Constructional engineering (Note (b))		Apprentices	60
Blacksmiths and their strikers, burners, caulkers, chippers, drillers, erectors, fitters, holders up, markers off, platers, riggers, riveters, rivet heaters, scaffolders, sheeters, template workers, turners and welders	140	All other workers	140
		Iron mining	
		Fillers, miners and underground workers	120
Banksmen labourers, shophelpers, slewers and straighteners	80	All other workers	100
Apprentices and storekeepers	60	**Leather**	
All other workers	100	Curriers (wet workers), fellmongering workers and tanning operatives (wet)	80
Electrical and electricity supply			
Those workers incurring laundry costs only	60	All other workers	60
All other workers	120	**Particular engineering** (Note (b))	
Engineering (trades ancillary to)		Pattern makers	140
Pattern makers	140	All chainmakers—cleaners, galvanisers, tinners and wire drawers in the wire drawing industry—toolmakers in the lockmaking industry	120
Labourers, supervisory and unskilled workers	80		
Apprentices and storekeepers	60	Apprentices and storekeepers	60
Motor mechanics in garage repair shops	120	All other workers	80

Income tax fixed rate employee expense allowances

	2008/09 onwards £
Police force	
Uniformed police officers (ranks up to and including Chief Inspector) and community support officers (£110 for 2007/08 only)	140
Precious metals—all workers	100
Printing	
Letterpress section—electrical engineers (rotary presses), electrotypers, ink and roller markers, machine minders (rotary), maintenance engineers (rotary presses) and stereotypers	140
Benchhands (periodical and bookbinding section), compositors and readers (letterpress section), telecommunication and electronic section wireroom operators, warehousemen (paperbox making section)	60
All other workers	100
Prisons	
Uniformed prison officers	80
Public service	
Dock and inland waterways:	
Dockers, dredger drivers and hopper steerers	80
All other workers	60
Public transport:	
Garage hands (including cleaners)	80
Conductors and drivers	60
Quarrying — all workers	100
Railways	
All workers except craftsmen	100
For craftsmen see the appropriate category (eg engineers)	

	2008/09 onwards £
Seamen	
Carpenters (passenger liners)	165
Carpenters (cargo vessels, tankers, coasters and ferries)	140
Shipyards	
Blacksmiths and their strikers, boilermakers, burners, carpenters, caulkers, drillers, furnacemen (platers), holders up, fitters, platers, plumbers, riveters, sheet iron workers, shipwrights, tubers and welders	140
Labourers	80
Apprentices and storekeepers	60
All other workers	100
Textiles and textile printing	
Carders, carding engineers, overlookers and technicians in spinning mills	120
All other workers	80
Vehicles	
Builders, railway vehicle repairers, and railway wagon lifters	140
Railway vehicle painters, letterers and builders' and repairers' assistants	80
All other workers	60
Wood and furniture	
Carpenters, cabinet makers, joiners, wood carvers and woodcutting machinists	140
Artificial limb makers (other than in wood), organ builders and packing-case makers	120
Coopers not providing own tools, labourers, polishers and upholsterers	60
All other workers	100

Notes

(a) The table above is reproduced from the HMRC Employment Income Manual, EIM 32712 and sets out the flat rate expenses agreed under *ITEPA 2003, s 367*. An employee may instead request a deduction under *ITEPA 2003, s 336* for the actual expenses incurred but should then retain evidence to demonstrate the expenditure.

(b) In the table above: (i) in the entry relating to aluminium, 'firemen' means persons engaged to light and maintain furnaces; (ii) 'constructional engineering' means engineering undertaken on a construction site, including buildings, shipyards, bridges, roads and other similar operations; and (iii) 'particular engineering' means engineering undertaken on a commercial basis in a factory or workshop for the purposes of producing components such as wire, springs, nails and locks.

(c) For flat rate expenses for uniformed airline pilots, co-pilots and other flight deck crew see HMRC Employment Income Manual EIM 50051 and for cabin crew see EIM 50070. For flat rate laundry expenses allowances for armed forces personnel (other than officers) see EIM 50125.

Income tax fixed rate adjustments for trades, professions and vocations

Business use of own vehicle

Vehicle	Rate per business mile
Car or goods vehicle	45p for the first 10,000 miles
	25p after that
Motor cycle	24p

Notes

(a) For 2013/14 onwards, if in computing the profits of a trade, profession or vocation carried on by an individual or partnership of individuals, a deduction would otherwise by allowable for qualifying expenditure in relation to a car, goods vehicle or motor cycle, a fixed rate deduction can be made in respect of the expenditure. This applies also where the expenditure would be allowable but for the fact that it is capital expenditure. If a fixed rate deduction is made no other deduction is allowed for the expenditure for that or any other period. No capital allowances (or no further capital allowances) can be claimed on a vehicle once a fixed rate deduction is made.

(b) Qualifying expenditure is expenditure incurred in respect of the acquisition, ownership, hire, leasing or other use of a vehicle, other than incidental expenses incurred in connection with a particular journey.

(c) The 10,000 mile band for which 45p per mile is available is shared between all the vehicles used for the trade etc. and in relation to which a fixed rate deduction is made for the period.

[ITTOIA 2005, ss 94B–94G; FA 2013, Sch 5]

Business use of home

Number of hours worked per month	Applicable amount per month £
25 or more	10
51 or more	18
101 or more	26

Notes

(a) For 2013/14 onwards, where, in computing the profits of a trade, profession or vocation for a period, a deduction would otherwise be allowable for the use of the trader's home for the purposes of the trade etc., a fixed rated deduction can be made instead. The amount of the deduction for a period is the sum of the applicable amounts for each month, or part of a month, falling in the period.

(b) The fixed rate deduction can be used by individuals and partnerships of individuals.

[ITTOIA 2005, s 94H; FA 2013, Sch 5]

Private use of business premises

Number of occupants	Disallowable amount per month £
1	350
2	500
3 or more	650

Notes

(a) For 2013/14 onwards, where a person carries on a trade, profession or vocation at a premises and the premises are used mainly for the purposes of the trade etc. but are also used by the person as a home, a fixed rate adjustment can be used in calculating taxable profits for expenses incurred in relation to the premises mainly for the purposes of the trade etc. The amount of the deduction in respect of the expenses is the amount of expenses incurred less an amount representing non-business use. The restriction for non-business use is the sum of the disallowable amounts for each month, or part of a month, falling in the period concerned. 'Occupants' are individuals who at any time in the month under review either occupy the premises as a home or stay at the premises otherwise than in the case of the trade etc.

(b) The fixed rate deduction can be used by individuals and partnerships of individuals.

[ITTOIA 2005, s 94I; FA 2013, Sch 5]

Bonus payments to employees [ITEPA 2003, ss 312A-312I; FA 2014, Sch 37]

An exemption from income tax applies to qualifying bonus payments made to employees on or after 1 October 2014 by a company which is owned directly or indirectly by an employee-ownership trust. The bonus must be paid to all employees on equal terms, although they can be paid by reference to a percentage of salary, length of service or hours worked, and are subject to a cap of £3,600 per employee for each tax year.

Cap on tax reliefs [ITA 2007, s 24A; FA 2013, Sch 3]

For 2013/14 onwards a limit applies to the aggregate amount of certain income tax reliefs that may be claimed against general income by an individual in a tax year. The limit is the greater of £50,000 and 25% of the individual's adjusted total income for the tax year. The cap applies to:

- trade loss relief against general income (ITA 2007, s 64);
- early trade losses relief (ITA 2007, s 72);
- post-cessation trade relief (ITA 2007, s 96);
- property loss relief against general income (ITA 2007, s 120);
- post-cessation property relief (ITA 2007, s 125);
- employment loss relief against general income (ITA 2007, s 128);
- former employees deduction for liabilities (ITEPA 2003, s 555);
- share loss relief on non-enterprise investment scheme/seed enterprise investment scheme shares (ITA 2007, Pt 4 Ch 6);
- losses on deeply discounted securities (ITTOIA 2005, ss 446, 454); and
- qualifying loan interest (ITA 2007, Pt 8 Ch 1).

Charitable giving

Gift Aid scheme [ITA 2007, ss 413–430; FA 2012, s 50]

Relief is available for qualifying donations to charity. The charity claims basic rate relief on the grossed up amount of the donation and the donor claims higher rate relief on the grossed up amount against income tax and capital gains tax by extension of the basic rate band. The donor may elect to treat any donation as made in the preceding tax year for higher rate relief purposes. The basic rate tax deemed to have been deducted by the donor at source is clawed back if he has insufficient liability (to income tax and capital gains tax) to match it. Following the reduction of the basic rate to 20% for 2008/09 onwards, a transitional relief supplement of 2% of grossed up qualifying donations is payable to charities for 2008/09 to 2010/11. The scheme also applies to gifts to Community Amateur Sports Clubs.

Before 6 April 2012, taxpayers could nominate a charity to receive all or part of any tax repayment due to them. The nomination is made on the taxpayer's self-assessment return, with an indication of whether Gift Aid should apply to the donation. This facility is withdrawn for repayments made after 5 April 2012.

Gifts in kind [CAA 2001, s 63(2)–(4); ITTOIA 2005, ss 107–109; CTA 2009, ss 105–108; FA 2002, Sch 18 para 9(3)]

Relief is available for gifts by traders, etc. to charities, community amateur sports clubs or educational establishments of goods produced or sold or of plant and machinery used in the donor's trade, etc.

Gifts of land, shares and securities etc. [ITA 2007, ss 431–446; CTA 2010, ss 203–217]

Relief is available where a person disposes of listed shares and securities, unit trust units, AIM shares etc. or of freehold or leasehold interests in land to a charity by way of gift or sale at an undervalue. The amount deductible in calculating net income is the market value of the shares etc. on the date of disposal plus incidental disposal costs less any consideration or value of benefits received by the donor or a connected person.

Payroll giving scheme [ITEPA 2003, ss 713–715]

An employee may make charitable donations of any amount by tax allowable deduction from earnings subject to PAYE.

Gifts of pre-eminent objects to the nation [FA 2012, s 49, Sch 14]

Under the cultural gift scheme from 1 April 2012, individuals who donate pre-eminent objects, or collections of objects, to the nation may qualify for an income tax reduction of 30% of the value of the objects. The taxpayer can spread the reduction forward across up to five years starting with the tax year in which the object is offered.

Child trust funds [SI 2004 No 1450, Regs 24–38]

The child trust fund scheme operates to provide savings funds for eligible children born after 31 August 2002 and before 3 January 2011. HMRC made an initial contribution in the form of a voucher, worth £250 (£500 for children in lower income families) for children born before 3 August 2010, and £50 (£100) for children born on or after that date but before 3 January 2011. The voucher is then used to open an account. Anyone may then pay money into the account up to a yearly limit of £4,080 (£4,000 before 6 April 2015; £3,840 before 1 July 2014; £3,720 before 6 April 2014; £3,600 before 6 April 2013; £1,200 before 1 November 2011) and HMRC also make further contributions in certain cases. The account provider invests the funds in a limited range of qualifying investments. Normally no withdrawals are permitted before the fund matures when the child reaches 18. No tax is chargeable in respect of interest, dividends, distributions, alternative financial arrangement return or building society bonus on account investments. Income from account investments is not regarded as income for any income tax purposes. See also page 21.

Community investment tax credit [ITA 2007, ss 333–382; FA 2002, s 57, Sch 16; FA 2013, s 74, Sch 27]

A tax relief worth up to 25% is available for qualifying investments in disadvantaged communities by individuals and companies via accredited intermediaries (Community Development Finance Institutions). The investment may be a loan or a subscription for shares or securities. The relief is given by way of tax reductions over a five-year period, the relief for each year being 5% of the invested amount (i.e. the average capital balance outstanding) but restricted, if necessary, to the amount which reduces the investor's tax liability to nil. For investments made on or after 6 April 2013, any tax reduction so restricted is carried forward to increase the tax reduction for subsequent years (but not beyond the five-year period).

Employee share schemes

Share incentive plans *ITEPA 2003, ss 488–515, Sch 2; ITA 2007, ss 488–490; FA 2014, Sch 8]*

Under a share incentive plan ('SIP') (open to all employees)

- a company may give an employee shares worth up to £3,600 per tax year (£3,000 for 2013/14 and earlier years) for which performance targets may be set) ('free shares');
- an employee may purchase shares worth up to £1,800 per tax year (£1,500 for 2013/14 and earlier years) or 10% of annual salary if lower by deductions from salary ('partnership shares'), these being allowable deductions for income tax and NICs; and
- the company may give an employee up to two free shares ('matching shares') for each partnership share purchased.

Shares are free of tax and NICs if held in the plan for five years. With some exceptions (e.g. on death, disability, retirement, redundancy or, from 17 July 2013, certain cash takeovers), if shares are withdrawn within between three and five years, liability arises on the lower of their value on entering the plan and their value on leaving it. With similar exceptions, if shares are withdrawn within three years, liability is on their value on leaving the plan. Dividends which are reinvested in shares are tax-free subject, for 2012/13 and earlier years, to a maximum of £1,500 per employee per tax year. No capital gains tax is payable on withdrawal of shares from the plan at any time; the shares withdrawn are treated as acquired by the employee at their market value at that time.

Employee shareholder shares *[ITEPA 2003, ss 226A–226D; FA 2013, Sch 23]*

A special employment status, known as 'employee shareholder' status, was introduced by *Growth and Infrastructure Act 2013, s 31*. Employee shareholders are issued or allotted at least £2,000 worth of shares in consideration of an employee shareholder agreement. For shares received from 1 September 2013, subject to meeting certain conditions, no income tax (and NIC) is chargeable on the first £2,000 of share value received when an individual becomes an employee shareholder. Relief is given by deeming that the individual had paid £2,000 for the shares. See also pages 5, 21.

Enterprise management incentives *[ITEPA 2003, ss 527–541, Sch 5; FA 2014, Sch 8]*

Certain independent trading companies with gross assets not exceeding £30 million and with fewer than 250 full-time equivalent employees may grant options over shares then worth up to £250,000 (£120,000 for options granted before 16 June 2012) to an eligible employee without income tax or NIC consequences (except to the extent that the option is to acquire shares at less than their then market value). The total value of shares in respect of which unexercised qualifying options exist must not exceed £3 million. Any gain on sale of the shares is chargeable to capital gains tax (but, for disposals on or after 6 April 2013, may qualify for entrepreneurs' relief; see page 22).

Approved profit sharing schemes *[ICTA 1988, ss 186, 187, Schs 9, 10; FA 2000, s 49]*

Before 1 January 2003, shares of value up to 10% of earnings (within PAYE but excluding benefits and after deducting superannuation contributions) for the year of assessment (or preceding year if greater) could be allocated to an individual in that year free of tax subject to a minimum of £3,000 and a maximum of £8,000. On disposal of the shares, income tax is chargeable on the following percentage of the initial market value when allocated (or sale proceeds if less).

Before 3rd anniversary of allocation	100%*
On or after 3rd anniversary	0%

* Reduced to 50%: employee leaves due to injury/disability/redundancy/reaching an age between 60–75 as specified by the scheme.

SAYE option schemes *[ITEPA 2003, ss 516–520, Sch 3; FA 2003, Sch 21; FA 2014, Sch 8]*

No income tax charge arises on the receipt of the options or any increase in value of the shares between the date of grant of the option and its exercise provided certain conditions are met.

Maximum monthly contribution	£500 (before 6 April 2014, £250)
Minimum monthly contribution	£5
Maximum discount	20% of market value at time of grant

Seven year savings-period contracts cannot be entered into on or after 23 July 2013.

Savings arrangement bonus rates

Date contract started	Monthly payment multiple		
	3-year contract	5-year contract	7-year contract
27.12.14–	0	0	—
28.7.14–26.12.14	0	0.6	—
1.8.12–27.7.14	0	0	0
23.9.11–31.7.12	0	0	1.6
12.8.11–22.9.11	0	0.9	3.5
27.2.11–11.8.11	0.1	1.7	4.8
12.9.10–26.2.11	0	0.9	3.2
14.5.10–11.9.10	0	1.8	4.9
29.5.09–13.5.10	0.3	2.2	5.2
17.2.09–28.5.09	0.6	2.6	5.6
27.12.08–16.2.09	1.5	4.8	9.3
1.9.08–26.12.08	2.4	7.0	12.7
4.4.08–31.8.08	1.6	5.1	9.8
1.9.07–3.4.08	2.4	7.2	13.3
1.9.06–31.8.07	1.8	5.5	10.3

Savings arrangement effective interest rates

Date contract started	3-year contract	5-year contract	7-year contract	Early withdrawal rate
27.12.14–	0%	0%	—	0%
28.7.14–26.12.14	0%	0.39%	—	0%
1.8.12–27.7.14	0%	0%	0%	0%
23.9.11–31.7.12	0%	0%	0.58%	0%
12.8.11–22.9.11	0%	0.59%	1.25%	0%
27.2.11–11.8.11	0.18%	1.1%	1.7%	0.12%
12.9.10–26.2.11	0%	0.59%	1.15%	0%
14.5.10–11.9.10	0%	1.16%	1.74%	0%
29.5.09–13.5.10	0.54%	1.42%	1.84%	0.36%
17.2.09–28.5.09	1.08%	1.67%	1.98%	0.5%
27.12.08–16.2.09	2.67%	3.04%	3.2%	2%
1.9.08–26.12.08	4.23%	4.36%	4.28%	3%
4.4.08–31.8.08	2.84%	3.22%	3.36%	2%
1.9.07–3.4.08	4.23%	4.48%	4.46%	3%
1.9.06–31.8.07	3.19%	3.46%	3.52%	2%

CSOP (company share option plan) schemes [*ITEPA 2003, ss 521–526, Sch 4; FA 2003, Sch 21; FA 2014, Sch 8*]

No income tax charge arises

(a) when option granted provided the exercise price is not manifestly less than the market value of the shares at the date of the grant (i.e. not at a discount);

(b) when option exercised between 3 and 10 years after grant.

Options exercised within three years of the grant by reason of injury, disability, redundancy or retirement or, from 17 July 2013, where there are certain cash takeovers of constituent companies do not lose their tax-exempt status.

Maximum value (at time of grant) of shares subject to options is £30,000.

Enterprise investment scheme [*ITA 2007, ss 156–257*]

The EIS applies to investments in qualifying unquoted companies trading in the UK. Eligible shares must be held for 3 years from issue date or commencement of trade if later. Subject to this and other conditions relief is given by way of a tax reduction equal to 30% (20% for shares issued before 6 April 2011) of the amount invested.

Maximum investment	2012/13 onwards – £1,000,000
	2008/09 to 2011/12 – £500,000
Minimum investment	2012/13 onwards – no minimum
	2011/12 and earlier years – £500
Carry back to preceding year	For 2009/10 onwards, no restrictions (subject to annual maximum).
	For 2008/09, ½ amount invested between 6 April and 5 October (maximum £50,000).

Any loss on a disposal of EIS shares (net of income tax relief) may be relieved against income or capital gains. See also page 21.

Foster carers and shared lives carers [*ITTOIA 2005, ss 803–828; F(No 3)A 2010, s 1, Sch 1*]

In general, to the extent that local authority payments made to a foster carer or shared lives carer do no more than meet the actual costs of caring, the payments are not taxable. In other cases, if gross receipts from foster care or, for 2010/11 onwards, shared lives care do not exceed an 'individual limit' the carer is treated as having a nil profit and nil loss for the tax year concerned. Where gross receipts exceed the individual limit, the carer can choose to be either taxed on the excess or compute profit or loss using the normal business rules. The 'individual limit' is made up of a fixed amount of £10,000 per residence for a full tax year and an additional amount per placement per week, or part week, that the individual provides care. The amounts are £200 per week for a child under 11 and £250 per week for a child of 11 or over or an adult. Relief for shared lives care is not available if more than three adults are placed with the carer at any time. For 2010/11 only, shared lives carers can opt to use the previous non-statutory arrangements.

Individual savings accounts ('ISAs') [*ITTOIA 2005, ss 694–701; SI 1998 No 1870*]

Savers can subscribe to an ISA up to the following limits per tax year

	Overall limit	Cash limit	Junior ISA limit
2015/16	£15,240	£15,240	£4,080
2014/15			
1.7.14 onwards	£15,000	£15,000	£4,000
Before 1.7.14	£11,880	£5,940	£3,840
2013/14	£11,520	£5,760	£3,720
2012/13	£11,280	£5,640	£3,600
2011/12	£10,680	£5,340	£3,600
2010/11	£10,200	£5,100	N/A
2009/10			
Age over 50	£10,200	£5,100	N/A
Under 50	£7,200	£3,600	N/A

For 2009/10, the over 50 limits apply only from 6 October 2009.

Savings are exempt from income tax and capital gains tax. Withdrawals may be made at any time without loss of tax relief. Shares acquired under a share incentive plan, profit sharing scheme or SAYE option scheme (see above) may be transferred to an ISA within 90 days without tax consequences. See also page 22.

Help to buy ISAs are to be introduced from 1 December 2015. The Government will provide a 25% top-up on savings of up to £200 per month (plus an initial investment of up to £1,000), subject to a maximum total top up of £3,000. The top-up will be paid when the savings are used to make a first-time house purchase. The house must be valued at no more than £450,000 in London and £250,000 elsewhere in the UK. Top-up payments and interest will be tax free.

Insurance benefits in event of sickness etc [*ITTOIA 2005, ss 735–743*]

Certain insurance benefits paid in the event of accident, sickness, disability, infirmity or unemployment are exempt, including benefits payable during convalescence or rehabilitation or to top-up earned income reduced following such disabilities.

Interest received

The following interest is exempt.

(a) On damages for personal injury or death. [*ITTOIA 2005, s 751*].

(b) On government securities held by persons not resident (before 6 April 2013, not ordinarily resident) in the UK. [*ITTOIA 2005, ss 713–716*]. See page 58.

(c) On certain national savings income.

(d) On SAYE certified contractual savings schemes. (Bonuses are also exempt.) [*ITTOIA 2005, ss 702–707*].

(e) Repayment interest and interest on overpaid tax (including income tax, capital gains tax, VAT and inheritance tax but not interest payable by HMRC in cases of official error under *VATA 1994, s 78*). [*IHTA 1984, s 235; ITTOIA 2005, ss 54, 749, 869*].

Income tax exemptions and reliefs

Landlord's energy-saving allowance [*ITTOIA, ss 312–314; SI 2007 No 831*]

A deduction is available in computing the profits of a property business for capital expenditure incurred before 6 April 2015 on the acquisition, and installation in a dwelling house, of a qualifying energy-saving item. The deduction is limited to a maximum of £1,500 per dwelling house.

Qualifying items are cavity wall insulation, loft insulation, solid wall insulation, draught proofing and insulation for hot water systems and floor insulation.

Maintenance payments [*ITA 2007, ss 453–456; ICTA 1988, s 347B*]

Payments are made gross and are not subject to tax in the hands of the recipient.

Where either party to the marriage was born before 6 April 1935, the payer obtains relief on qualifying maintenance payments (as defined) by means of a tax reduction on the lesser of the amount paid and the minimum married couple's allowance for the year (see page 60) at the rate of 10%.

Miscellaneous

The following income is exempt from income tax.

(a) **Adoption etc. allowances.** [*ITTOIA 2005, ss 744–747; F(No 3)A 2010, s 2*]. A similar exemption for allowances to special guardians and certain kinship carers applies for 2010/11 onwards.
(b) **Awards for bravery.** [*ITEPA 2003, s 638*].
(c) **Compensation for mis-sold pensions.** [*FA 1996, s 148; HMRC ESC A99*].
(d) **Compensation on unclaimed bank accounts of Holocaust victims.** [*HMRC ESC A100; FA 2006, s 64*].
(e) **Continuity of education allowances** (for 2012/13 onwards).
(f) **Damages and compensation for personal injury.** [*ITTOIA 2005, ss 731–734*].
(g) **Foreign service allowances.** [*ITEPA 2003, s 299*].
(h) **German and Austrian** pensions and annuities for victims of Nazi persecution. [*ITEPA, s 642*].
(i) **Housing grants.** [*ITTOIA 2005, s 769*].
(j) **Members of Parliament.** Certain accommodation allowances and reimbursed costs paid to MPs. [*ITEPA 2003, ss 292–295; F(No 2)A 2010, Sch 4; FA 2011, s 37; FA 2013, s 10*].
(k) **Miners'** free coal or cash in lieu. [*ITEPA 2003, ss 306, 646*].
(l) **Non-resident competitors in certain sporting events.** Subject to conditions, the income arising to non-resident competitors from certain sporting events. For example, the 2013 Champions League Final, the London Anniversary Games and the 2014 Commonwealth Games and Glasgow Grand Prix. [*FA 2012, s 13; FA 2013, ss 8–9*].
(m) **Sandwich courses.** Payments to an employee for periods of attendance provided (i) course lasts at least one academic year with an average of at least 20 weeks per year full-time attendance, and (ii) rate of payment does not exceed greater of £7,000 p.a. and rate of payment receivable in similar circumstances by way of public grant. (HMRC SP 4/86).
(n) **Scholarship** income and bursaries. [*ITTOIA 2005, s 766*]. See also page 7.

See also benefits in kind on pages 4 to 8.

'Rent a room' relief [*ITTOIA 2005, ss 785–802*]

The *gross* rents on letting of rooms in a private residence are exempt up to £4,250. Where gross rents exceed the exempt amount, the taxpayer can elect to pay tax on the excess instead of the profits computed under the normal rules. The exemption limit will increase to £7,500 for 2016/17 onwards.

Seed enterprise investment scheme [*ITA 2007 ss 257A-HJ; FA 2012, Sch 6*]

The SEIS applies to investments made on or after 6 April 2012 in small qualifying companies carrying on or preparing to carry on a new business. Subject to conditions, relief is given by way of a tax reduction equal to 50% of the amount invested, up to a maximum investment of £100,000 per tax year. Relief may be claimed as if all or part of the investment had been made in the preceding tax year (subject to the annual maximum). Relief cannot be carried back from 2012/13.

Gains on shares within the scope of the SEIS are exempt from capital gains tax. See also page 24.

Social investment relief [*ITA 2007 ss 257J-257TE; FA 2014, Sch 11*]

Income tax relief is available for investments made on or after 6 April 2014 in qualifying shares or debentures in a social enterprise. Subject to conditions, relief is given by way of a tax reduction equal to 30% of the amount invested, up to a maximum investment of £1,000,000 per tax year. Relief may be claimed as if all or part of the investment had been made in the preceding tax year (subject to the annual maximum). Relief cannot be carried back from 2014/15.

Gains on investments to which income tax relief is attributable are exempt from capital gains tax if the investments are held for at least three years. See also page 24.

Social security benefits

Certain social security benefits are not taxable. See page 105.

Termination payments [*ITEPA 2003, ss 401–416*]

Provided payment is not taxable under general employment earnings rules, termination payments (including non-contractual payments in lieu of notice and genuine non-statutory redundancy payments) fall to be taxed under *ITEPA 2003, ss 401–416* subject to the following exemptions.

(a) The first £30,000 of the payments.
(b) Payments where cessation arises from death, injury or disability.
(c) Payments for foreign service where this comprised (i) three-quarters of the whole period of service, or (ii) the last 10 years, or (iii) where employment exceeded 20 years, one half of the whole, including 10 of the last 20 years. (Proportional relief in other cases.)
(d) Certain benefits under retirement schemes.

Venture capital trusts [*ITA 2007, ss 258–332; ITTOIA 2005, ss 709–712; FA 2014, Sch 10*]

An individual who *subscribes* for ordinary shares in a VCT obtains income tax relief at 30% on an investment limit of £200,000 in any tax year. The shares must be held for at least five years. Any dividends received from a VCT are exempt from income tax to the extent that the shares *acquired* each year do not exceed the investment limit and provided the main purpose of acquiring the shares is not the avoidance of tax; tax credits are not repayable. See also page 24.

Income tax self-assessment

Payment of tax

1st interim payment. On or before 31 January in tax year

2nd interim payment. On or before 31 July following tax year

Interim payments are normally half the net income tax liability (including Class 4 NIC) of the previous year. Interim payments are not required if either the previous year's liability (net of tax at source) was less than £1,000 (£500 for 2008/09 and earlier years) or tax at source covered more than 80% of the gross liability. (Tax at source includes PAYE.) The taxpayer may make a claim to reduce (or dispense with) interim payments if the current year liability will be less than that of the previous year (or will be nil).

Final payment. Where necessary, 31 January following tax year except that

(a) where a person has given notice of chargeability to tax within six months of the tax year but was not given notice to deliver a return until after 31 October following the tax year, the due date is 3 months after the date of notice; and

(b) where a person's self-assessment is amended, the due date is deferred as regards any tax payable by virtue of the amendment until, if later, 30 days after the date of notice of amendment or closure notice following an enquiry (but not so as to defer the date from which interest on overdue tax runs).

The final payment (or repayment) is the total net liability for income tax (including Class 4 NIC and, for 2015/16 onwards, Class 2 NIC) and capital gains tax less any interim payments on account of income tax.

Surcharge. Where any income tax or capital gains tax for 2010/11 or earlier year is payable before 6 April 2010 and remains outstanding more than 28 days after the due date, a surcharge of 5% of the unpaid tax will be levied. A further 5% surcharge will be levied on any tax unpaid more than six months after the due date. Surcharges can be suspended where the taxpayer has agreed a time to pay arrangement with HMRC. Surcharges have been replaced by the penalty for late payment of tax — see page 95.

Returns

The deadline for delivering the completed self-assessment return is determined as follows.

* If the return is an electronic return, it must be delivered to HMRC on or before **31 January** following the tax year to which it relates or, if later, within three months beginning with the date of HMRC's notice to deliver the return.
* If the return is a non-electronic return, it must be delivered to HMRC on or before **31 October** following the tax year to which it relates or, if later, within three months beginning with the date of HMRC's notice to deliver the return.

For earlier years, the deadline for delivering the completed return is as for electronic returns above.

An individual or trustee who has received a notice to make a return for 2012/13 or a later year may request HMRC to withdraw the notice. If HMRC agree to do so they issue a withdrawal notice and any corresponding penalty for failing to make a return is cancelled.

See pages 96, 98 for penalties for late filing of returns.

Basis of assessment

Property income	All UK property income arising in the current tax year, calculated as for trading profits and using ordinary accounting principles. A restriction on relief for finance costs to the basic rate is to be phased in with effect from 2017/18 onwards.
Trading income	*Year 1* — Actual
	Year 2 — 12 months ending with accounting date in Year 2 *or* (if period from commencement to accounting date in Year 2 is less than 12 months) the first 12 months *or* (if no accounting date in Year 1 or Year 2) actual
	Year 3 — Current year basis (unless Year 3 is the first year in which there is an accounting date falling not less than 12 months after commencement, when assessment based on 12 months ending with the accounting date)
	Intermediate years — Current year basis
	Closing year — Period from end of basis period in the penultimate year to date of cessation (subject to transitional rules covering overlap profits for 1997/98)
	Current year basis normally means that assessment is based on the profits shown by the annual accounts ended within the current tax year
Savings/investment income	Income arising in the current tax year
Foreign income	As for UK property, trading or savings/investment income above
	See the table on page 69 for determining whether income is assessed on an arising or remittance basis
Other income	Income arising in the current tax year
Employment income	See the table on page 69 for determining whether earnings are assessed on a receipts or remittance basis
Income taxed at source	Dividends, interest, etc. receivable

Income tax foreign income and employment income

Foreign income

The table below shows whether foreign income is assessed on an arising or, where claimed, a remittance basis.

Resident	Ordinarily resident (before 6.4.13 only)	Domiciled	British subject	Trades, etc.	Pensions	Other income
No	N/A	N/A	N/A	Exempt	Exempt	Exempt
Yes	Yes	Yes	Yes	Arising	90% arising	Arising
Yes	No	Yes	Yes	Remittance	Remittance	Remittance
Yes	Yes/No	No	Yes	Remittance	Remittance	Remittance
Yes	Yes/No	Yes	No	Arising	90% arising	Arising
Yes	Yes/No	No	No	Remittance	Remittance	Remittance

Employment income

2013/14 and subsequent years. The table below shows whether employment income is taxed on a receipts or, where claimed, a remittance basis.

Domiciled	Resident	Meeting three-year non-residence requirement (note (b))	UK employer	Foreign employer	Wholly UK income	Wholly overseas income (note (c))	Partly UK/partly overseas duties	
							UK duties	Overseas duties (note (c))
Yes	Yes	N/A	Immaterial	Immaterial	Receipts	Receipts	Receipts	Receipts
Yes	No	N/A	Immaterial	Immaterial	Receipts	Exempt	Receipts	Exempt
No	Yes	No	Yes	N/A	Receipts	Receipts	Receipts	Receipts
No	Yes	No	N/A	Yes	Receipts	Remittances	Receipts	Remittances
No	Yes	Yes	Yes	N/A	Receipts	Remittances	Receipts	Remittances
No	Yes	Yes	N/A	Yes	Receipts	Remittances	Receipts	Remittances
No	No	Yes/No	Yes	N/A	Receipts	Exempt	Receipts	Exempt
No	No	Yes/No	N/A	Yes	Receipts	Exempt	Receipts	Exempt

2012/13 and earlier years. The table below shows whether employment income is taxed on a receipts or, where claimed, a remittance basis.

Domiciled	Resident	Ordinarily resident	UK employer	Foreign employer	Wholly UK income	Wholly overseas income (note (c))	Partly UK/partly overseas duties	
							UK duties	Overseas duties (note (c))
Yes	Yes	Yes	Immaterial	Immaterial	Receipts	Receipts	Receipts	Receipts
Yes	Yes	No	Immaterial	Immaterial	Receipts	Remittances	Receipts	Remittances
Yes	No	Yes/No	Immaterial	Immaterial	Receipts	Exempt	Receipts	Exempt
No	Yes	Yes	Yes	N/A	Receipts	Receipts	Receipts	Receipts
No	Yes	Yes	N/A	Yes	Receipts	Remittances	Receipts	Receipts
No	Yes	No	Yes	N/A	Receipts	Remittances	Receipts	Remittances
No	Yes	No	N/A	Yes	Receipts	Remittances	Receipts	Remittances
No	No	Yes/No	Yes	N/A	Receipts	Exempt	Receipts	Exempt
No	No	Yes/No	N/A	Yes	Receipts	Exempt	Receipts	Exempt

Notes

(a) For 2013/14 onwards, an individual's residence status is determined by a statutory residence test and the concept of ordinary residence is abolished.

(b) An employee meets the requirement for a three-year period of non-residence for a tax year (X) if he has been non-resident for three consecutive tax years and year X is any of the three tax years immediately following that non-resident period.

(c) Where such duties are performed by seafarers in the course of a qualifying period of 365 days or more, emoluments for those duties receive a 100% deduction. [*ITEPA 2003, s 378*].

(d) An individual who claims to use the remittance basis for a tax year is not entitled to any income tax personal allowances or the capital gains tax annual exemption for that year. This does not apply if the individual's unremitted foreign income and gains for the year are less than £2,000. [*ITA 2007, s 809G*].

(e) Individuals aged over 18 who have been resident in the UK for at least seven years of the past nine years can claim the remittance basis for a tax year only if they pay a £30,000 tax charge in respect of the foreign income and gains they leave outside the UK. For 2012/13 onwards, the charge is increased for those resident in the UK for at least 12 of the last 14 years: to £60,000 for 2015/16 onwards and to £50,000 for 2012/13 to 2014/15. For 2015/16 onwards the charge is £90,000 for those resident in the UK for at least 17 of the last 20 years. The charge does not apply if the individual's unremitted foreign income and gains for the year are less than £2,000. [*ITA 2007, s 809H; FA 2015, s 24*]. For 2017/18 onwards, an individual will be deemed UK-domiciled for tax purposes if he has been UK-resident for at least 15 of the last 20 tax years (and therefore ineligible to claim the remittance basis).

Chargeable lifetime transfers

(a) Tax on gross transfers			Cumulative totals		(b) Grossing-up of net lifetime transfers		Cumulative totals	
Cumulative transfers (gross)	Rate	Tax on band	Taxable transfers	Tax thereon	Net values	Tax payable thereon	Net values	Gross equivalent
£	%	£	£	£	£	%	£	£
6.4.15 onwards					**6.4.15 onwards**			
0–325,000	Nil	Nil	325,000	Nil	0–325,000	Nil	325,000	325,000
Over 325,000	20%				Over 325,000	Nil+ ¼ for each £1 over £325,000		
6.4.14–5.4.15					**6.4.14–5.4.15**			
0–325,000	Nil	Nil	325,000	Nil	0–325,000	Nil	325,000	325,000
Over 325,000	20%				Over 325,000	Nil+ ¼ for each £1 over £325,000		
6.4.13–5.4.14					**6.4.13–5.4.14**			
0–325,000	Nil	Nil	325,000	Nil	0–325,000	Nil	325,000	325,000
Over 325,000	20%				Over 325,000	Nil+ ¼ for each £1 over £325,000		
6.4.12–5.4.13					**6.4.12–5.4.13**			
0–325,000	Nil	Nil	325,000	Nil	0–325,000	Nil	325,000	325,000
Over 325,000	20%				Over 325,000	Nil+ ¼ for each £1 over £325,000		
6.4.11–5.4.12					**6.4.11–5.4.12**			
0–325,000	Nil	Nil	325,000	Nil	0–325,000	Nil	325,000	325,000
Over 325,000	20%				Over 325,000	Nil+ ¼ for each £1 over £325,000		
6.4.10–5.4.11					**6.4.10–5.4.11**			
0–325,000	Nil	Nil	325,000	Nil	0–325,000	Nil	325,000	325,000
Over 325,000	20%				Over 325,000	Nil+ ¼ for each £1 over £325,000		
6.4.09–5.4.10					**6.4.09–5.4.10**			
0–325,000	Nil	Nil	325,000	Nil	0–325,000	Nil	325,000	325,000
Over 325,000	20%				Over 325,000	Nil+ ¼ for each £1 over £325,000		
6.4.08–5.4.09					**6.4.08–5.4.09**			
0–312,000	Nil	Nil	312,000	Nil	0–312,000	Nil	312,000	312,000
Over 312,000	20%				Over 312,000	Nil+ ¼ for each £1 over £312,000		
6.4.07–5.4.08					**6.4.07–5.4.08**			
0–300,000	Nil	Nil	300,000	Nil	0–300,000	Nil	300,000	300,000
Over 300,000	20%				Over 300,000	Nil+ ¼ for each £1 over £300,000		
6.4.06–5.4.07					**6.4.06–5.4.07**			
0–285,000	Nil	Nil	285,000	Nil	0–285,000	Nil	285,000	285,000
Over 285,000	20%				Over 285,000	Nil+ ¼ for each £1 over £285,000		

Inheritance tax rates

Transfers on death

(a) Tax on transfers

Cumulative transfers (gross) £	Rate %	Tax on band £	Taxable transfers £	Tax thereon £
6.4.15 onwards				
0–325,000	Nil	Nil	325,000	Nil
Over 325,000	40%			
6.4.14–5.4.15				
0–325,000	Nil	Nil	325,000	Nil
Over 325,000	40%			
6.4.13–5.4.14				
0–325,000	Nil	Nil	325,000	Nil
Over 325,000	40%			
6.4.12–5.4.13				
0–325,000	Nil	Nil	325,000	Nil
Over 325,000	40%			
6.4.11–5.4.12				
0–325,000	Nil	Nil	325,000	Nil
Over 325,000	40%			
6.4.10–5.4.11				
0–325,000	Nil	Nil	325,000	Nil
Over 325,000	40%			
6.4.09–5.4.10				
0–325,000	Nil	Nil	325,000	Nil
Over 325,000	40%			
6.4.08–5.4.09				
0–312,000	Nil	Nil	312,000	Nil
Over 312,000	40%			
6.4.07–5.4.08				
0–300,000	Nil	Nil	300,000	Nil
Over 300,000	40%			
6.4.06–5.4.07				
0–285,000	Nil	Nil	285,000	Nil
Over 285,000	40%			

(b) Grossing-up of net lifetime transfers that do not bear their own tax

Net values £	Tax payable thereon %	Net values £	Gross equivalent £
6.4.15 onwards			
0–325,000	Nil	325,000	325,000
Over 325,000	Nil + ²/₃ for each £1 over £325,000		
6.4.14–5.4.15			
0–325,000	Nil	325,000	325,000
Over 325,000	Nil + ²/₃ for each £1 over £325,000		
6.4.13–5.4.14			
0–325,000	Nil	325,000	325,000
Over 325,000	Nil + ²/₃ for each £1 over £325,000		
6.4.12–5.4.13			
0–325,000	Nil	325,000	325,000
Over 325,000	Nil + ²/₃ for each £1 over £325,000		
6.4.11–5.4.12			
0–325,000	Nil	325,000	325,000
Over 325,000	Nil + ²/₃ for each £1 over £325,000		
6.4.10–5.4.11			
0–325,000	Nil	325,000	325,000
Over 325,000	Nil + ²/₃ for each £1 over £325,000		
6.4.09–5.4.10			
0–325,000	Nil	325,000	325,000
Over 325,000	Nil + ²/₃ for each £1 over £325,000		
6.4.08–5.4.09			
0–312,000	Nil	312,000	312,000
Over 312,000	Nil + ²/₃ for each £1 over £312,000		
6.4.07–5.4.08			
0–300,000	Nil	300,000	300,000
Over 300,000	Nil + ²/₃ for each £1 over £300,000		
6.4.06–5.4.07			
0–285,000	Nil	285,000	285,000
Over 285,000	Nil + ²/₃ for each £1 over £285,000		

Notes

(a) Any nil-rate band which is unused on a person's death can be transferred to their surviving spouse or civil partner for the purposes of the charge to tax on the death of the survivor on or after 9 October 2007. [*IHTA 1984, ss 8A–8C*].

(b) For deaths on or after 6 April 2012, the rate of inheritance tax is 36% where 10% or more of the net estate (after deducting exemptions, reliefs and the nil-rate band) is left to charity. [*IHTA 1984, Sch 1A; FA 2012, s 209, Sch 33*].

(c) The nil rate band will be frozen at £325,000 until 2020/21. An additional nil rate band for main residences is to be introduced for deaths on or after 6 April 2017. The band will apply where the main residence is passed on to one or more direct descendants. Initially the band will be £100,000, increasing to £175,000 for deaths on or after 6 April 2020. The band will be progressively withdrawn for estates valued at more than £2 million. Unused nil-rate band can be transferred to any surviving spouse or civil partner.

	Delivery of account	Payment of tax	
Chargeable lifetime transfers	Within later of (a) 12 months from the end of the month in which the transfer is made; and (b) 3 months beginning with the date on which the person delivering the account first becomes liable for tax No account need be delivered where: (i) the transfer is of cash or quoted shares or securities and the value of the transfer and other chargeable transfers made in the preceding seven years does not exceed the IHT threshold; or (ii) the value of the transfer and other chargeable transfers made in the preceding seven years does not exceed 80% of the IHT threshold and the value of the transfer does not exceed the net amount of the threshold available to the transferor at the time of the transfer.	6 April–30 September 1 October–5 April	30 April in following year Six months after end of month of transfer
PETs which prove to be chargeable	Within 12 months from the end of the month in which the transferor dies	6 months after the end of the month in which death occurs	
Gifts with reservation chargeable on death	Within 12 months from the end of the month in which death occurs	6 months after the end of the month in which death occurs	
Transfers on death	Within later of (a) 12 months from the end of the month in which death occurs; and (b) 3 months beginning with the date on which the personal representatives first act or the person liable first has reason to believe he is required to deliver an account *Excepted estates.* No account need be delivered in respect of an estate falling into one of the following categories. (a) Where the deceased was never domiciled in the UK and the value of the UK estate is wholly attributable to cash or quoted shares or securities not exceeding £150,000. (b) Where the deceased died domiciled in the UK and (i) of the value of the estate, not more than £150,000 consisted of settled property and not more than £100,000 of overseas property; (ii) there were no chargeable transfers in the 7 years before death other than 'specified transfers' not exceeding £150,000; and (iii) the aggregate of the gross estate, specified transfers and 'specified exempt transfers' did not exceed the appropriate IHT threshold. (c) Where the deceased died domiciled in the UK and (i) the conditions in (b)(i) and (ii) above are satisfied; (ii) the aggregate of gross estate, specified transfers and specified exempt transfers did not exceed £1,000,000; and (iii) the aggregate in (ii) less any exempt spouse, civil partner or charity transfers and total estate liabilities did not exceed the appropriate IHT threshold. For deaths after 31 March 2014, total estate liabilities do not include certain liabilities not deductible in calculating the value of the estate. For deaths after 28 February 2011, it is also a condition that the transfers on death include exempt spouse, civil partner or charity transfers. Where the whole of a person's nil-rate band has been transferred to a spouse or civil partner (see note (a) on page 71) and the spouse or partner dies after 5 April 2010, for the purposes of (b) and (c) above, the normal appropriate IHT threshold is doubled (subject to further conditions). '*Specified transfers*' are transfers of cash, personal chattels or corporeal moveable property, quoted shares and securities, and interests in or over land. '*Specified exempt transfers*' are transfers in the seven years before death between spouses or civil partners, gifts to charities, political parties or housing associations, transfers to maintenance funds for historic buildings etc., or to employee trusts. For the purposes of (b)(ii)(iii) and (c)(ii) above, for deaths after 28 February 2011, transfers exempt as normal expenditure out of income exceeding £3,000 per tax year are treated as chargeable transfers.	6 months after end of the month in which death occurs or on delivery of account by personal representatives if earlier	
National heritage property	Within 6 months from the end of the month in which the charge arises on the ending of conditional exemption	6 months after end of the month in which chargeable event occurs	

Inheritance tax reliefs

Exempt transfer	Limits and conditions		Reference
Lifetime only			
Potentially exempt transfers	Unless provided to the contrary (e.g. gifts with reservation)		
	(a) transfers by individuals to other individuals;		
	(b) transfers by individuals to certain trusts for the disabled;		
	(c) transfers on or after 22 March 2006 by an individual to a bereaved minor's trust on the coming to an end of an immediate post-death interest;		
	(d) transfers before 22 March 2006 by an individual to an accumulation and maintenance trust;		
	(e) transfers by an individual into interest in possession trusts in which, for transfers on or after 22 March 2006, the beneficiary has a disabled person's interest; and		
	(f) (in restricted circumstances following *FA 2006*) certain transfers on the termination or disposal of an individual's beneficial interest in possession in settled property		*IHTA 1984, s 3A*
	are potentially exempt transfers. Such transfers made seven years or more before the death of the transferor are exempt transfers		*FA 2006, Sch 20 para 9*
Annual gifts	Transfers of value per fiscal year not exceeding	£3,000	*IHTA 1984, s 19*
	Any shortfall in usage can be carried forward to the next year and added to the allowance for that year only		
Gifts in consideration of marriage or civil partnership	Parent of either party to marriage or partnership	£5,000	*IHTA 1984, s 22*
	Grandparent or remoter ancestor of either party to marriage or partnership; or by one party to the other	£2,500	
	Any other person	£1,000	
Normal expenditure out of income	Exempt if		*IHTA 1984, s 21*
	(a) transfer made out of post-tax income taking one year with another; and		
	(b) transferor left with sufficient income to maintain usual standard of living		
Small gifts	All gifts to the same person in the same year not exceeding	£250	*IHTA 1984, s 20*
Lifetime and on death			
Charities	Wholly exempt. Community Amateur Sports Clubs are treated as charities		*IHTA 1984, s 23*
National purposes	Property may be given or bequeathed to any of the bodies listed in the Schedule to the Act (British Museum, National Gallery, local authorities etc.)		*IHTA 1984, s 25, Sch 3*
Political parties	Wholly exempt		*IHTA 1984, s 24*
Shares to an employee trust by individuals	Exempt if trustees hold, within one year of transfer, over 50% of the ordinary shares trust by individuals and have voting control. Beneficiaries must include most of the employees		*IHTA 1984, s 28*
Spouse/civil partner	Wholly exempt unless spouse or civil partner non-UK-domiciled when limit is	£325,000	*IHTA 1984, s 18; FA 2013, s 178*
	For transfers of value before 6 April 2013, the limit was £55,000.		
	For transfers of value made on or after 6 April 2013, individuals who are domiciled outside the UK can elect to be treated as domiciled in the UK for inheritance tax purposes if, at any time on or after 6 April 2013 and during the period of seven years ending with the date on which the election is made, they have a UK-domiciled spouse or civil partner. An election can also be made following the death of a UK-domiciled spouse or civil partner. The election has effect from the date specified in it, which must be on or after 6 April 2013 and within the seven years ending with the date on which the election is made or the spouse or civil partner dies.		*IHTA 1984, ss 267ZA, 267ZB; FA 2013, s 177*
	An election is irrevocable but will cease to have effect if the individual is not resident in the UK for income tax purposes for four successive tax years beginning after the election is made.		
	See also note (a) on page 71.		

Agricultural property relief [IHTA 1984, ss 115–124B]

	Rates for disposals After 31.8.95
Vacant possession or right to obtain it within 12 months	100%
Entitled to 50% relief at 9 March 1981 and from that date beneficially entitled to interest but without vacant possession rights	100%
Agricultural land let on tenancy starting after 31 August 1995	100%
Other transfers	50%

The agricultural property must (inter alia) have been (i) *occupied* by the transferor for agricultural purposes throughout the 2 years before the transfer; or (ii) owned by him for the 7 years before the transfer and occupied (by him or another) for agricultural purposes throughout that period. With effect, broadly, from 22 April 2009, relief is extended to agricultural property within the European Economic Area.

Business property relief [IHTA 1984, ss 103–114]

	Rates for disposals After 5.4.96
Unincorporated business or interest in	100%
Shares in unquoted company	
— over 25% voting control	100%
— 25% or less	100%
Shares in quoted company giving control	50%
Shares in AIM or USM company	
— controlling interest	100%
— over 25% voting control	100%
— 25% or less	100%
Settled property comprising a life tenant's business or interest in a business	100%
Land, buildings, machinery or plant in a partnership or in a controlled company or in a settlement	50%

The property must (inter alia) (i) have been owned by the transferor for at least the 2 years immediately before the transfer; or (ii) have replaced other qualifying property and the qualifying properties together have been owned by the transferor for at least 2 out of the 5 years immediately before the transfer.

Transfers within seven years of death [IHTA 1984, s 7, Sch 2 paras 1A, 2]

Where a transferor dies within seven years of a lifetime transfer, IHT is recomputed at the death rates applying at the time of death but the tax rates (not the value of the lifetime transfer) are, subject to below, tapered as follows.

Years between transfer and death	Percentage of full tax rate
Not more than 3	100%
Over 3 but not more than 4	80%
Over 4 but not more than 5	60%
Over 5 but not more than 6	40%
Over 6 but not more than 7	20%

In the case of a chargeable lifetime transfer, the IHT payable cannot be reduced below that originally chargeable at half death rates.

Quick succession relief [IHTA 1984, s 141]

Where there is a later transfer of property within 5 years of an earlier transfer ('the first transfer') which increased the transferor's estate and the later transfer arises on death, the IHT payable on the later transfer is reduced by

$$\text{Percentage} \times \frac{(G - T)}{G} \times T$$

where

G = gross (chargeable) first transfer

T = IHT on first transfer

The percentages are as follow

Years between transfers	Percentage
One year or less	100%
Over 1 but not more than 2	80%
Over 2 but not more than 3	60%
Over 3 but not more than 4	40%
Over 4 but not more than 5	20%

Relief also applies where the later transfer is settled property in which the transferor had an interest in possession and the first transfer was the making of the settlement or was made after that time.

Interest on tax paid by companies

Corporation tax self assessment:
accounting periods ending after 30.6.99

Interest on unpaid tax

Interest on unpaid tax runs from the due date (generally nine months and one day after the end of the accounting period, see page 40) to the actual date of payment. It is deductible from profits.

Rates of interest		Days
6.9.05 – 5.9.06	6.5%	365
6.9.06 – 5.8.07	7.5%	334
6.8.07 – 5.1.08	8.5%	153
6.1.08 – 5.11.08	7.5%	305
6.11.08 – 5.12.08	6.5%	30
6.12.08 – 5.1.09	5.5%	31
6.1.09 – 26.1.09	4.5%	21
27.1.09 – 23.3.09	3.5%	28
24.3.09 – 28.9.09	2.5%	189
29.9.09 –	3%	

Interest on overpaid tax

Interest on overpaid tax runs from the later of

(a)   the date on which the tax was paid, and
(b)   the due date (generally nine months and one day after the end of the accounting period, see page 40)

to the date the repayment order is issued. The interest is taxable.

Rates of interest		Days
6.9.05 – 5.9.06	3%	365
6.9.06 – 5.8.07	4%	334
6.8.07 – 5.1.08	5%	153
6.1.08 – 5.11.08	4%	305
6.11.08 – 5.12.08	3%	30
6.12.08 – 5.1.09	2%	31
6.1.09 – 26.1.09	1%	21
27.1.09 – 28.9.09	0%	245
29.9.09	0.5%	

Interest on unpaid instalments

Interest on unpaid instalments for 'large companies' (see page 40) is paid from the due date to the earlier of

(a)   the date of payment, and
(b)   nine months after the end of the accounting period

(whereafter the normal interest rate provisions apply). The interest is deductible from profits.

Rates of interest		Days
20.4.00 – 18.2.01	7%	305
19.2.01 – 15.4.01	6.75%	56
16.4.01 – 20.5.01	6.5%	35
21.5.01 – 12.8.01	6.25%	84
13.8.01 – 30.9.01	6%	49
1.10.01 – 14.10.01	5.75%	14
15.10.01 – 18.11.01	5.5%	35
19.11.01 – 16.2.03	5%	455
17.2.03 – 20.7.03	4.75%	154
21.7.03 – 16.11.03	4.5%	119
17.11.03 – 15.2.04	4.75%	91
16.2.04 – 16.5.04	5%	91
17.5.04 – 20.6.04	5.25%	35
21.6.04 – 15.8.04	5.5%	56
16.8.04 – 14.8.05	5.75%	364
15.8.05 – 13.8.06	5.5%	364
14.8.06 – 19.11.06	5.75%	98
20.11.06 – 21.1.07	6%	63
22.1.07 – 20.5.07	6.25%	119
21.5.07 – 15.7.07	6.5%	56
16.7.07 – 16.12.07	6.75%	154
17.12.07 – 17.2.08	6.5%	63
18.2.08 – 24.4.08	6.25%	63
21.4.08 – 19.10.08	6%	182
20.10.08 – 16.11.08	5.5%	28
17.11.08 – 14.12.08	4%	28
15.12.08 – 18.1.09	3%	35
19.1.09 – 15.2.09	2.5%	28
16.2.09 – 15.3.09	2%	28
16.3.09 –	1.5%	

Interest on overpaid instalments and early payments

Interest on overpaid instalments for 'large companies' (see page 40) and on early payments by other companies is paid from the date the excess arises (but not earlier than the due date of the first instalment) to the earlier of

(a)   the date of repayment, and
(b)   nine months after the end of the accounting period

(whereafter the normal interest rate provisions apply). The interest is taxable.

Rates of interest		Days
19.2.01 – 15.4.01	5.5%	56
16.4.01 – 20.5.01	5.25%	35
21.5.01 – 12.8.01	5%	84
13.8.01 – 30.9.01	4.75%	49
1.10.01 – 14.10.01	4.50%	14
15.10.01 – 18.11.01	4.25%	35
19.11.01 – 16.2.03	3.75%	455
17.2.03 – 20.7.03	3.5%	154
21.7.03 – 16.11.03	3.25%	119
17.11.03 – 15.2.04	3.5%	91
16.2.04 – 16.5.04	3.75%	91
17.5.04 – 20.6.04	4%	35
21.6.04 – 15.8.04	4.25%	56
16.8.04 – 14.8.05	4.5%	364
15.8.05 – 13.8.06	4.25%	364
14.8.06 – 19.11.06	4.5%	98
20.11.06 – 21.1.07	4.75%	63
22.1.07 – 20.5.07	5%	119
21.5.07 – 15.7.07	5.25%	56
16.7.07 – 16.12.07	5.5%	154
17.12.07 – 17.2.08	5.25%	63
18.2.08 – 20.4.08	5%	63
21.4.08 – 19.10.08	4.75%	182
20.10.08 – 16.11.08	4.25%	28
17.11.08 – 14.12.08	2.75%	28
15.12.08 – 18.1.09	1.75%	35
19.1.09 – 15.2.09	1.25%	28
16.2.09 – 15.3.09	0.75%	28
16.3.09 – 20.9.09	0.25%	189
21.9.09 –	0.5%	

Interest on tax paid by companies

Corporation tax pay and file:

accounting periods ending before 1.7.99

Interest on unpaid tax

Interest on unpaid tax runs from the due date (generally nine months and one day after the end of the accounting period, see page 40) to the actual date of payment. It is not deductible from profits.

Rates of interest		Days
6.1.94 – 5.10.94	5.5%	273
6.10.94 – 5.3.95	6.25%	151
6.3.95 – 5.2.96	7%	337
6.2.96 – 5.8.97	6.25%	547
6.8.97 – 5.1.99	7.5%	518
6.1.99 – 5.3.99	6.5%	59
6.3.99 – 5.2.00	5.75%	337
6.2.00 – 5.5.01	6.75%	455
6.5.01 – 5.11.01	6%	184
6.11.01 – 5.8.03	5%	638
6.8.03 – 5.12.03	4.25%	122
6.12.03 – 5.9.04	5.25%	274
6.9.04 – 5.9.05	6%	365
6.9.05 – 5.9.06	5.25%	365
6.9.06 – 5.8.07	6%	334
6.8.07 – 5.1.08	6.75%	153
6.1.08 – 5.11.08	6%	305
6.11.08 – 5.12.08	5%	30
6.12.08 – 5.1.09	4.25%	31
6.1.09 – 26.1.09	3.5%	21
27.1.09 – 23.3.09	2.75%	28
24.3.09 – 28.9.09	1.75%	189
29.9.09 –	3%	

Interest on overpaid tax

Interest on overpaid tax runs from the later of

(a)   the date on which the tax was paid, and
(b)   the due date (generally nine months and one day after the end of the accounting period, see page 40

to the date the repayment order is issued. The interest is tax-free.

Rates of interest		Days
6.1.94 – 5.10.94	2.5%	273
6.10.94 – 5.3.95	3.25%	151
6.3.95 – 5.2.96	4%	337
6.2.96 – 5.8.97	3.25%	547
6.8.97 – 5.1.99	4%	518
6.1.99 – 5.3.99	3.25%	59
6.3.99 – 5.2.00	2.75%	337
6.2.00 – 5.5.01	3.5%	455
6.5.01 – 5.11.01	2.75%	184
6.11.01 – 5.8.03	2%	638
6.8.03 – 5.12.03	1.25%	122
6.12.03 – 5.9.04	2%	274
6.9.04 – 5.9.05	2.75%	365
6.9.05 – 5.9.06	2%	365
6.9.06 – 5.8.07	2.75%	334
6.8.07 – 5.1.08	3.5%	153
6.1.08 – 5.11.08	2.75%	305
6.11.08 – 5.12.08	2%	30
6.12.08 – 5.1.09	1.25%	31
6.1.09 – 26.1.09	0.5%	21
27.1.09 – 28.9.09	0%	245
29.9.09 –	0.5%	

Income tax on company payments

Interest on unpaid tax is chargeable on income tax payable by companies from the due date to the actual date of payment.

Interest on tax repaid carries interest from the material date (see page 78) until the repayment order is issued.

Rates of interest		Days
Payment due before 14.10.99		
6.11.01 – 5.8.03	5%	638
6.8.03 – 5.12.03	4.25%	122
6.12.03 – 5.9.04	5%	274
6.9.04 – 5.9.05	5.75%	365
6.9.05 – 5.9.06	5%	365
6.9.06 – 5.8.07	5.75%	334
6.8.07 – 5.1.08	6.5%	153
6.1.08 – 5.11.08	5.75%	305
6.11.08 – 5.12.08	5%	30
6.12.08 – 5.1.09	4.25%	31
6.1.09 – 26.1.09	3.5%	21
27.1.09 – 23.3.09	2.75%	28
24.3.09 – 28.9.09	2%	189
29.9.09 –	3%	
Payment due after 13.10.99		
6.9.04 – 5.9.05	7.5%	365
6.9.05 – 5.9.06	6.5%	365
6.9.06 – 5.8.07	7.5%	334
6.8.07 – 5.1.08	8.5%	153
6.1.08 – 5.11.08	7.5%	305
6.11.08 – 5.12.08	6.5%	30
6.12.08 – 5.1.09	5.5%	31
6.1.09 – 26.1.09	4.5%	21
27.1.09 – 23.3.09	3.5%	28
24.3.09 – 28.9.09	2.5%	189
29.9.09 –	3%	

Interest on tax and NIC *paid by individuals*

NICs Class 1 (until 5.4.14), 1A and 4, stamp duty, SDRT (until 31.12.14), SDLT and income tax and capital gains tax (until 30.10.11)

Interest on unpaid tax. Interest runs from the relevant date (see page 78) until the date of payment. Interest is payable gross and is not tax deductible. See page 78 for the harmonised interest regime which now applies to income tax, capital gains tax, Class 1 NICs and SDRT.

Rates of interest		Days
6.10.94 – 5.3.95	6.25%	151
6.3.95 – 5.2.96	7%	337
6.2.96 – 30.1.97	6.25%	360
31.1.97 – 5.8.97	8.5%	187
6.8.97 – 5.1.99	9.5%	518
6.1.99 – 5.3.99	8.5%	59
6.3.99 – 5.2.00	7.5%	337
6.2.00 – 5.5.01	8.5%	455
6.5.01 – 5.11.01	7.5%	184
6.11.01 – 5.8.03	6.5%	638
6.8.03 – 5.12.03	5.5%	122
6.12.03 – 5.9.04	6.5%	274
6.9.04 – 5.9.05	7.5%	365
6.9.05 – 5.9.06	6.5%	365
6.9.06 – 5.8.07	7.5%	334
6.8.07–5.1.08	8.5%	153
6.1.08 – 5.11.08	7.5%	305
6.11.08 – 5.12.08	6.5%	30
6.12.08 – 5.1.09	5.5%	31
6.1.09 – 26.1.09	4.5%	21
27.1.09 – 23.3.09	3.5%	56
24.3.09 – 28.9.09	2.5%	189
29.9.09	3%	

Interest on overpaid tax: repayment supplement

For 1996/97 onwards, interest runs from the date of payment (or, for income tax deducted at source, from 31 January following the year of assessment) to the date the repayment order is issued. See page 78 for the harmonised interest regime which now applies to income tax, capital gains tax, Class 1 NICs and SDRT.

Rates of interest		Days
6.10.94 – 5.3.95	6.25%	151
6.3.95 – 5.2.96	7%	337
6.2.96 – 30.1.97	6.25%	360
31.1.97 – 5.8.97	4%	187
6.8.97 – 5.1.99	4.75%	518
6.1.99 – 5.3.99	4%	59
6.3.99 – 5.2.00	3%	337
6.2.00 – 5.5.01	4%	455
6.5.01 – 5.11.01	3%	184
6.11.01 – 5.8.03	2.25%	638
6.8.03 – 5.12.03	1.5%	122
6.12.03 – 5.9.04	2.25%	274
6.9.04 – 5.9.05	3%	365
6.9.05 – 5.9.06	2.25%	365
6.9.06 – 5.8.07	3%	334
6.8.07 – 5.1.08	4%	153
6.1.08 – 5.11.08	3%	305
6.11.08 – 5.12.08	2.25%	30
6.12.08 – 5.1.09	1.5%	31
6.1.09 – 26.1.09	0.75%	21
27.1.09 – 28.9.09	0%	245
29.9.09 –	0.5%	

Inheritance tax

Unpaid tax

Interest is chargeable on unpaid inheritance tax from the due date for payment (see page 72) to the actual date of payment at the rates shown below. Interest is payable gross and is not deductible in computing income, profits or losses for tax purposes.

Rates of interest		Days
6.12.92 – 5.1.94	5%	396
6.1.94 – 5.10.94	4%	273
6.10.94 – 5.3.99	5%	1,612
6.3.99 – 5.2.00	4%	337
6.2.00 – 5.5.01	5%	455
6.5.01 – 5.11.01	4%	184
6.11.01 – 5.8.03	3%	638
6.8.03 – 5.12.03	2%	122
6.12.03 – 5.9.04	3%	274
6.9.04 – 5.9.05	4%	365
6.9.05 – 5.9.06	3%	365
6.9.06 – 5.8.07	4%	334
6.8.07 – 5.1.08	5%	153
6.1.08 – 5.11.08	4%	305
6.11.08 – 5.1.09	3%	61
6.1.09 – 26.1.09	2%	21
27.1.09 – 23.3.09	1%	56
24.3.09 – 28.9.09	0%	189
29.9.09 –	3%	

Interest on tax repaid

Any repayment of inheritance tax or interest paid carries interest from the date of payment to the date the repayment order is issued at the rates shown below. The interest is tax-free. Before 29.9.09, the rates of interest were the same as for unpaid tax.

Rates of interest		Days
29.9.09 –	0.5%	

Interest on tax and NIC

Relevant dates for unpaid tax

The relevant dates from which interest on unpaid tax and NIC runs are as follows.

(a) **IT, CGT, Class 4 NIC**
1996/97 and subsequent years and assessments raised after 5.4.98 (From 1997/98 and subsequent years for partnerships set up before 6.4.94)
Interim payments (see page 68) – due date for payment.
Any other case – 31 January after the year of assessment or, where taxpayer gave notice of chargeability before 5 October following the year of assessment and the return was not issued until after 31 October, three months after notice to deliver the return, if later.
In practice, where a return is submitted by 30 September for calculation by the Revenue of the tax due, interest runs from 30 days after notification of the liability to the taxpayer if after 31 December.

(b) **PAYE and Class 1 NIC.** See page 91.
(c) **Class 1A NIC.** 19 July after the end of the relevant tax year.
(d) **PAYE settlement agreement.** 19 October after the end of the relevant tax year.
(e) **Class 1B NIC.** 19 October after the end of the relevant tax year.
(f) **Corporation tax** – see page 75.
(g) **Income tax on company payments.** 14 days after the end of the relevant return period.
(h) **SDLT.** 30 days after the effective date of the transaction.

Material dates for repayment supplements

The material dates from which interest repayment supplements run are as follows.

(a) **Corporation tax**
Accounting periods ending after 30.9.93 and before 1.7.99. Later of nine months after the end of the accounting period and the actual date of payment.
Accounting periods ending after 30.6.99. For instalment payments by 'large companies' and early payments by other companies, see page 75.

(b) **Tax credits and income tax on company payments.**
Accounting periods ending after 30.6.99. The day after the end of the accounting period in which the payments/franked investment income were received.
Accounting periods ending before 1.7.99. Nine months after the end of the accounting period in which the payments/franked investment income were received.

(c) **Close company loan repayment/release/write-off.** Later of the date tax was paid and nine months after the end of the accounting period in which the loan was repaid, released or written off.

Harmonised interest regime

FA 2009, ss 101–105, Schs 53–54A created a harmonised interest regime for all taxes and duties administered by HMRC. The new regime applies with effect from 31.10.11 for income tax and capital gains tax self-assessment purposes, including penalties and with effect from 6.4.14 for PAYE, Class 1 NICs and construction industry scheme in-year amounts for 2014/15 onwards (from 6.10.14 for in-year late filing penalties for employers with 50 or more employees (6.3.15 for in-year late filing penalties for employers with fewer than 50 employees)) and 6.4.15 for in-year late payment penalties). It does not yet apply to corporation tax or inheritance tax (but it is expected to be extended to IHT in 2015 or 2016). The regime also applies to bank payroll tax (from 31.8.10); machine games duty (from 1.2.13); annual tax on enveloped dwellings (from 1.10.13); stamp duty reserve tax (from 1.1.15); remote gambling taxes (from 1.1.15); diverted profits tax (from 1.4.15); Class 2 NIC (from 6.4.15) and penalties relating to construction industry scheme late returns (from 6.10.11) and dishonest tax agents (from 1.4.13). The regime provides for 'late payment interest' and 'repayment interest' at differential rates. Where interest is already accruing immediately before the applicable start date, it will accrue on and after that date under the new regime.

Late payment interest. A late payment of tax (or associated penalty) carries interest at the late payment interest rate from the date on which that amount becomes due and payable until the date on which payment is made. A special rule applies to determine the interest start date if:

(i)   there is an amendment or correction to an assessment or self-assessment; or
(ii)   HMRC make one in place of, or in addition to, an assessment made by a taxpayer; or
(iii) HMRC make an assessment in place of one that a taxpayer ought to have made.

In such a case, the late payment interest start date is what it would have been if:

- the original assessment or self-assessment had been complete and accurate and had been made on the date (if any) by which it was required to be made; and
- accordingly, the amount had been due and payable as a result of that original assessment or self-assessment.

Rates of interest		Days
31.10.11 –	3%	

Repayment interest. A repayment of tax (or associated penalty) carries interest at the repayment interest rate from the 'repayment interest start date' until the date on which the repayment is made. The *'repayment interest start date'* is arrived at as set out below.

- Where the repayment is of an amount which has been paid to HMRC, the repayment interest start date is the *later* of date A and date B, where:
    date A = the date on which the amount was paid to HMRC; and
    date B = the date on which payment of the amount to HMRC became due and payable to HMRC (where it was paid in connection with a liability to make a payment to HMRC).
- Where the repayment is of an amount which has not been paid to HMRC but is payable by them by virtue of a return having been filed or a claim having been made, the repayment interest start date is the *later* of date C and date D, where:
    date C = the date (if any) on which the return was required to be filed or the claim was required to be made; and
    date D = the date on which the return was in fact filed or the claim was in fact made.
- Where the repayment is the result of a loss relief claim affecting two or more years, the repayment interest start date is 31 January following the *later* year in relation to the claim, i.e. on a claim to carry back a loss, the tax year in which the loss arises.

Rates of interest		Days
31.10.11 –	0.5%	

Mileage allowances car, cycling and motor cycling allowances

Car or van mileage rates (note (a))

	Mileage allowance	
	First 10,000	Over 10,000
2011/12 onwards	45p	25p
2006/07 – 2010/11	40p	25p

Car or van passengers (note (b))

	Mileage allowance
2006/07 onwards	5p

Cycling allowance (note (c))

	Mileage allowance
2006/07 onwards	20p

Motorcycle allowance (note (c))

	Mileage allowance
2006/07 onwards	24p

Advisory fuel rates for company cars (notes (d), (e))

	Fuel cost per mile		
	Petrol	Diesel	LPG
1.6.15 onwards			
Up to 1,400 cc	12p	—	8p
Up to 1,600 cc	—	10p	—
1,401–2,000 cc	14p	—	9p
1,601–2,000 cc	—	12p	—
Over 2,000 cc	21p	14p	14p
1.3.15 – 31.5.15			
Up to 1,400 cc	11p	—	8p
Up to 1,600 cc	—	9p	—
1,401–2,000 cc	13p	—	10p
1,601–2,000 cc	—	11p	—
Over 2,000 cc	20p	14p	14p
1.12.14 – 28.2.15			
Up to 1,400 cc	13p	—	9p
Up to 1,600 cc	—	11p	—
1,401–2,000 cc	16p	—	11p
1,601–2,000 cc	—	13p	—
Over 2,000 cc	23p	16p	16p
1.9.14 – 30.11.14			
Up to 1,400 cc	14p	—	9p
Up to 1,600 cc	—	11p	—
1,401–2,000 cc	16p	—	11p
1,601–2,000 cc	—	13p	—
Over 2,000 cc	24p	17p	16p
1.6.14 – 31.8.14			
Up to 1,400 cc	14p	—	9p
Up to 1,600 cc	—	12p	—
1,401–2,000 cc	16p	—	11p
1,601–2,000 cc	—	14p	—
Over 2,000 cc	24p	17p	16p

Notes

(a) The mileage allowances that can be paid free of tax and NICs to employees who use their own cars for business travel are statutory. Where employers pay less than the statutory rate, employees can claim tax relief on the difference. Employees cannot claim actual business motoring costs if these are above the statutory rates. [ITEPA 2003, ss 229–232, 235, 236].

(b) Tax and NIC free allowance for each fellow employee passenger carried. [ITEPA 2003, ss 233, 234].

(c) Employers can pay employees up to the mileage allowance tax free for using their own cycles/motorcycles for business travel. Employees can claim tax relief on the mileage allowance if their employer pays no cycle/motorcycle allowance (or on the balance up to the mileage allowance if the employer pays less than this rate). [ITEPA 2003, ss 229–232, 235, 236].

(d) The advisory fuel rates for company cars can be used to negotiate dispensations for mileage payments for business motoring in company cars and may be used for reimbursement by employees of fuel used for private motoring. The advisory rates will not be binding where the employer can demonstrate that the cost of business motoring is higher than the advisory rates or where a lower rate would cover the full cost of private fuel. HMRC will accept that, for one month from the date of change, employers may use either the previous or new current rates.

(e) The advisory fuel rates can also be used to reclaim VAT on fuel costs reimbursed for business travel by employees in company cars. The employer must obtain and keep a valid VAT invoice.

Miscellaneous levies and taxes

Aggregates levy [FA 2001 ss 16–49, Schs 4–10]

Aggregates levy applies to any aggregate that is subjected to commercial exploitation unless specifically exempt or previously used for construction purposes. Aggregate is rock, gravel or sand, together with whatever substances are incorporated in the rock, gravel or sand or naturally occur mixed with it. The rate of tax (apportioned on amounts less than one tonne) is:

1.4.09 onwards	£2.00 per tonne
1.4.08 – 31.3.09	£1.95 per tonne

Annual tax on enveloped dwellings [FA 2013, ss 94-174, Schs 33-35]

The annual tax on enveloped dwellings applies to companies, collective investment schemes and partnerships with company members which have a chargeable interest in land in the UK which consists of a dwelling at any time in a chargeable period. See also pages 20, 39.

Property value	Annual charge 1.4.13–31.3.14	1.4.14–31.3.15	1.4.15–31.3.16
£1,000,001 to £2,000,000	N/A	N/A	£7,000
£2,000,001 to £5,000,000	£15,000	£15,400	£23,350
£5,000,001 to £10,000,000	£35,000	£35,900	£54,450
£10,000,001 to £20,000,000	£70,000	£71,850	£109,050
£20,000,001 or more	£140,000	£143,750	£218,200

Notes

(a) Where the taxpayer does not have the chargeable interest throughout the chargeable period the annual charge is reduced accordingly on a daily basis.

(b) For chargeable periods beginning on or after 1 April 2016, an annual charge of £3,500 will apply to chargeable interests valued at more than £500,000 but not more than £1,000,000.

Bank levy [FA 2011, s 73, Sch 19]

Bank levy is a tax based upon the total chargeable equity and liabilities as reported in the relevant balance sheets of banks, banking and building society groups at the end of each chargeable period. The levy is collected through the corporation tax self-assessment system. The rates are as follows:

Rate (notes (a)(b))	1.3.11 – 30.4.11	1.5.11 – 31.12.11	1.1.12 – 31.12.12	1.1.13 – 31.12.13	1.1.14 – 31.3.15	1.4.15 – 31.12.15
Long term chargeable equity and liabilities	0.05%	0.0375%	0.044%	0.065%	0.078%	0.105%
Short term chargeable liabilities	0.1%	0.075%	0.088%	0.130%	0.156%	0.21%

Notes

(a) Where the chargeable period straddles any of the above periods, the chargeable equity and liabilities are apportioned between the periods on a time basis and the levy is charged accordingly.

(b) The first £20 billion of the chargeable equity and liabilities is exempt from the levy. The £20 billion is apportioned between the long-term equity and liabilities and the short-term liabilities.

Climate change levy [FA 2000, s 30, Sch 6; FA 2006, ss 171, 172]

Climate change levy (CCL) is a single stage tax chargeable on taxable supplies of taxable commodities. A supply is excluded from the levy if it is for domestic use or for use by a charity otherwise than in the course or furtherance of a business. With effect from 1 April 2013 separate carbon price support rates apply outside Northern Ireland to solid fossil fuels, gas and liquid petroleum gas used in most forms of electricity generation. The rates are as follows:

Taxable commodity	Main rates (note (a))			
	1.4.12 – 31.3.13	1.4.13 – 31.3.14	1.4.14 – 31.3.15	1.4.15 – 31.3.16
Electricity	0.509p per kWh	0.524p per kWh	0.541p per kWh	0.554p per kWh
Gas supplied by a gas utility or supplied in a gaseous state that is of a kind supplied by a gas utility	0.177p per kWh	0.182p per kWh	0.188p per kWh	0.193p per kWh
Gas (NI rate)	0.062p per kWh	0.064p per kWh (note (d))	N/A	N/A
Petroleum gas or other gaseous hydrocarbon supplied in a liquid state	1.137p per kg	1.172p per kg	1.21p per kg	1.24p per kg
Coal and lignite, coke and semi-coke of coal or lignite and petroleum coke	1.387p per kg	1.429p per kg	1.476p per kg	1.512p per kg
Carbon price support rates				
Natural gas	N/A	0.091p per kWh	0.175p per kWh	0.334p per kWh
Liquid petroleum gas	N/A	1.46p per kg	2.822p per kg	5.307p per kg
Coal and other taxable solid fossil fuels	N/A	44.264p per gross gigajoule	81.906p per gross gigajoule	156.86p per gross gigajoule

Notes

(a) This is the rate at which CCL is payable if the supply is not a reduced-rate supply and the carbon price support rates do not apply.

(b) A 65% reduction in the CCL main rates (80% for supplies before 1 April 2011) applies for energy intensive industries that have entered into a negotiated energy efficiency CCL agreement. The reduction is 90% for supplies of electricity on or after 1 April 2013. Energy intensive users are those that operate a Part A process listed in *Pollution Prevention and Control (England and Wales) Regulations 2000 (SI 2000/1973), Sch 1*. An 80% reduction applies for supplies of taxable commodities used in the recycling of steel and aluminium made on or after 1 April 2012 and before 1 April 2014. Before 1 April 2012 and after 31 March 2014 such supplies are exempt. Increased main rates will apply with effect from 1 April 2016: 0.559p per kWh for electricity; 0.195p per kWh for gas; 1.251p per kg for petroleum gas etc.; and 1.526p per kg for coal, coke etc. Carbon price support rates will be 0.331p per kWh for natural gas; 5.28p per kg for liquid petroleum gas; and 154.79p per gross gigajoule for coal etc.

(c) NI rate applies on or before 31 October 2013; the main rate applies thereafter.

Miscellaneous levies and taxes

Insurance premium tax [FA 1994, ss 48–74, Schs 6A, 7, 7A]

IPT is a tax on insurance premiums received under taxable insurance contracts. Insurance risk located in the UK is taxable unless specifically exempted by relating to one or more of (i) risks outside the UK; (ii) reinsurance; (iii) long-term business; (iv) commercial ships; (v) contracts relating to the Channel Tunnel; (vi) lifeboats and lifeboat equipment; (vii) commercial aircraft; (viii) international railway rolling stock; (ix) goods in foreign or international transit; (x) export finance related insurance; or (xi) contracts relating to motor vehicles for use by handicapped persons. The rates of tax are as follows:

	Standard rate	Higher rate (note (a))
From 1.11.2015	9.5% (Tax fraction 19/219)	20% (Tax fraction 1/6)
4.1.2011–31.10.2015	6% (Tax fraction 3/53)	20% (Tax fraction 1/6)
1.7.1999–3.1.2011	5% (Tax fraction 1/21)	17.5% (Tax fraction 7/47)

Note

(a) The higher rate applies to insurance sales in three trading sectors where insurance is sold in relation to goods and services which are subject to VAT. These are (i) sales of motor cars, light vans or motorcycles; (ii) sales of electrical or mechanical domestic appliances; and (iii) sales of travel insurance.

Landfill tax [FA 1996 ss 39–71, Sch 5]

Landfill tax applies to all waste disposed of by way of landfill at a licensed landfill site unless the waste is specifically exempt. Exemption applies to (i) waste removed from inland waterways and harbours by dredging; (ii) waste arising from mining and quarrying operations; (iii) pet cemeteries; (iv) waste arising from the clearance of contaminated land (where the exemption certificate application was made before 1 December 2008); and (v) (before 1 September 2009) inactive waste which is used for the purposes of restoring to use a landfill site. The rates of tax are as follows:

	Active waste per tonne	Inactive waste per tonne
1.4.15 – 31.3.16	£82.60	£2.60
1.4.14 – 31.3.15	£80	£2.50
1.4.13 – 31.3.14	£72	£2.50
1.4.12 – 31.3.13	£64	£2.50
1.4.11 – 31.3.12	£56	£2.50
1.4.10 – 31.3.11	£48	£2.50
1.4.09 – 31.3.10	£40	£2.50

The lower rate applies to those inactive wastes listed in the *Landfill Tax (Qualifying Material) Order 2011 (SI 2011 No 1017)* and the standard rate to all other taxable waste.

Notes

(a) From 1 April 2016 the rates will be £84.40 per tonne for active waste and £2.65 per tonne for inactive waste.
(b) Landfill site operators can claim a tax credit of 90% of contributions made to approved environmental bodies, subject to a maximum percentage of the liability during the contribution year.
(c) With effect from 1 April 2015, landfill tax does not apply in Scotland. Scottish landfill tax applies with effect from that date. Initially the standard rate is £82.60, and the lower rate £2.60.

Vehicle excise duty [VERA 1994, Sch 1; FA 2009, ss 13, 14; FA 2011, ss 21, 22]

VED ('car tax' or 'road tax') is a duty charged in respect of any mechanically-propelled vehicle which is used or kept on a public road in the UK. The duty is paid on a licence taken out by the person in whose name the vehicle is registered or by its keeper. Annual rates are as follows:

Band	CO₂ emissions g/km	1.4.13–31.3.14	1.4.14–31.3.15	1.4.15–31.3.16
Light passenger vehicles registered on or after 1 March 2001 (notes (a)(b))				
A	Up to 100	£0	£0	£0
B	101–110	£20	£20	£20
C	111–120	£30	£30	£30
D	121–130	£105	£110	£110
E	131–140	£125	£130	£130
F	141–150	£140	£145	£145
G	151–165	£175	£180	£180
H	166–175	£200	£205	£205
I	176–185	£220	£225	£225
J	186–200	£260	£265	£265
K (note (c))	201–225	£280	£285	£290
L	226–255	£475	£485	£490
M	Over 255	£490	£500	£505
First year rate (note (d))				
A	Up to 100	£0	£0	£0
B	101–110	£0	£0	£0
C	111–120	£0	£0	£0
D	121–130	£0	£0	£0
E	131–140	£125	£130	£130
F	141–150	£140	£145	£145
G	151–165	£175	£180	£180
H	166–175	£285	£290	£295
I	176–185	£335	£345	£350
J	186–200	£475	£485	£490
K	201–225	£620	£635	£640
L	226–255	£840	£860	£870
M	Over 255	£1,065	£1,090	£1,100
Light passenger vehicles registered before 1 March 2001				
Engine size below 1,550cc		£140	£145	£145
Over 1,549cc		£225	£230	£230
Motorcycles				
Engine size up to 150cc		£17	£17	£17
151–400cc		£37	£38	£38
401–600cc		£57	£58	£59
Over 600cc		£78	£80	£81
Light goods vehicles registered on or after 1 March 2001 (note (e))				
Standard rate		£220	£225	£225
Euro 4 & 5		£140	£140	£140

Notes

(a) Reduced rates apply to certain vehicles powered by alternative fuels.
(b) Duty can also be paid for a six-month licence. The charge is 55% of the equivalent annual rate. With effect from 1 October 2014 it is possible to pay the charge monthly or biannually by direct debit, subject to a 5% surcharge.
(c) Band K includes cars that have a CO₂ figure over 225g/km but were registered before 23 March 2006.
(d) First-year rates are payable for a vehicle's first licence taken out at first registration on or after 1 April 2010. The standard rate applies to subsequent licences.
(e) The reduced rate applies to Euro 4 vehicles registered between 1 March 2003 and 31 December 2006 inclusive and to Euro 5 vehicles registered between 1 January 2009 and 31 December 2010 inclusive. For light goods vehicles registered before 1 March 2001 the same rates apply as for light passenger vehicles registered before that date.
(f) A revised banding system is to be introduced for cars registered on or after 1 April 2017.

Motor cars car benefit

Benefit for 2011/12 to 2014/15 | Benefit for 2015/16

2011/12	2012/13	2013/14	2014/15	% of list price Petrol	Diesel	2015/16	% of list price Petrol	Diesel
75	75	75	75	5%	8%	50	5%	8%
120	99	94	N/A	10%	13%	75	9%	12%
N/A	100	95	94	11%	14%	94	13%	16%
N/A	105	100	95	12%	15%	95	14%	17%
N/A	110	105	100	13%	16%	100	15%	18%
N/A	115	110	105	14%	17%	105	16%	19%
125	120	115	110	15%	18%	110	17%	20%
130	125	120	115	16%	19%	115	18%	21%
135	130	125	120	17%	20%	120	19%	22%
140	135	130	125	18%	21%	125	20%	23%
145	140	135	130	19%	22%	130	21%	24%
150	145	140	135	20%	23%	135	22%	25%
155	150	145	140	21%	24%	140	23%	26%
160	155	150	145	22%	25%	145	24%	27%
165	160	155	150	23%	26%	150	25%	28%
170	165	160	155	24%	27%	155	26%	29%
175	170	165	160	25%	28%	160	27%	30%
180	175	170	165	26%	29%	165	28%	31%
185	180	175	170	27%	30%	170	29%	32%
190	185	180	175	28%	31%	175	30%	33%
195	190	185	180	29%	32%	180	31%	34%
200	195	190	185	30%	33%	185	32%	35%
205	200	195	190	31%	34%	190	33%	36%
210	205	200	195	32%	35%	195	34%	37%
215	210	205	200	33%	35%	200	35%	37%
220	215	210	205	34%	35%	205	36%	37%
225	220	215	210	35%	35%	210	37%	37%

Notes

(a) The cash equivalent of a car benefit is treated as earnings from employment of directors and 'P11D' employees i.e. employees with earnings, including benefits etc. to be entered on form P11D (including VAT), at the rate of £8,500 p.a. or more.

(b) The car benefit is linked to the car's CO_2 emissions. For all cars registered on or after 1 March 2001, the definitive CO_2 emissions figure for tax purposes is recorded on the vehicle registration document (V5). For cars first registered after 31 December 1997 and before 1 March 2001, the Vehicle Certification Agency supply CO_2 emissions and other relevant information on their website at carfueldata.direct.gov.uk.

For cars registered after 31 December 1997 with no approved CO_2 emissions figure, the tax charge is 15% of the list price for engines up to 1,400 cc, 25% for engines of 1,401 to 2,000 cc and 37% (35% for 2014/15 and earlier years) for engines above 2,000 cc or cars without a cylinder capacity. For 2016/17 onwards, the 15% and 25% figures will be increased to 16% and 27% respectively.

For cars registered after 31 December 1997

(i) cars which are incapable of producing carbon dioxide engine emissions when driven are charged to tax on 5%% of the list price (0% for 2010/11 to 2014/15; 7% for 2016/17); and

(ii) automatic cars made available to disabled drivers are taxable on the equivalent manual car, if less.

(c) For cars registered before 1 January 1998, the tax charge is 15% of the list price for engines up to 1,400 cc, 22% for engines of 1,401 to 2,000 cc and 32% for engines above 2,000 cc. For 2016/17 onwards, the percentages will be increased to 16%, 27% and 37% respectively. Cars without a cylinder capacity are taxed on 32% of the car's price (37% for 2016/17).

(d) The general rule is that where a car's CO_2 emissions figure is not a multiple of 5g/km, it is rounded down to the nearest 5. This rule does not apply in determining whether a car qualifies for the 5%/8%, 9%/12%, 10%/13% and, for 2014/15 only, the 11%/14% rates; in such cases, the emissions figure must not exceed the appropriate figure shown in the table. For 2015/16, the 13%/16% and 14%/17% rates apply only where the emissions figure does not exceed the appropriate figure.

(e) The 'list price' is the price published by the manufacturer, importer or distributor (inclusive of delivery charges and taxes) at the time of registration. It includes any optional extras supplied with the car when first made available to the employee, together with any further accessory costing £100 or more, but does not include certain security enhancements for employees whose employment creates a threat to personal security. Where a car is converted to run on road fuel gas, the equipment is not regarded as an accessory. Where an employee makes a capital contribution to the initial cost of the car, the price of the car for the year of contribution and subsequent years is reduced by that contribution or £5,000 if less.

(f) The value of the benefit is reduced proportionately if the car is 'unavailable' for part of the year. It is unavailable before and after it is made available to the employee and on any day in a period of 30 consecutive days throughout which it is not available.

(g) The cash equivalent (after any reductions under (e) above) is reduced (or extinguished) by the amount of contributions which an employee is required to make for private use. For 2014/15 onwards, the reduction is available only if contributions are paid in the tax year in which the private use is undertaken.

(h) Where a car is more than 15 years old at the end of the tax year and has a market value of at least £15,000, market value, if greater, is substituted for list price.

(i) Employers also pay Class 1A national insurance contributions on the scale charge.

(j) For 2016/17, the benefit for petrol cars registered after 31 December 1997 will be 7% of the list price for cars emitting not more than 50g/km, 11% for cars emitting more than 50g/km but not more than 75g/km and 15% for cars emitting more than 75g/km but less than 95g/km, and this increases by one percentage point for each additional 5g/km up to a maximum of 37%. The diesel supplement will be abolished for 2016/17 onwards.

[ITEPA 2003, ss 114–148; FA 2011, s 51; FA 2012, ss 14, 17; FA 2013, s 23; FA 2014, ss 24, 25; FA 2015, ss 7–9].

Motor cars Car fuel benefit

2011/12		
CO$_2$ emissions (g/km)	Petrol (£)	Diesel (£)
75	940	1,504
120	1,880	2,444
125	2,820	3,384
130	3,008	3,572
135	3,196	3,760
140	3,384	3,948
145	3,572	4,136
150	3,760	4,324
155	3,948	4,512
160	4,136	4,700
165	4,324	4,888
170	4,512	5,076
175	4,700	5,264
180	4,888	5,452
185	5,076	5,640
190	5,264	5,828
195	5,452	6,016
200	5,640	6,204
205	5,828	6,392
210	6,016	6,580
215	6,204	6,580
220	6,392	6,580
225	6,580	6,580

2012/13		
CO$_2$ emissions (g/km)	Petrol (£)	Diesel (£)
75	1,010	1,616
99	2,020	2,626
100	2,222	2,828
105	2,424	3,030
110	2,626	3,232
115	2,828	3,434
120	3,030	3,636
125	3,232	3,838
130	3,434	4,040
135	3,636	4,242
140	3,838	4,444
145	4,040	4,646
150	4,242	4,848
155	4,444	5,050
160	4,646	5,252
165	4,848	5,454
170	5,050	5,656
175	5,252	5,858
180	5,454	6,060
185	5,656	6,262
190	5,858	6,464
195	6,060	6,666
200	6,262	6,868
205	6,464	7,070
210	6,666	7,070
215	6,868	7,070
220	7,070	7,070

2013/14		
CO$_2$ emissions (g/km)	Petrol (£)	Diesel (£)
75	1,055	1,688
94	2,110	2,743
95	2,321	2,954
100	2,532	3,165
105	2,743	3,376
110	2,954	3,587
115	3,165	3,798
120	3,376	4,009
125	3,587	4,220
130	3,798	4,431
135	4,009	4,642
140	4,220	4,853
145	4,431	5,064
150	4,642	5,275
155	4,853	5,486
160	5,064	5,697
165	5,275	5,908
170	5,486	6,119
175	5,697	6,330
180	5,908	6,541
185	6,119	6,752
190	6,330	6,963
195	6,541	7,174
200	6,752	7,385
205	6,963	7,385
210	7,174	7,385
215	7,385	7,385

Motor cars   Car fuel benefit

2014/15

CO$_2$ emissions (g/km)	Petrol (£)	Diesel (£)
75	1,085	1,736
94	2,387	3,038
95	2,604	3,255
100	2,821	3,472
105	3,038	3,689
110	3,255	3,906
115	3,472	4,123
120	3,689	4,340
125	3,906	4,557
130	4,123	4,774
135	4,340	4,991
140	4,557	5,208
145	4,774	5,425
150	4,991	5,642
155	5,208	5,859
160	5,425	6,076
165	5,642	6,293
170	5,859	6,510
175	6,076	6,727
180	6,293	6,944
185	6,510	7,161
190	6,727	7,378
195	6,944	7,595
200	7,161	7,595
205	7,378	7,595
210	7,595	7,595

2015/16

CO$_2$ emissions (g/km)	Petrol (£)	Diesel (£)
50	1,105	1,768
75	1,989	2,652
94	2,873	3,536
95	3,094	3,757
100	3,315	3,978
105	3,536	4,199
110	3,757	4,420
115	3,978	4,641
120	4,199	4,862
125	4,420	5,083
130	4,641	5,304
135	4,862	5,525
140	5,083	5,746
145	5,304	5,967
150	5,525	6,188
155	5,746	6,409
160	5,967	6,630
165	6,188	6,851
170	6,409	7,072
175	6,630	7,293
180	6,851	7,514
185	7,072	7,735
190	7,293	7,956
195	7,514	8,177
200	7,735	8,177
205	7,956	8,177
210	8,177	8,177

Notes

(a) The cash equivalent of the benefit of car fuel is taxable as earnings of directors and 'P11D' employees (i.e. employees with earnings, including benefits, etc. to be entered on form P11D, including VAT, at the rate of £8,500 p.a. or more) provided with free fuel for private use of company cars. [*ITEPA 2003, ss 149, 217*]. The £8,500 threshold will be abolished for 2016/17 onwards, so that all employees will be taxed on benefits and expenses in the same way. Exemptions will apply for minsters of religion earning less than £8,500.

(b) The same percentage figure on page 82 used to calculate the car benefit charge for the company car, which is directly linked to the car's CO$_2$ emissions, is used to calculate the benefit charge for fuel provided for private motoring. The relevant percentage figure is multiplied by £22,100 for 2015/16; £21,700 for 2014/15; £21,100 for 2013/14; £20,200 for 2012/13; and £18,800 for 2011/12.

(c) The benefit is reduced to nil if the employee is required to, and does, make good all fuel provided for private use, including journeys between home and normal place of work. There is no taxable benefit where the employer only provides fuel for business travel. The charge is proportionately reduced where the employee stops receiving free fuel part way through the tax year, but where free fuel is subsequently provided in the same tax year, the full year's charge is payable. [*ITEPA 2003, ss 151, 152*].

(d) The benefit is proportionately reduced where a car is not available or is incapable of being used for part of a year (being at least 30 days). [*ITEPA 2003, s 152*].

(e) Fuel provided for private motoring of a director or 'P11D' employee but not for a company car and fuel provided for lower-paid employees (e.g. by paying garage bills or by use of credit tokens or vouchers) is taxable on the cost to the employer less any contributions from the employee.

(f) Employers pay Class 1A national insurance contributions on the amount of the benefit shown.

National insurance contributions Class 1

Class 1 (earnings related)		2015/16	
Lower earnings limit	— per week	£112	
	— per month	£486	
	— per year	£5,824	
Primary earnings threshold	— per week	£155	
	— per month	£672	
	— per year	£8,060	
Secondary earnings threshold	— per week	£156	
	— per month	£676	
	— per year	£8,112	
Upper accruals point	— per week	£770	
	— per month	£3,337	
	— per year	£40,040	
Upper earnings limit/Upper secondary threshold	— per week	£815	
	— per month	£3,532	
	— per year	£42,385	

Not contracted out

Employee (note (a))	First £155 pw	Nil
	From £155 pw to £815 pw	12%
	Balance above £815 pw	2%

Employer (notes (c), (f))	First £156 pw	Nil
	Balance above £156 pw	13.8%

Contracted out — salary related schemes

Employee (notes (a), (d))	First £155 pw	Nil
	From £155 pw to £770 pw	10.6%
	From £770 pw to £815 pw	12%
	Balance above £815 pw	2%
— rebate (note (b))	From £112 pw to £155 pw	1.4%

Employer (notes (c), (d), (f))	First £156 pw	Nil
	From £156 pw to £770 pw	10.4%
	Balance above £770 pw	13.8%
— rebate	From £112 pw to £156 pw	3.4%

Women at reduced rate

Employee (note (a))	First £155 pw	Nil
	From £155 pw to £815 pw	5.85%
	Balance above £815 pw	2%

Notes

(a) For 2015/16, NICs are not payable on earnings up to and including the primary earnings threshold. Employees' rates are nil for employees of pensionable age although normal employers' contributions are still payable. Pensionable age is, in the case of a man born before 6 December 1953, 65, and in the case of a woman born before 6 April 1950, 60. For women born after 5 April 1950 and before 6 October 1954, and for men born after 5 December 1953 and before 6 October 1954, pensionable age rises on a sliding scale contained in *Pensions Act 1995, Sch 4 Pt 1*. For men and women born after 5 October 1954 and before 6 April 1960 pensionable age is 66. A sliding scale under *Sch 4 Pt 1* again applies to gradually increase the pensionable age for men and women born after 5 April 1960 and before 6 April 1961, so that for men and women born after 5 April 1961 pensionable age is 67. A further phased increase applies to those born on or after 6 April 1977 and before 6 April 1978, so that the pensionable age for those born after 5 April 1978 will be 68.

(b) Where insufficient employee contributions are paid to cover the rebate, it is offset against employers' contributions to the extent of the shortfall.

(c) For 2015/16, NICs are not payable on earnings up to and including the secondary earnings threshold. For employees below the age of 21, NICs are not payable on earnings up to and including the upper secondary earning threshold and, if the scheme is contracted-out, the rebate of 3.4% is payable for earnings from £112 per week to £770 per week. For 2016/17 onwards, NICs will not be payable up to and including the upper secondary threshold for apprentices under 25.

(d) Contracting out is to be abolished for salary related schemes with effect from 6 April 2016.

(e) See page 77 for interest on Class 1 NIC.

(f) For 2015/16 employers may claim an employment allowance of £2,000. The allowance is given effect by offset against the employer's liability for secondary Class 1 NICs. For 2016/17 the allowance will be £3,000 but it will not be available to companies whose only employee is the director.

National insurance contributions Class 1

Class 1 (earnings related)			2014/15		2013/14	
Lower earnings limit		— per week	£111		£109	
		— per month	£481		£473	
		— per year	£5,772		£5,668	
Primary earnings threshold		— per week	£153		£149	
		— per month	£663		£646	
		— per year	£7,956		£7,755	
Secondary earnings threshold		— per week	£153		£148	
		— per month	£663		£641	
		— per year	£7,956		£7,696	
Upper accruals point		— per week	£770		£770	
		— per month	£3,337		£3,337	
		— per year	£40,040		£40,040	
Upper earnings limit		— per week	£805		£797	
		— per month	£3,489		£3,454	
		— per year	£41,865		£41,450	

Not contracted out

Employee (note (a))			First £153 pw	Nil	First £149 pw	Nil
			From £153 pw to £805 pw	12%	From £149 pw to £797 pw	12%
			Balance above £805 pw	2%	Balance above £797 pw	2%
Employer (notes (c), (g))			First £153 pw	Nil	First £148 pw	Nil
			Balance above £153 pw	13.8%	Balance above £148 pw	13.8%

Contracted out — salary related schemes

Employee (notes (a), (d))			First £153 pw	Nil	First £149 pw	Nil
			From £153 pw to £770 pw	10.6%	From £149 pw to £770 pw	10.6%
			From £770 pw to £805 pw	12%	From £770 pw to £797 pw	12%
			Balance above £805 pw	2%	Balance above £797 pw	2%
— rebate (note (b))			From £111 pw to £153 pw	1.4%	From £109 pw to £149 pw	1.4%
Employer (notes (c), (d), (g))			First £153 pw	Nil	First £148 pw	Nil
			From £153 pw to £770 pw	10.4%	From £148 pw to £770 pw	10.4%
			Balance above £770 pw	13.8%	Balance above £770 pw	13.8%
— rebate			From £111 pw to £153 pw	3.4%	From £109 pw to £148 pw	3.4%

Women at reduced rate

Employee (note (a))			First £153 pw	Nil	First £149 pw	Nil
			From £153 pw to £805 pw	5.85%	From £149 pw to £797 pw	5.85%
			Balance above £805 pw	2%	Balance above £797 pw	2%

Notes

(a) For 2013/14 and 2014/15, NICs are not payable on earnings up to and including the primary earnings threshold. Employees' rates are nil for employees of pensionable age although normal employers' contributions are still payable.

(b) Where insufficient employee contributions are paid to cover the rebate, it is offset against employers' contributions to the extent of the shortfall.

(c) For 2013/14 and 2014/15, NICs are not payable on earnings up to and including the secondary earnings threshold.

(d) See page 77 for interest on Class 1 NIC.

(e) An NIC 'holiday' was available for new businesses in Northern Ireland, Scotland, Wales and six English regions. Under the scheme, an employer did not have to pay the first £5,000 of its employer NICs for each of its first ten employees hired in its first year of business. The scheme applied to businesses starting up in the period from 22 June 2010 to 5 September 2013, but only to NICs in respect of earnings paid on or after 6 September 2010 and before 6 September 2013.

(f) For 2014/15 employers may claim an employment allowance of £2,000. The allowance is given effect by offset against the employer's liability for secondary Class 1 NICs.

National insurance contributions Class 1

Class 1 (earnings related)		2012/13		2011/12	
Lower earnings limit	— per week	£107		£102	
	— per month	£464		£442	
	— per year	£5,564		£5,304	
Primary earnings threshold	— per week	£146		£139	
	— per month	£634		£602	
	— per year	£7,605		£7,225	
Secondary earnings threshold	— per week	£144		£136	
	— per month	£624		£589	
	— per year	£7,488		£7,072	
Upper accruals point	— per week	£770		£770	
	— per month	£3,337		£3,337	
	— per year	£40,040		£40,040	
Upper earnings limit	— per week	£817		£817	
	— per month	£3,540		£3,540	
	— per year	£42,475		£42,475	
Not contracted out					
Employee (note (a))		First £146 pw	Nil	First £139 pw	Nil
		From £146 pw to £817 pw	12%	From £139 pw to £817 pw	12%
		Balance above £817 pw	2%	Balance above £817 pw	2%
Employer (note (c))		First £144 pw	Nil	First £136 pw	Nil
		Balance above £144 pw	13.8%	Balance above £136 pw	13.8%
Contracted out					
Employee (note (a))		First £146 pw	Nil	First £139 pw	Nil
		From £146 pw to £770 pw	10.6%	From £139 pw to £770 pw	10.4%
		From £770 pw to £817 pw	12%	From £770 pw to £817 pw	12%
		Balance above £817 pw	2%	Balance above £817 pw	2%
— rebate (note (b))		From £107 pw to £146 pw	1.4%	From £102 pw to £139 pw	1.6%
Employer — salary related schemes (note (c))		First £144 pw	Nil	First £136 pw	Nil
		From £144 pw to £770 pw	10.4%	From £136 pw to £770 pw	10.1%
		Balance above £770 pw	13.8%	Balance above £770 pw	13.8%
— rebate		From £107 pw to £144 pw	3.4%	From £102 pw to £136 pw	3.7%
Employer — money purchase scheme (notes (c), (d))		N/A		First £136 pw	Nil
				From £136 pw to £770 pw	12.4%
				Balance above £770 pw	13.8%
— rebate				From £102 pw to £136 pw	1.4%
Women at reduced rate					
Employee (note (a))		First £146 pw	Nil	First £139 pw	Nil
		From £146 pw to £817 pw	5.85%	From £139 pw to £817 pw	5.85%
		Balance above £817 pw	2%	Balance above £817 pw	2%

Notes

(a) For 2011/12 and 2012/13, NICs are not payable on earnings up to and including the primary earnings threshold. Employees' rates are nil for employees of pensionable age although normal employers' contributions are still payable.

(b) Where insufficient employee contributions are paid to cover the rebate, it is offset against employers' contributions to the extent of the shortfall.

(c) For 2011/12 and 2012/13, NICs are not payable on earnings up to and including the secondary earnings threshold.

(d) Contracting out is abolished for money purchase schemes with effect from 6 April 2012.

(e) See page 77 for interest on Class 1 NIC.

(f) An NIC 'holiday' is available for new businesses in Northern Ireland, Scotland, Wales and six English regions. Under the scheme, an employer does not have to pay the first £5,000 of its employer NICs for each of its first ten employees hired in its first year of business. The scheme applies to businesses starting up in the period from 22 June 2010 to 5 September 2013, but only to NICs in respect of earnings paid on or after 6 September 2010 (and before 6 September 2013).

National insurance contributions Class 1

Class 1 (earnings related)		2010/11		2009/10	
Lower earnings limit	— per week	£97		£95	
	— per month	£421		£412	
	— per year	£5,044		£4,940	
Primary/secondary earnings threshold	— per week	£110		£110	
	— per month	£476		£476	
	— per year	£5,715		£5,715	
Upper accruals point	— per week	£770		£770	
	— per month	£3,337		£3,337	
	— per year	£40,040		£40,040	
Upper earnings limit	— per week	£844		£844	
	— per month	£3,656			
	— per year	£43,875		£43,875	
Not contracted out					
Employee (note (a))		First £110 pw	Nil	First £110 pw	Nil
		From £110 pw to £844 pw	11%	From £110 pw to £844 pw	11%
		Balance above £844 pw	1%	Balance above £844 pw	1%
Employer (note (c))		First £110 pw	Nil	First £110 pw	Nil
		Balance above £110 pw	12.8%	Balance above £110 pw	12.8%
Contracted out					
Employee (note (a))		First £110 pw	Nil	First £110 pw	Nil
		From £110 pw to £770 pw	9.4%	From £110 pw to £770 pw	9.4%
		From £770 pw to £844 pw	11%	From £770 pw to £844 pw	11%
		Balance above £844 pw	1%	Balance above £844 pw	1%
— rebate (note (b))		From £97 pw to £110 pw	1.6%	From £95 pw to £110 pw	1.6%
Employer — salary related schemes (note (c))		First £110 pw	Nil	First £110 pw	Nil
		From £110 pw to £770 pw	9.1%	From £110 pw to £770 pw	9.1%
		Balance above £770 pw	12.8%	Balance above £770 pw	12.8%
— rebate		From £97 pw to £110 pw	3.7%	From £95 pw to £110 pw	3.7%
Employer — money purchase scheme (note (c))		First £110 pw	Nil	First £110 pw	Nil
		From £110 pw to £770 pw	11.4%	From £110 pw to £770 pw	11.4%
		Balance above £770 pw	12.8%	Balance above £770 pw	12.8%
— rebate		From £97 pw to £110 pw	1.4%	From £95 pw to £110 pw	1.4%
Women at reduced rate					
Employee (note (a))		First £110 pw	Nil	First £110 pw	Nil
		From £110 pw to £844 pw	4.85%	From £110 pw to £844 pw	4.85%
		Balance above £844 pw	1%	Balance above £844 pw	1%

Notes

(a) For 2009/10 and 2010/11, NICs are not payable on earnings up to and including the primary earnings threshold. Employees' rates are nil for employees of pensionable age although normal employers' contributions are still payable.

(b) Where insufficient employee contributions are paid to cover the rebate, it is offset against employers' contributions to the extent of the shortfall.

(c) For 2009/10 and 2010/11, NICs are not payable on earnings up to and including the secondary earnings threshold.

(d) See page 77 for interest on Class 1 NIC.

(e) An NIC 'holiday' is available for new businesses in Northern Ireland, Scotland, Wales and six English regions. Under the scheme, an employer does not have to pay the first £5,000 of its employer NICs for each of its first ten employees hired in its first year of business. The scheme applies to businesses starting up in the period from 22 June 2010 to 5 September 2013, but only to NICs in respect of earnings paid on or after 6 September 2010 (and before 6 September 2013).

National insurance contributions Classes 1A, 1B, 2, 3 and 4

	2015/16	2014/15	2013/14	2012/13	2011/12	2010/11	2009/10
Class 1A (note (a))	13.8%	13.8%	13.8%	13.8%	13.8%	12.8%	12.8%
Class 1B (PSAs) (note (b))	13.8%	13.8%	13.8%	13.8%	13.8%	12.8%	12.8%
Class 2 (self-employed, flat rate)							
Small profits threshold/small earnings exemption—per year	£5,965	£5,885	£5,725	£5,595	£5,315	£5,075	£5,075
Contributions —per week	£2.80	£2.75	£2.70	£2.65	£2.50	£2.40	£2.40
Share fishermen	£3.45	£3.40	£3.35	£3.30	£3.15	£3.05	£3.05
Volunteer development workers	£5.60	£5.55	£5.45	£5.35	£5.10	£4.85	£4.75
Class 3 (voluntary contributions)							
Contributions —per week	£14.10	£13.90	£13.55	£13.25	£12.60	£12.05	£12.05
Class 4 (self-employed, profits related) (note (c))							
Lower annual limit	£8,060	£7,956	£7,755	£7,605	£7,225	£5,715	£5,715
Upper annual limit	£42,385	£41,865	£41,450	£42,475	£42,475	£43,875	£43,875
Percentage rate between lower and upper annual limits	9%	9%	9%	9%	9%	8%	8%
Percentage rate above upper annual limit	2%	2%	2%	2%	2%	1%	1%
Maximum contributions (note (d))							
Class 1 or Class 1/Class 2	£4,197.60	£4,146.72	£4,121.28	£4,267.56	£4,312.08	£4,279.22	£4,279.22
Class 4 limiting amount	£3,237.65	£3,197.56	£3,175.65	£3,278.75	£3,305.00	£3,180.00	£3,180.00

Notes

(a) **Class 1A contributions.** Class 1A contributions are payable by employers on the provision of cars and private fuel to employees and most other benefits in kind provided by employers. Employees' contributions are not payable. The income tax rules are used to determine the chargeable amount (see pages 82 to 84). Contributions are payable by 19 July following the tax year to which they relate. If private fuel is provided for use in an employee's own car, Class 1A contributions do not apply but there may be a liability for both employer's and employee's Class 1 contributions depending upon how the fuel is provided.
For the provisions relating to interest on unpaid and overpaid Class 1A contributions, see page 77.

(b) **Class 1B contributions.** Class 1B contributions are payable by employers by reference to the value of any items included in a PAYE settlement agreement (PSA) which would otherwise be earnings for Class 1 or Class 1A, including the amount of tax paid.
Employees' contributions are not payable. Income tax and Class 1B contributions on a PSA are payable by 19 October following the end of the tax year to which the PSA applies.

(c) **Class 2 and Class 4 contributions.** The provisions relating to interest on unpaid tax and interest on overpaid tax also apply to Class 4 contributions. See page 77.
Where Class 4 contributions are due, the same penalties for failure to make a return within the required period or making an incorrect return apply as for income tax purposes. See pages 96, 97.
The same interest and penalty provisions apply to Class 2 contributions for 2015/16 onwards.

(d) **Maximum contributions.** Where an earner is employed in more than one employment (whether employed earners' employments or self-employments) liability for Class 1 or Class 1 and Class 2 contributions cannot exceed a maximum figure. Similarly, where Class 4 contributions are payable in addition to Class 1 and/or Class 2 contributions, liability for Class 4 contributions cannot exceed a limiting amount.
Subject to below, the Class 1/Class 2 maximum is the equivalent of 53 primary Class 1 contributions at the maximum standard rate. The Class 4 maximum is such amount as, when added to the Class 1/Class 2 contributions payable (after applying the maximum if appropriate), equals the limiting amount shown above (this being the maximum Class 4 contributions payable at 9%/8% plus 53 Class 2 contributions).
Because of the open-ended Class 1 and Class 4 contributions at 2%/1%, each person has, in effect, their own 'personalised maximum'. Further adjustments to the figures quoted in the table above are required for any contributions payable at the 2% or 1% rate on earnings over the upper earnings limit and profits over the upper annual limit.

National insurance contributions Class 3A

Age on payment date (October 2015 to April 2017)	Rate for each additional pension unit of £1 per week	Age on payment date (October 2015 to April 2017)	Rate for each additional pension unit of £1 per week	Age on payment date (October 2015 to April 2017)	Age on payment date (October 2015 to April 2017)
62 (women only)	£956	75	£674	88	£314
63 (women only)	£934	76	£646	89	£291
64 (women only)	£913	77	£625	90	£270
65	£890	78	£596	91	£251
66	£871	79	£574	92	£232
67	£847	80	£544	93	£216
68	£827	81	£514	94	£200
69	£801	82	£484	95	£185
70	£779	83	£454	96	£172
71	£761	84	£424	97	£159
72	£738	85	£394	98	£148
73	£719	86	£366	99	£137
74	£694	87	£339	100	£127

Notes

(a) An extra category of voluntary contributions will be available for an 18-month period from 12 October 2015 as a state pension top up. Payment will allow existing pensioners, and those entitled to a state pension and reaching state pension age before 6 April 2016, the opportunity to gain additional state pension. Contribution amounts vary according to the age of the payer as shown in the table above. See *SI 2014 No 3240*.

(b) Class 3A contributions cannot provide more than £25 per week additional pension.

PAYE

PAYE thresholds

2015/16	£204 per week	£883 per month

Payment by quarterly instalments

Employers whose average monthly liability for PAYE and NIC is less than £1,500 can choose to pay quarterly instead. Payments are due 14 days after the end of the relevant quarter (extended to 17 days where payment is made by electronic means).

PAYE codes

Code suffix	Meaning
L	Basic personal allowance
M	Marriage allowance transferred from spouse or civil partner
N	Marriage allowance transferred to spouse or civil partner
Y	Full personal allowance for those born before 6.4.1938
T	Other calculations included to work out the personal allowance
K	Total allowances in the code are less than total deductions
D0	Tax to be deducted at higher rate
D1	Tax to be deducted at additional rate
BR	Tax to be deducted at basic rate; no allowances given
NT	No tax to be deducted
0T	No allowances available; tax to be deducted at appropriate rate
M1	Tax to be deducted on a month 1 basis
W1	Tax to be deducted on a week 1 basis

Penalties—P14, P35, P38 and P38A

Failure to submit returns. For returns for 2013/14 and earlier years not submitted by due date (i.e. 19 May following the tax year)

(a) an automatic penalty of the 'monthly amount' for each month (or part month) the failure continues, up to 12 months; and

(b) for failure beyond 12 months, a penalty of up to the amount of the PAYE or NIC payable which was unpaid after 19 April following the tax year.

The 'monthly amount' is £100 for every 50 employees or subcontractors (or part thereof).

Real time information. The above penalties apply for failure to submit the final full payment submission (FPS) or employer payment summary (EPS) for 2012/13 and 2013/14 by 19 May following the tax year.

For penalties for late filing of FPSs and EPSs for 2014/15 onwards see page 96.

Penalties—P9D and P11D

Failure to submit returns. For returns not submitted by 6 July following the tax year

(a) a penalty of up to £300 per form;

(b) if failure continues after penalty under (a) imposed, continuing penalty of up to £60 per form per day.

PAYE

Gross pay for PAYE and NIC purposes (HMRC Guide CWG2 (2015))

The following payments should be entered as pay on the employee's payroll record/deduction working sheet (as opposed to being returned at the year end on forms P9D or P11D or included in a PAYE settlement agreement).

Childcare vouchers not meeting the qualifying conditions (NIC only).

Christmas boxes in cash.

Clothing or uniforms—(i) Payments to employees for non-durable items such as tights or stockings (PAYE only); and (ii) other payments to employees to purchase clothing or uniforms whether this can be worn at any time or (for PAYE only) only at work.

Council tax paid on employee's living accommodation except where the value does not have to be included on forms P9D or P11D (NICs only).

Credit cards, charge cards, etc.—employees' use of an employer's card for expenditure, *other than* goods or services bought on the employer's behalf, on readily convertible assets (see below), and (for NICs) where no reimbursement made.

Credit card reward payments for detecting/withdrawing lost/stolen cards made by employer.

Damages or similar payments made to an employee injured at work if there is a contractual liability to make it.

Directors' remuneration, salary, bonuses, fees etc. including any advance or anticipatory payments paid, voted or credited.

Employment income provided through third parties when taxable under disguised remuneration rules in *ITEPA 2003, Pt 7A*.

Employment Tribunal awards under an order for re-instatement or re-engagement or for continuation of employment, or a protective award.

Guarantee payments under *Employment Rights Act 1996*.

Honoraria

Incentive awards made by cash or vouchers exchangeable for cash including (for NICs) those made by third parties.

Inducement payments such as 'golden hellos' to recruit or retain employees.

Loans written off (NICs only.)

Long service awards in cash or cash vouchers or readily convertible assets (see below).

Lost time payments other than those made by, or by the employer on behalf of, a third party.

Maternity suspension payments made under the *Employment Rights Act 1996*.

Meal allowances and vouchers comprising (i) cash payments for meals; and (ii) vouchers redeemable for food and drink or cash alternative (but not vouchers redeemable for food and drink only or for food and drink on business premises or any canteen where meals are generally provided for employer's staff).

Medical suspension payments made under the *Employment Rights Act 1996*.

Mortgage payments (for NICs only) on a contract between the employee and mortgagee.

Payments in kind (other than readily convertible assets for which see below) which can be turned into cash *by surrender*, e.g. premium bonds.

Payments made to an employee pursuing a claim for *damages against a third party* for loss of earnings following an accident if the employee is not required to repay the employer.

Pensions (PAYE only)

Personal bills paid for goods and services supplied to employees and directors, club memberships, etc. where the payments are made or reimbursed direct to the employee, and (for NICs only) where made direct to the provider or via an overdrawn director's loan account into which director's earnings normally paid.

Personal incidental expenses (other than benefits in kind) exceeding the prescribed limit or failing the qualifying conditions (the whole amount is liable to tax and NICs).

Prize money paid in cash to employees for competitions the employer runs in connection with its business and which are not open to the public.

Readily convertible assets i.e. assets which are (i) capable of being sold on a recognised investment exchange, London Bullion market or New York Stock Exchange (other than shares under an approved scheme); (ii) a right over a money debt; (iii) subject to a fiscal warehousing regime; (iv) give rise to a right to enable an employee to obtain money; (v) subject to trading arrangements; (vi) already owned by the employee and whose value is enhanced by the employer.

Relocation payments that are non-qualifying.

Round sum allowances unless otherwise agreed with HMRC.

Sickness, maternity and other absence from work payments.

Statutory adoption (SAP), **maternity** (SMP), **paternity** (SPP), **shared parental** (ShPP), **sick pay** (SSP).

Subscriptions or fees to professional bodies: (i) paid directly by the employer but not allowable under *ITEPA 2003, ss 343, 344* (NIC only);(ii) reimbursed by the employer and allowable under *ITEPA 2003, ss 343, 344* (PAYE only) or not so allowable .

Suggestion scheme awards to employees (see *ITEPA 2003, s 321* for exemption).

Telephone bills — NICs on full amount of rental and on private calls where telephone used for business and private calls, the employee is the subscriber and the employer pays for the calls and/or rental. See also *Personal bills* above where the telephone is used exclusively for private calls.

Termination payments — (i) payments made under the terms and conditions of employment (such as compensation for loss of office, accrued pay and pay in lieu of notice); (ii) payments for a restrictive covenant; (iii) redundancy payments and payments made as damages (PAYE only) subject to a £30,000 relief under certain circumstances; (iv) certain payments made to unapproved retirement benefits schemes (NICs only).

Tips and service charges where a scheme is operated by the employer (if separate organised arrangements exist, for example, employees are paid out of a tronc, then the troncmaster is responsible for operating PAYE but not for NICs).

Training payments (for course fees, books, etc.) unless the training is work-related or is encouraged or required by the employer in connection with the employee's work.

Travelling time payments.

Trivial commutations from registered pension schemes (PAYE only)

Vouchers which can be redeemed or exchanged for (i) goods and cash or cash alone; (ii) goods alone or transport services (NICs only) or (iii) readily convertible assets.

Wages, salaries, fees, overtime, bonuses, commission, etc.

PAYE

PAYE settlement agreements (PSAs) [ITEPA 2003, ss 703–707; SI 2003 No 2682 Pt 6; HMRC SP 5/96]

PSAs cover arrangements under which employers can settle, in a single payment, the tax and Class 1B NICs (see page 89) liability on certain benefits in kind and expense payments. Expenses payments and benefits can be included in a PSA if they are minor or payable on an irregular basis or in circumstances where it is impracticable to apply PAYE or apportion the value of particular benefits which have been shared by employees.

The scope of the PSA must be finalised by 6 July, and any tax paid by 19 October, following the tax year to which the PSA applies.

Personal service companies etc. [ITEPA 2003, ss 48–61]

Where a worker who would otherwise have been an employee provides his services through an intermediary such as a service company, it must operate PAYE and pay NICs. For this purpose, the income from the worker's relevant engagements in the year, less the amounts provided to the worker as salary/benefits in kind and less allowable expenses, are deemed to have been paid to the worker as salary on 5 April. Allowable expenses include normal deductible employment expenses, employer's NICs and pension contributions and 5% of income from relevant engagements. From 6 April 2013 the provisions are extended to office holders.

Managed service companies [ITEPA 2003, ss 61A–61J; FA 2007, s 25, Sch 3]

Where a worker provides his services through an intermediary which is a managed service company (as defined), all payments received by him from the company on or after 6 April 2007 which are not otherwise employment income are deemed to be employment income. The company must operate PAYE and, from 6 August 2007, pay NICs on each such payment. PAYE and NIC debts which cannot be recovered from a managed service company will be collectible from certain other persons, primarily the company's director or the person who provided the company to the worker.

The personal service companies provisions above are disapplied where the managed service companies rules apply.

Student loan repayments [SI 2009 No 470]

Student loan repayments of employees are collected through the PAYE system. The employer must calculate and deduct student loan repayments due each pay period, based on the employee's earnings for that period. The deduction is 9% of earnings in excess of the threshold in the table below. If total earnings for a tax year do not exceed the yearly threshold, the employee can claim a refund of any repayments deducted in that tax year. Repayments must also be made by reference to other income (from self-employment, savings and investments etc.) through the self-assessment system where total income exceeds the yearly threshold.

Year	Percentage	Threshold		
		Per week	Per month	Per year
2015/16	9%	£333.00	£1,444.00	£17,335.00
2014/15	9%	£325.19	£1,409.16	£16,910.00
2013/14	9%	£314.71	£1,363.75	£16,365.00
2012/13	9%	£303.75	£1,316.25	£15,795.00
2005/06 to 2011/12	9%	£288.46	£1,250.00	£15,000.00

National minimum wage

Age	Hourly rate				
	1.10.11–30.9.12	1.10.12–30.9.13	1.10.13–30.9.14	1.10.14–30.9.15	1.10.15 onwards
Under 18	£3.68	£3.68	£3.72	£3.79	£3.87
18–20	£4.98	£4.98	£5.03	£5.13	£5.30
21 or over	£6.08	£6.19	£6.31	£6.50	£6.70
Apprentice rate	£2.60	£2.65	£2.68	£2.73	£3.30

Penalties general

Offence	Penalty
Error in taxpayer's document [FA 2007, Sch 24 para 1] Careless or deliberate error in document amounting to or leading to understatement of liability, overstatement or loss or false or inflated claim to repayment of tax. Applies to IT (including Class 4 NICs and, for 2015/16 onwards, Class 2 NICs), CIS, CGT, CT and VAT returns, statements, declarations, claims etc. relating to tax years, accounting periods and VAT periods beginning on or after 1 April 2008. No penalty can be charged in respect of any period for which a return is required before 1 April 2009. Applies to further taxes, including to IHT where the date of death is on or after 1 April 2009 or, in other cases, where the tax liability arises on or after 1 April 2010 and to SDLT where the liability arises on or after 1 April 2010. Also applies to annual tax on enveloped dwellings.	Deliberate and concealed action or omission: 100% of potential lost revenue. Deliberate but not concealed action or omission: 70% of potential lost revenue. Careless action or omission: 30% of potential lost revenue. *Reductions.* A statutory reduction in the amount of the penalty is made for disclosure of an inaccuracy. For an unprompted disclosure, a 100% penalty may be reduced to no less than 30%, a 70% penalty to no less than 20% and a 30% penalty to any percentage, including 0%. For a prompted disclosure, a 100% penalty may be reduced to no less than 50%, a 70% penalty to no less than 35% and a 30% penalty to no less than 15%. HMRC can also reduce a penalty in special circumstances. *Offshore evasion.* See page 97 for the increase in the amount of the penalty where the error involves an offshore matter.
Error in taxpayer's document attributable to another person [FA 2007, Sch 24 para 1A] Deliberately supplying false information to, or deliberately withholding information from, a person giving a document within the above provisions to HMRC resulting in document containing an inaccuracy amounting to or leading to understatement of liability, overstatement of loss or false or inflated claim to repayment of tax. Applies to tax years, accounting periods and VAT periods beginning on or after 1 April 2009 where the filing date is on or after 1 April 2010; to repayment claims for a tax period made on or after 1 April 2010; to inheritance tax accounts where the date of death is on or after 1 April 2009; and in any other case where the tax liability arises on or after 1 April 2010. Also applies to annual tax on enveloped dwellings.	100% of potential lost revenue, subject to the same reductions as above for disclosure or in special circumstances.
Failure to notify HMRC of error in assessment [FA 2007, Sch 24 para 2] Failure to take reasonable steps to notify HMRC of an under-assessment to IT, CT, CGT or VAT for a tax year, accounting period or VAT period beginning on or after 1 April 2008 within the 30 days beginning with the date of the assessment. Also applies to further taxes including IHT and SDLT for tax periods beginning on or after 1 April 2009 where the filing date is on or after 1 April 2010. Also applies to annual tax on enveloped dwellings.	30% of potential lost revenue, subject to the same reductions as above for disclosure or in special circumstances.
Failure to comply with notification obligations and VAT offences [FA 2008, Sch 41] Failure to comply with any of the following obligations: • to notify chargeability to IT or CGT within six months of tax year • to notify chargeability to CT within one year of accounting period • to notify liability to register for VAT • to notify acquisition of goods from another member state (for VAT purposes) Issue of invoice showing VAT by person not authorised to do so. Penalty applies to obligations arising on or after 1 April 2010 and to invoices issued on or after that date. Applies also to similar obligations in relation to insurance premium tax, diverted profits tax, aggregates levy, climate change levy, landfill tax, air passenger duty and certain other types of duty.	Deliberate and concealed failure: 100% of potential lost revenue. Deliberate but unconcealed failure: 70% of potential lost revenue. Any other case: 30% of potential lost revenue. *Reductions.* A statutory reduction in the amount of the penalty is made for disclosure of a failure. For an unprompted disclosure, a 100% penalty may be reduced to no less than 30%, a 70% penalty to no less than 20% and a 30% penalty to any percentage, including 0%, unless HMRC do not become aware of the failure until twelve months after the time tax first became unpaid because of the failure, in which case the penalty may be reduced to no less than 10%. For a prompted disclosure, a 100% penalty may be reduced to no less than 50%, a 70% penalty to no less than 35% and a 30% penalty to no less than 10% (20% where HMRC do not become aware of the failure until twelve months after the time tax first became unpaid because of the failure). HMRC can also reduce a penalty in special circumstances. *Offshore evasion.* See page 97 for the increase in the amount of the penalty where the failure to comply with an obligation involves an offshore matter.

Penalties general

Offence	Penalty
Failure to comply with HMRC investigatory powers [FA 2008, Sch 36 paras 39, 40] Failure to comply with an information notice within FA 2008, Sch 36 Pt 1 or deliberately obstructing an HMRC officer in the course of an inspection of premises under FA 2008, Sch 36 Pt 2 which has been approved by the First-tier Tribunal. Applies to (a) IT, CT, CGT, VAT and certain foreign taxes with effect from 1 April 2009; (b) further taxes, including IHT and SDLT, from 1 April 2010; (c) ATED (see page 80) from 17 July 2013; (d) pension scheme registration applications from 17 July 2014; (e) diverted profits tax from 1 April 2015.	(i) initial penalty of £300. (ii) if failure/obstruction continues, a further penalty up to £60 per day. (iii) if failure/obstruction continues after penalty under (i) imposed, a tax-related amount determined by the Upper Tribunal.
HMRC investigatory powers: inaccurate information etc [FA 2008, Sch 36 para 40A] Providing inaccurate information or document carelessly or deliberately or failing to take reasonable steps to notify HMRC of an inaccuracy discovered later. One penalty for each inaccuracy. Applies with effect from 21 July 2009.	Up to £3,000
Tax agents: dishonest conduct [FA 2012, Sch 38 para 26; SI 2013 No 279] HMRC also have the power to publish the names and details of tax agents who incur a penalty exceeding £5,000. Applies with effect from 1 April 2013.	Up to £50,000 (minimum £5,000) although HMRC have the discretion to apply a special reduction to a £5,000 penalty to reflect the quality of the disclosure and compliance with any access notice.
Tax agents: failure to comply with file access notice [FA 2012, Sch 38 paras 22, 23] Applies with effect from 1 April 2013.	(i) initial penalty of £300. (ii) if failure continues, a further penalty up to £60 per day.
Failure to make payments on time [FA 2009 Sch 56] Applies for 2010/11 onwards to income tax and Class 1 NICs collected through in-year PAYE and to Class 1A and Class 1B NICs and student loan deductions. Applies for 2011/12 onwards to income tax (including Class 4 NICs) and capital gains tax payable under self-assessment for 2010/11 onwards. Applies to annual tax on enveloped dwellings due on or after 31 October 2013. Applies to stamp duty reserve tax with effect from 1 January 2015 and to diverted profits tax for accounting periods beginning on or after 1 April 2015. Applies to Class 2 NICs for 2015/16 onwards. To be extended over a number of years to other taxes.	*In-year payments.* The first failure in a tax year does not count as a default. If there are one, two or three defaults during a tax year, penalty of 1% of total amount of defaults. If four, five or six defaults during a tax year, penalty of 2%; if seven, eight or nine defaults, penalty of 3%; if ten or more defaults in one tax year penalty 4%. If tax remains unpaid six months after penalty date a penalty of 5% of the unpaid amount applies; a further 5% penalty applies if tax is still unpaid after a further six months. *IT, CGT, Class 1A, 1B, 2, 4 NICs.* A 5% penalty applies if full amount not paid within 30 days of due date. If amount remains unpaid six months after due date a penalty of 5% applies; a further 5% penalty applies if amount is still unpaid after a further six months.

Penalties general

Offence	Penalty
Late filing of returns [*FA 2009, Sch 55*] Failure to make a return or deliver a specified document on or before the filing date. Applies to income tax (and CGT) returns and documents for 2010/11 onwards with effect from 6 April 2011; pension scheme returns for periods ending after 31 March 2011; construction industry scheme returns for which the filing date is on or after 19 October 2011; and annual tax on enveloped dwellings returns for which the filing date is on or after 1 October 2013. Applies to PAYE real time information monthly returns in relation to 2014/15 onwards from 6 October 2014 for employers with 50 or more employees and from 6 March 2015 for employers with fewer than 50 employees. Applies to Class 2 NICs for 2015/16 onwards. To be extended over a number of years to other taxes.	(i) initial penalty of £100. (ii) if failure continues two months after penalty date a penalty of £200 (CIS only). (iii) if failure continues three months after penalty date and HMRC give notice, a further penalty of £10 per day for each day failure continues in 90-day period beginning with date specified in notice. Penalty does not apply to CIS returns. (iv) if failure continues six months after penalty date, a further penalty of the greater of 5% of the tax liability and £300. (v) for returns other than CIS returns, if failure continues 12 months after penalty date and the withholding of information is deliberate and concealed a further penalty of the greater of 100% of the tax liability and £300; if the withholding is deliberate and not concealed, the greater of 70% of the liability and £300; or otherwise, greater of 5% of the liability and £300. (vi) for CIS returns, if failure continues 12 months after penalty date and the withholding of information is deliberate and concealed a further penalty of the greater of 100% of the tax liability and £3,000; if the withholding is deliberate and not concealed, the greater of 70% of the liability and £1,500; or otherwise, greater of 5% of the liability and £300. Where the information required in the return relates only to persons registered for gross payment, and the withholding of information is deliberate and concealed the penalty is £3,000; if the withholding is deliberate but not concealed the penalty is £1,500. For the first CIS return made by a contractor (together with any returns with an earlier filing date), the total fixed penalties cannot exceed £3,000 and any tax-geared penalty which would otherwise be the greater of £300 and 5% of the tax due is instead 5%. *Real time information.* No penalty for first failure in a tax year. Each subsequent failure:£100 for employer with 1–9 employees, £200 for 10–49 employees, £300 for 50–249 employees, £400 for 250 or more employees. Further penalty where failure continues for more than three months: 5% of tax due. No penalty for new employer for return received within 30 days of making the first payment to employee(s). *Reductions.* A statutory reduction in the amount of the penalty is made for disclosure of a failure. For an unprompted disclosure, a 100% penalty may be reduced to no less than 30% and a 70% penalty to no less than 20%. For a prompted disclosure, a 100% penalty may be reduced to no less than 50% and a 70% penalty to no less than 35%. HMRC can also reduce a penalty in special circumstances. *Offshore evasion.* See below.

Penalties general

Offence	Penalty
Offshore evasion [*FA 2010, Sch 10; FA 2015, Sch 20*] For documents, returns and assessments relating to periods beginning after 5 April 2011, penalties in respect of income tax or CGT under *FA 2007, Sch 24 para 1, FA 2008, Sch 41 para 1* and *FA 2009, Sch 55* are increased where the error or failure is linked to an offshore matter relating to a territory within category 2 or 3. No increase is made in relation to category 1 territories. With effect from a date to be fixed, expected to be 6 April 2016, the offshore penalty rules will be amended to include IHT and to apply to domestic offences where the proceeds are hidden offshore. The territory classification system will be updated to reflect the jurisdictions that adopt the new global standard of automatic tax information exchange; and to have four categories.	*Category 2 territories.* The amount of the penalty, and the statutory limits for reductions for disclosure are increased by 50%. *Category 3 territories.* The amount of the penalty, and the statutory limits for reductions for disclosure are increased by 100%.

The current categories are:

1: Anguilla; Aruba; Australia; Belgium; Bulgaria; Canada; Cayman Islands; Cyprus; Czech Republic; Denmark (excluding Faroe Islands and Greenland); Estonia; Finland; France; Germany; Greece; Guernsey; Hungary; Ireland; Isle of Man; Italy; Japan; Latvia; Liechtenstein (after 23 July 2013); Lithuania; Malta; Montserrat; Netherlands (excluding Bonaire, Sint Eustatius and Saba); New Zealand (excluding Tokelau); Norway; Poland; Portugal; Romania; Slovakia; Slovenia; South Korea; Spain; Sweden; Switzerland (after 23 July 2013); USA (excluding overseas territories and possessions).

2: All territories (except the UK) not within categories 1 or 3.

3: Albania; Algeria; Andorra; Bonaire, Sint Eustatius and Saba; Brazil; Cameroon; Cape Verde; Colombia; Republic of the Congo; Cook Islands; Costa Rica; Curaçao; Cuba; Democratic People's Republic of Korea; Dominican Republic; Ecuador; El Salvador; Gabon; Guatemala; Honduras; Iran; Iraq; Jamaica; Kyrgyzstan; Lebanon; Macau; Marshall Islands; Federated States of Micronesia; Monaco; Nauru; Nicaragua; Niue; Palau; Panama; Paraguay; Peru; Seychelles; Sint Maarten; Suriname; Syria; Tokelau; Tonga; Trinidad and Tobago; UAE; Uruguay. The following territories were in category 3 before 24 July 2013: Antigua and Barbuda, Armenia, Bahrain, Barbados, Belize, Dominica, Grenada, Mauritius, San Marino, Saint Kitts and Nevis, Saint Lucia, and Saint Vincent and the Grenadines.

Offshore asset move [*FA 2015, Sch 21; SI 2015 No 866*] Offshore asset moved on or after 27 March 2015 from a specified territory to a non-specified territory where IT, CGT or IHT penalty under *FA 2007, Sch 24 para 1, FA 2008, Sch 41,* or *FA 2009, Sch 55* above already applies for a deliberate failure. The specified territories are Albania, Andorra, Anguilla, Antigua and Barbuda, Argentina, Aruba, Australia, Austria, The Bahamas, Barbados, Belgium, Belize, Bermuda, Brazil, British Virgin Islands, Brunei Darussalam, Bulgaria, Canada, Cayman Islands, Chile, China, Colombia, Costa Rica, Croatia, Curaçao, Cyprus, Czech Republic, Denmark, Dominica, Estonia, Faroe Islands, Finland, France, Germany, Gibraltar, Greece, Greenland, Grenada, Guernsey, Hong Kong, Hungary, Iceland, India, Indonesia, Ireland, Isle of Man, Israel, Italy, Japan, Jersey, Korea (South), Latvia, Liechtenstein, Lithuania, Luxembourg, Macau, Malaysia, Malta, Marshall Islands, Mauritius, Mexico, Monaco, Montserrat, Netherlands (including Bonaire, Sint Eustatius and Saba) New Zealand (not including Tokelau), Niue, Norway, Poland, Portugal, Qatar, Romania, Russia, Saint Kitts and Nevis, Saint Lucia, Saint Vincent and the Grenadines, Samoa, San Marino, Saudi Arabia, Seychelles, Singapore, Sint Maarten, Slovak Republic, Slovenia, South Africa, Spain, Sweden, Switzerland, Trinidad and Tobago, Turkey, Turks and Caicos Islands, United Arab Emirates, United States of America (not including overseas territories and possessions), Uruguay.	50% of amount of original penalty

Penalties income tax, capital gains tax and corporation tax

Offence	Penalty
Failure to notify chargeability to tax [*TMA 1970, s 7; FA 1998, Sch 18 para 2*]	
(a) Failure to notify chargeability to IT or CGT within six months of tax year	Up to tax liability still outstanding after 31 January following tax year
(b) Failure to notify chargeability to CT within one year of accounting period.	Up to amount of CT unpaid one year after end of accounting period
Replaced by *FA 2008, Sch 41* penalty for obligations arising after 31 March 2010 (see page 94)	
Failure to maintain records [*TMA 1970, s 12B*]	
Failure to keep and preserve appropriate records supporting personal and trustees' returns or partnership returns	Up to £3,000
Failure to keep and preserve records supporting ATED return (see page 80) [*FA 2013, Sch 33*].	
Failure to render return [*TMA 1970, ss 93, 93A; FA 1998, Sch 18 paras 17, 18*]	
(a) Income tax and capital gains tax	(i) Automatic penalty of £100 (or tax due if less);
Replaced by penalty under FA 2009, Sch 55 for returns for 2010/11 onwards (see page 96)	(ii) For each day failure continues, a further penalty of up to £60 per day as directed by the tribunal or Commissioners on application by HMRC;
	(iii) If failure continues after six months from filing date and no penalty imposed under (ii), a further automatic penalty of £100 (or tax due if less);
	(iv) If failure continues after one year from filing date, a further penalty of up to the amount of tax due
(b) Corporation tax	(i) £100 if up to 3 months late (£500 if previous two returns also delivered late);
	(ii) £200 if over 3 months late (£1,000 if previous two returns also late);
Failure continuing at later of final day for delivery of return and 18 months after return period	Further penalty of 10% of tax unpaid 18 months after return period (20% of tax unpaid at that date if return not made within 2 years of return period)
Negligence or fraud	Up to amount of tax underpaid by reason of incorrectness for
Negligently or fraudulently making an incorrect statement in connection with a claim to reduce payments on account [*TMA 1970, s 59A*]	Up to the amount (or additional amount) payable on account if a correct statement had been made
Failure to notify within charge to corporation tax [*TMA 1970, s 98; FA 2004, s 55*]	(i) Initial penalty of £300;
Failure to notify within three months after the beginning of the first accounting period and any subsequent accounting period not following on immediately from the end of a previous accounting period. Repealed for obligations arising after 31 March 2010	(ii) If failure continues after penalty in (i) imposed, additional penalty up to £60 per day
Other returns, etc. [*TMA 1970, ss 98, 98A*]	(i) up to £300 (£3,000 in certain specified cases)
Failure to comply with a notice to deliver any return or other document, to furnish any particulars, to produce any document or record, to make anything available for inspection or give any certificate under the provisions listed in *TMA 1970, s 98*	(ii) if failure continues after penalty under (i) imposed, continuing penalty of up to £60 (£600) per day
Failure to submit PAYE returns (P14, P35, P38 and P38A) or returns of sub-contractors in the construction industry	See under PAYE (page 91) which provisions also apply to returns of sub-contractors
Sub-contractors in the Construction Industry Scheme	
Fraudulent attempt by sub-contractor to obtain or misuse a sub-contractor's certificate (pre-6 April 2007 scheme) [*ICTA 1988, s 561(10), (11)*]	Up to £3,000
Making false statements etc. for the purpose of becoming registered for gross payment (post-5 April 2007 scheme) [*FA 2004, s 72*]	Up to £3,000
Assisting in preparation of incorrect returns, accounts and other documents [*TMA 1970, s 99*]	Up to £3,000
Repealed from 1 April 2013 and replaced by penalty under *FA 2012, Sch 38*. See page 95.	
Certificates of non-liability to income tax [*TMA 1970, s 99A*]	Up to £3,000
Fraudulently or negligently giving such a certificate in connection with receiving bank or building society interest gross or failing to comply with an undertaking in the certificate	
Refusal to allow deduction of income tax at source [*TMA 1970, s 106*]	£50
Falsification of documents [*TMA 1970, s 20BB*]	On summary conviction, a penalty not exceeding the statutory maximum (currently £5,000). On conviction on indictment, imprisonment for up to 2 years or a fine or both
Intentionally falsifying, concealing or destroying documents	
Advance pricing agreements [*TIOPA 2010, s 227; FA 1999, s 86*]	Up to £10,000
Fraudulently or negligently making a false or misleading statement in the preparation of, or application to enter into, any advance pricing agreement	
Fraudulent evasion of income tax [*TMA 1970, s 106A; FA 2000, s 144*]	On summary conviction, imprisonment for up to 6 months or a fine not exceeding the statutory maximum (currently £5,000). On conviction on indictment, imprisonment for up to 7 years or a fine or both

Penalties inheritance tax and stamp duty land tax

Offence	Penalty
Failure to deliver inheritance tax account [*IHTA 1984, s 245*]	(i) An initial penalty of £100 (or tax payable if less);
Failure to deliver an account within 12 months of death	(ii) A further penalty up to £60 for each day on which the failure continues (where failure is declared by court, tribunal or Special Commissioners);
	(iii) If failure continues after six months after the date on which account is due, and proceedings under (ii) not commenced, a further penalty of £100 (or tax payable if less);
	(iv) If failure continues one year after end of the period in which account is due, and tax is payable, a penalty up to £3,000
Failure to notify instrument varying disposition on death [*IHTA 1984, s 245A(1A)(1B)*]	(i) An initial penalty up to £100;
Failure to notify HMRC within six months after the date of the instrument (where additional tax is payable)	(ii) A further penalty up to £60 for each day on which the failure continues (where failure is declared by court, tribunal or Special Commissioners);
	(iii) If failure continues one year after end of the period in which notification is due, a penalty up to £3,000
Negligence or fraud (IHT) [*IHTA 1984, s 247*]	
Taxpayer negligently or fraudulently delivering, furnishing or producing incorrect account, information or document. Replaced by penalty under *FA 2007, Sch 24* where the date of death is on or after 1 April 2009 or, in other cases, where the tax liability arises on or after 1 April 2010 (see page 94)	Up to amount of tax underpaid by reason of incorrectness
Person other than taxpayer negligently or fraudulently furnishing or producing incorrect information or document	Up to £3,000
Assisting in or inducing the delivery, furnishing or production of any account, information or document knowing it to be incorrect. Repealed from 1 April 2013.	Up to £3,000
Failure to deliver SDLT return [*FA 2003, Sch 10 paras 3, 4*]	(i) £100 if return delivered within three months of filing date, otherwise £200;
Failure to deliver return within 30 days after the effective date of the land transaction	(ii) If return not delivered within 12 months after filing date, a penalty up to the tax chargeable
Failure to comply with notice to deliver SDLT return [*FA 2003, Sch 10 para 5*]	Up to £60 for each day on which the failure continues after notification of penalty decision by tribunal or General or Special Commissioners
Failure to comply within period specified in notice	
Negligence or fraud (SDLT) [*FA 2003, Sch 10 para 8, Sch 11 para 3*]	
Purchaser negligently or fraudulently delivering an incorrect return or failing to remedy an error without unreasonable delay. Replaced by penalty under *FA 2007, Sch 24* for liabilities arising on or after 1 April 2010 (see page 94)	Up to amount of tax understated
Failure to keep and preserve records [*FA 2003, Sch 10 para 11, Sch 11 para 6*]	
Failure to keep and preserve such records as may be needed to enable delivery of correct return or certificate for required period	Up to £3,000 unless information is provided by other documentary evidence

Pensions

Registered pension schemes [FA 2004, ss 149–284, Schs 28–36; FA 2013, ss 47-49]]

Individual contributions. An individual may make unlimited contributions but tax relief is only available on contributions up to the higher of 100% of relevant earnings and £3,600 gross (provided the scheme operates tax relief at source). There is no provision for the carry-back or carry-forward of contributions to tax years other than the year of payment.

Special annual allowance charge. This charge applies with effect from 22 April 2009 to 5 April 2011 to individuals with incomes of £130,000 or more. Broadly, the effect of the charge is to restrict tax relief on pension savings above the individual's special annual allowance to basic rate by taxing the excess relief. An individual's special annual allowance is the higher of their regular pension savings and £20,000 (£30,000 where money purchase scheme contributions have been paid less regularly than quarterly).

Employer contributions are deductible for tax purposes, with exceptionally large contributions being spread over a period of up to 4 years. The contributions are not treated as taxable income of the employee (although, for 2013/14 onwards, this exemption does not extend to contributions for the benefit of family members).

'Tax-free' lump sum. The maximum 'tax-free' lump sum that can be paid out is 25% of the fund, subject to an overriding maximum of 25% of the lifetime allowance. There is transitional protection of lump sum rights accrued before 6 April 2006.

Lifetime allowance. Each individual has a lifetime allowance as follows.

2015/16	£1,250,000	2013/14	£1,500,000	2011/12	£1,800,000
2014/15	£1,250,000	2012/13	£1,500,000	2010/11	£1,800,000

If benefits are withdrawn in excess of the allowance, tax is charged on the excess at 55% if taken as a lump sum and at 25% if used to buy a pension. Any tax due may be deducted from the individual's benefits. The lifetime allowance is to be reduced to £1 million from 6 April 2016.

Annual allowance. Each individual has an annual allowance for maximum 'pension inputs' (i.e. contributions paid to money purchase schemes and/or increases in accrued benefits under final salary schemes) as follows.

2015/16	£40,000	2013/14	£50,000	2011/12	£50,000
2014/15	£40,000	2012/13	£50,000	2010/11	£255,000

If pension inputs exceed the annual allowance, the excess is chargeable at the individual's marginal tax rate (40% for 2010/11 and earlier years). The individual is liable for the tax subject, for 2011/12 onwards, to an election for the scheme to pay the charge if it exceeds £2,000 (in which event scheme benefits are proportionately reduced). For 2011/12 onwards, an individual can carry forward unused annual allowance for up to three tax years. Unused allowances for 2008/09 to 2010/11 can be carried forward to 2011/12, but only on the assumption that for each of those years the annual allowance was £50,000. For 2015/16 onwards there are special rules for taxpayers who flexibly access a money purchase arrangement. Such taxpayers are, in certain circumstances, restricted to a £10,000 annual allowance in respect of money purchase pension savings. If the £10,000 money purchase annual allowance limit is exceeded, the taxpayer has a reduced £30,000 annual allowance for the remainder of their pension savings (in addition to the £10,000 money purchase annual allowance).

For 2016/17 onwards, the annual allowance will be reduced for individuals whose annual income exceeds £150,000 (including pension contributions). The allowance will be reduced by £1 for every £2 of income over £150,000 down to a minimum allowance of £10,000. The reduction will not normally apply where annual income excluding pension contributions is less than £110,000 (subject to anti-avoidance provisions).

Minimum pension age. The minimum pension age is 55 (50 before 6 April 2010) with earlier retirement permitted on ill-health grounds. Those with existing contractual rights to draw a pension earlier will have those rights protected and there is special protection for members of pre-6 April 2006 approved schemes with early retirement ages. The available lifetime allowance for these protected groups will, however, be reduced.

Maximum benefit age. There is no maximum age at which benefits must be taken with effect from 6 April 2011. Previously, benefits had to be taken at latest at age 77 (75 for those reaching that age before 22 June 2010). A member of a money purchase scheme could take a pension from the age of 77 (75) by way of income withdrawal ('alternatively secured pension'). The maximum alternatively secured pension was 70% of a comparable annuity and, after 5 April 2007, the minimum was 55% of a comparable annuity.

With effect from 6 April 2015, everyone aged 55 or over with defined contribution pension savings is able to access them as they wish, regardless of the total amount of their pension savings, and are charged to income tax as pension income at their marginal rate for the tax year of access. Previously, for 2011/12 onwards, individuals who were members of a defined contribution scheme were able to leave their pension funds invested in a drawdown arrangement and to make withdrawals throughout their retirement, subject to an annual cap. The maximum withdrawal of income that an individual could make from most drawdown funds on reaching minimum pension age was capped at 150% of the equivalent annuity that could have been bought with the fund value (120% for drawdown pension years beginning before 27 March 2014; 100% for drawdown pension years beginning before 26 March 2013). The maximum capped amount was determined every three years until the end of the year in which the member reached the age of 75, after which reviews to determine the maximum capped withdrawal were carried out annually. Individuals able to demonstrate that they had a secure pension income for life of at least £12,000 a year (£20,000 for applications before 27 March 2014) could apply for access to their drawdown funds without any annual cap. All withdrawals from drawdown funds are chargeable to income tax as pension income.

Retail price index Capital gains—indexation

Year	Jan	Feb	Mar	Apr	May	Jun	Jul	Aug	Sep	Oct	Nov	Dec
1982	78.7	78.8	79.44	81.04	81.62	81.85	81.88	81.90	81.85	82.26	82.66	82.51
1983	82.61	82.97	83.12	84.28	84.64	84.84	85.30	85.68	86.06	86.36	86.67	86.89
1984	86.84	87.20	87.48	88.64	88.97	89.20	89.10	89.94	90.11	90.67	90.95	90.87
1985	91.20	91.94	92.80	94.78	95.21	95.41	95.23	95.49	95.44	95.59	95.92	96.05
1986	96.25	96.60	96.73	97.67	97.85	97.79	97.52	97.82	98.30	98.45	99.29	99.62
1987	100.0	100.4	100.6	101.8	101.9	101.9	101.8	102.1	102.4	102.9	103.4	103.3
1988	103.3	103.7	104.1	105.8	106.2	106.6	106.7	107.9	108.4	109.5	110.0	110.3
1989	111.0	111.8	112.3	114.3	115.0	115.4	115.5	115.8	116.6	117.5	118.5	118.8
1990	119.5	120.2	121.4	125.1	126.2	126.7	126.8	128.1	129.3	130.3	130.0	129.9
1991	130.2	130.9	131.4	133.1	133.5	134.1	133.8	134.1	134.6	135.1	135.6	135.7
1992	135.6	136.3	136.7	138.8	139.3	139.3	138.8	138.9	139.4	139.9	139.7	139.2
1993	137.9	138.8	139.3	140.6	141.1	141.0	140.7	141.3	141.9	141.8	141.6	141.9
1994	141.3	142.1	142.5	144.2	144.7	144.7	144.0	144.7	145.0	145.2	145.3	146.0
1995	146.0	146.9	147.5	149.0	149.6	149.8	149.1	149.9	150.6	149.8	149.8	150.7
1996	150.2	150.9	151.5	152.6	152.9	153.0	152.4	153.1	153.8	153.8	153.9	154.4
1997	154.4	155.0	155.4	156.3	156.9	157.5	157.5	158.5	159.3	159.5	159.6	160.0
1998	159.5	160.3	160.8	162.6	163.5	163.4	163.0	163.7	164.4	164.5	164.4	164.4
1999	163.4	163.7	164.1	165.2	165.6	165.6	165.1	165.5	166.2	166.5	166.7	167.3
2000	166.6	167.5	168.4	170.1	170.7	171.1	170.5	170.5	171.7	171.6	172.1	172.2
2001	171.1	172.0	172.2	173.1	174.2	174.4	173.3	174.0	174.6	174.3	173.6	173.4
2002	173.3	173.8	174.5	175.7	176.2	176.2	175.9	176.4	177.6	177.9	178.2	178.5
2003	178.4	179.3	179.9	181.2	181.5	181.3	181.3	181.6	182.5	182.6	182.7	183.5
2004	183.1	183.8	184.6	185.7	186.5	186.8	186.8	187.4	188.1	188.6	189.0	189.9
2005	188.9	189.6	190.5	191.6	192.0	192.2	192.2	192.6	193.1	193.3	193.6	194.1
2006	193.4	194.2	195.0	196.5	197.7	198.5	198.5	199.2	200.1	200.4	201.1	202.7
2007	201.6	203.1	204.4	205.4	206.2	207.3	206.1	207.3	208.0	208.9	209.7	210.9
2008	209.8	211.4	212.1	214.0	215.1	216.8	216.5	217.2	218.4	217.7	216.0	212.9
2009	210.1	211.4	211.3	211.5	212.8	213.4	213.4	214.4	215.3	216.0	216.6	218.0
2010	217.9	219.2	220.7	222.8	223.6	224.1	223.6	224.5	225.3	225.8	226.8	228.4
2011	229.0	231.3	232.5	234.4	235.2	235.2	234.7	236.1	237.9	238.0	238.5	239.4
2012	238.0	239.9	240.8	242.5	242.4	241.8	242.1	243.0	244.2	245.6	245.6	246.8
2013	245.8	247.6	248.7	249.5	250.0	249.7	249.7	251.0	251.9	251.9	252.1	253.4
2014	252.6	254.2	254.8	255.7	255.9	256.3	256.0	257.0	257.6	257.7	257.1	257.5
2015	255.4	256.7	257.1	258.0	258.5	258.9						

Notes

(a)   The index was re-referenced in January 1987 from 394.5 to 100.
(b)   The figures above which relate to months before January 1987 have been recomputed from the new base.

Social security taxable benefits

Weekly rates from weeks commencing	6.4.15	7.4.14	8.4.13	9.4.12	11.4.11	12.4.10	6.4.09
Retirement pensions (note (a))	£	£	£	£	£	£	£
Category A or B	115.95	113.10	110.15	107.45	102.15	97.65	95.25
Category B (lower)	69.50	67.80	66.00	64.40	61.20	58.50	57.05
Category C or D (non-contributory)	69.50	67.80	66.00	64.40	61.20	58.50	57.05
Category C (lower)	41.50	40.50	39.45	38.50	36.60	35.00	34.15
Increase for adult dependant (note (b))	65.70	64.90	63.20	61.85	58.80	57.05	57.05
Age addition—over 80	0.25	0.25	0.25	0.25	0.25	0.25	0.25
Bereavement benefit (note (a))							
Widowed parent's allowance	112.55	111.20	108.30	105.95	100.70	97.65	95.25
Bereavement allowance (standard rate) (note (c))	112.55	111.20	108.30	105.95	100.70	97.65	95.25
Carer's allowance (previously invalid care allowance)(note (a))							
Basic	62.10	61.35	59.75	58.45	55.55	53.90	53.10
Increase for adult dependant (note (b))	36.55	36.10	35.15	34.40	32.70	31.70	31.70
Employment and support allowance (notes (f)(g)(k))							
Under 25	57.90	57.35	56.80	56.25	53.45	51.85	50.95
25 or over	73.10	72.40	71.70	71.00	67.50	65.45	64.30
Incapacity benefit (note (f))							
Long term (after 52 weeks)	105.35	104.10	101.35	99.15	94.25	91.40	89.80
—increase for adult dependant	61.20	60.45	58.85	57.60	54.75	53.10	53.10
Increase of long term benefit for age							
—higher rate (under 35)	11.15	11.00	10.70	11.70	13.80	15.00	15.65
—lower rate (35 to under 45)	6.20	6.15	6.00	5.90	5.60	5.80	6.55
Short term (over pension age)							
—higher rate (from week 29 to 52) (note (f))	105.35	104.10	101.35	99.15	94.25	91.40	89.80
—increase for adult dependant	58.90	58.20	56.65	55.45	52.70	51.10	51.10
Short term (under pension age)							
—higher rate (from week 29 to 52)	94.05	92.95	90.50	88.55	84.15	81.60	80.15
—increase for adult dependant	47.65	47.10	45.85	44.85	42.65	41.35	41.35
Industrial death benefit (deaths before 11.4.88 only) (note (a))							
Widow's pension (higher permanent rate)	115.95	113.10	110.15	107.45	102.15	97.65	95.25
Widow's pension (lower permanent rate)	34.79	33.93	33.05	32.24	30.65	29.30	28.58
Widower's pension	115.95	113.10	110.15	107.45	102.15	97.65	95.25
Statutory adoption pay (note (d))							
Higher rate— ⁹/₁₀ths of average weekly earnings	Varies	—	—	—	—	—	—
Standard rate (note (j))	139.58	138.18	136.78	135.45	128.73	124.88	123.06
Earnings threshold	112.00	111.00	109.00	107.00	102.00	97.00	95.00

Social security taxable benefits

Weekly rates from weeks commencing	6.4.15	7.4.14	8.4.13	9.4.12	11.4.11	12.4.10	6.4.09
Statutory maternity pay (note (d))	£	£	£	£	£	£	£
Higher rate— $^9/_{10}$ths of average weekly earnings	Varies	Varies	Varies	Varies	Varies	Varies	Varies
Standard rate	139.58	138.18	136.78	135.45	128.73	124.88	123.06
Earnings threshold	112.00	111.00	109.00	107.00	102.00	97.00	95.00
Statutory paternity pay (note (d))							
Standard rate (note (j))	139.58	138.18	136.78	135.45	128.73	124.88	123.06
Earnings threshold	112.00	111.00	109.00	107.00	102.00	97.00	95.00
Statutory shared parental pay (note (d))							
Standard rate (note (j))	139.58	—	—	—	—	—	—
Earnings threshold	112.00	—	—	—	—	—	—
Statutory sick pay (note (d))							
Standard rate	88.45	87.55	86.70	85.85	81.60	79.15	79.15
Earnings threshold	112.00	111.00	109.00	107.00	102.00	97.00	95.00
Invalidity allowances when paid with retirement pensions (note (f))							
Higher rate (under 40 when first taken ill)	21.50	21.25	20.70	20.25	19.25	18.65	18.65
Middle rate (40–49 when first taken ill)	13.90	13.70	13.30	13.00	12.40	12.00	12.00
Lower rate (50 to pension age when first taken ill)	6.95	6.85	6.65	6.50	6.20	6.00	6.00
Jobseekers allowance (notes (e)(k))							
Single —under 25	57.90	57.35	56.80	56.25	53.45	51.85	50.95
—25 or over	73.10	72.40	71.70	71.00	67.50	65.45	64.30
Couple —both under 18	57.90	57.35	56.80	56.25	53.45	51.85	50.95
—both under 18, with child responsibility	87.50	86.65	85.80	84.95	80.75	78.30	76.90
—one under 18, one 18–24	57.90	57.35	56.80	56.25	53.45	51.85	50.95
—one under 18, one over 25	73.10	72.40	71.70	71.00	67.50	65.45	64.30
—both over 18	114.85	113.70	112.55	111.45	105.95	102.75	100.95

Notes

(a) Any increase for a child dependant paid with retirement pension, bereavement benefit, carer's allowance, incapacity benefit and higher rate industrial death benefit is non-taxable.

(b) Adult dependency increases to state pension and carer's allowance are paid after 5 April 2010 only to claimants receiving the increase at that date. The increase is to be withdrawn completely with effect from 6 April 2020.

(c) Reduced rates apply if the claimant/widow aged below 55 at the time of spouse's/husband's death.

(d) Rates for statutory sick pay, statutory maternity pay, statutory paternity pay, statutory shared parental pay and statutory adoption pay apply from 6 April each year.

(e) Jobseekers allowance applies to claimants who are required to be both available for and actively seeking employment. Where the amount of a jobseekers allowance paid exceeds the figure shown above, the excess is not taxable.

(f) Employment and support allowance replaces incapacity benefit for new claimants on or after 27 October 2008. Existing claimants continue to receive incapacity benefit. Incapacity benefit itself replaced invalidity allowance from April 1995: invalidity allowances still payable are for a transitional period.

(g) Only contributory employment and support allowance is taxable. Income related allowance is not taxable.

(h) Incapacity benefit is taxable except for benefits paid in the first 28 weeks of incapacity and benefits paid to persons already receiving invalidity benefit on 13 April 1995 so long as they remain incapable of work.

(i) The short-term, higher rate of incapacity benefit for over pension age is not a taxable benefit for those eligible to receive the benefit before 13 April 1995.

(j) $^9/_{10}$ths of average weekly earnings, if less.

(k) Income support, income-based jobseeker's allowance, income based employment and support allowance, housing benefit, child tax credits and working tax credits are being replaced by universal credit (see page 106). Universal credit was initially introduced in certain areas of England in April 2013 and is being introduced nationally over the period to the end of 2017.

(l) A cap applies to limit the total amount of benefit that most people aged 16 to 64 can receive. The cap was introduced between April and September 2013 and applies to the total amount that the individuals in a household receive from specified benefits. Initially, the cap operates by reducing the amount of housing benefit paid by local authorities. From October 2013 the cap applies directly to all new claims to universal credit including those migrated from existing benefits. For 2013/14 to 2015/16 the cap is £500 a week for couples and for single parents whose children live with them and £350 a week for single adults with no children or whose children do not live with them. Where the cap is applied directly to universal credit, the restriction is made on a monthly basis: £2,167 a month for couples and for single parents, and £1,517 a month for single adults without children. The Government has announced that the cap is to be reduced to an annual limit of £20,000 (£23,000 in Greater London).

Social security taxable benefits

Total benefit if received for full tax year (52 weeks)	2015/16	2014/15	2013/14	2012/13	2011/12	2010/11	2009/10
Retirement pensions	£	£	£	£	£	£	£
Category A or B	6,029	5,881	5,727	5,587	5,311	5,077	4,953
Category B (lower)	3,614	3,525	3,432	3,348	3,182	3,042	2,966
Category C or D (non-contributory)	3,614	3,525	3,432	3,348	3,182	3,042	2,966
Category C (lower)	2,158	2,106	2,051	2,002	1,903	1,820	1,775
Increase for adult dependant	3,416	3,374	3,286	3,216	3,057	2,966	2,966
Age addition—over 80 (each)	13	13	13	13	13	13	13
Bereavement benefit							
Widowed parent's (mother's) allowance	5,852	5,782	5,631	5,509	5,236	5,077	4,953
Bereavement allowance (widow's pension)	5,852	5,782	5,631	5,509	5,236	5,077	4,953
Carer's allowance (previously invalid care allowance)							
Basic	3,229	3,190	3,107	3,039	2,888	2,802	2,761
Increase for adult dependant	1,900	1,877	1,827	1,788	1,700	1,648	1,648
Incapacity benefit							
Long term (after 52 weeks)	5,478	5,413	5,270	5,155	4,901	4,752	4,669
—increase for adult dependant	3,182	3,143	3,060	2,995	2,847	2,761	2,761
Increase of long term benefit for age							
—higher rate (under 35)	579	572	556	608	717	780	814
—lower rate (35 to under 45)	322	319	312	306	291	301	340
Industrial death benefit (deaths before 11.4.88 only)							
Widow's pension (higher permanent rate)	6,029	5,881	5,727	5,587	5,311	5,077	4,953
Widow's pension (lower permanent rate)	1,809	1,764	1,718	1,676	1,593	1,523	1,486
Widower's pension	6,029	5,881	5,727	5,587	5,311	5,077	4,953
Invalidity allowances when paid with retirement pensions							
Higher rate	1,118	1,105	1,076	1,053	1,001	969	969
Middle rate	722	712	691	676	644	624	624
Lower rate	361	356	345	338	322	312	312

Notes

(a)   See notes on previous page.

(b)   All figures are exclusive of additional benefits in respect of graduated pension, additional pension, etc. which vary with the individual. Certain benefits may be subject to reduction or withdrawal occasioned by earnings of the individual or of an adult dependant. See note (d) below for the basis of assessment.

(c)   Retirement pension may be deferred. The following rules apply to those reaching state pension age before 6 April 2016. For periods of deferral after 5 April 2005, subject to conditions, either the benefit finally payable is increased or a taxable lump sum is payable. Increased benefit is calculated by adding 0.2% of the pension otherwise payable for each full week of deferral, subject to a minimum deferral of 5 weeks. The lump sum is equal to the pension that would have been payable in the deferral period plus interest at a rate at least 2% above the Bank of England base rate, subject to a minimum deferral of 12 months. For deferral periods before 6 April 2005, benefit finally payable is increased by 1/7th% for each full week of deferral, subject to a minimum deferral of 7 weeks and a maximum of 5 years (and there is no lump sum option).

(d)   Benefits are assessed on the 'accruals' basis rather than on a receipts basis. HMRC consider that where a person is entitled to receive 53 weekly payments within a single tax year, the taxable amount is 53 times the weekly amount, rather than the amount shown in the above table. This applies also where the benefit is paid four-weekly and 14 payments are made in the tax year.

Social security non-taxable benefits

Weekly rates from weeks commencing		6.4.15	7.4.14
Attendance allowance		£	£
Higher rate (day and night)		82.30	81.30
Lower rate (day or night)		55.10	54.45
Child benefit (see note (a))			
Eldest child		20.70	20.50
Each subsequent child		13.70	13.55
Child dependency addition			
Paid with retirement pension, bereavement benefit, carer's allowance, incapacity benefit, severe disablement unemployability supplement		11.35	11.35
Council tax reduction (income related)		Varies	Varies
Disability living allowance (DLA)/personal independence payment			
Care/daily living component	higher rate	82.30	81.30
	middle rate	55.10	54.45
	lower rate (DLA only)	21.80	21.55
Mobility component	higher rate	57.45	56.75
	lower rate	21.80	21.55
Guardian's allowance		16.55	16.35
Housing benefit (income related) (note (b))		Varies	Varies
Incapacity benefit (short-term)			
Over pension age—lower rate (first 28 weeks)		101.10	99.90
—increase for adult dependant		58.90	58.20
Under pension age—lower rate (first 28 weeks)		79.45	78.50
—increase for adult dependant		47.65	47.10
Income support (income related) (note (b))		Varies	Varies
Non-taxable in hands of those not available for employment and not involved in a trade dispute			

Weekly rates from weeks commencing		6.4.15	7.4.14
Industrial injuries disablement benefit			
Standard rate	Disablement %		
	100%	168.00	166.00
	90%	151.20	149.40
	80%	134.40	132.80
	70%	117.60	116.20
	60%	100.80	99.60
	50%	84.00	83.00
	40%	67.20	66.40
	30%	50.40	49.80
	20%	33.60	33.20
Unemployability supplement		103.85	102.60
— increase for early incapacity:			
higher rate		21.50	21.25
middle rate		13.90	13.70
lower rate		6.95	6.85
Constant attendance allowance			
— exceptional rate		134.40	132.80
— intermediate rate		100.80	99.60
— normal maximum rate		67.20	66.40
— part-time rate		33.60	33.20
Exceptionally severe disablement allowance		67.20	66.40
Maternity allowance (where SMP not available)			
Standard rate		139.58	138.18
MA threshold		30.00	30.00
Severe disablement allowance			
Basic rate		74.65	73.75
Age-related addition	under 40	11.15	11.00
—(age when disabled)	under 50	6.20	6.15
	under 60	6.20	6.15
Increase for adult dependant		36.75	36.30

Notes

(a) **High income child benefit charge.** With effect on and after 7 January 2013, an income tax charge (the 'high income child benefit charge') is imposed on an individual whose adjusted net income exceeds £50,000 in a tax year and who is, or whose partner is, in receipt of child benefit. In the event that both partners have an adjusted net income that exceeds £50,000, the charge applies only to the partner with the highest income. The amount of the charge is 1% of the amount of the child benefit for every £100 of income above £50,000. If the individual's adjusted net income exceeds £60,000, the charge is on the full amount of the child benefit. *'Adjusted net income'* is, broadly, taxable income before deducting personal reliefs but adjusted by deducting the gross equivalent of any gift aid donations or any pension contributions paid net of basic rate tax. For 2013/14, child benefit to

which a person is entitled for a week beginning before 7 January 2013 is excluded. A person (P) who is entitled to child benefit for one or more children can elect not to receive that benefit if P reasonably expects that, in the absence of an election, P or another person would be liable to a high income child benefit charge.

(b) Income support, income-based jobseeker's allowance, income based employment and support allowance, housing benefit, child tax credits and working tax credits are being replaced by universal credit (see page 106). Universal credit was initially introduced in certain areas of England on 29 April 2013 and is being introduced nationally over the period to the end of 2017.

(c) A cap applies to limit the total benefits that most people aged 16 to 64 can receive. The cap was introduced between April and September 2013 and applies to the total amount that the indi-

viduals in a household receive from specified benefits. Initially, the cap operates by reducing the amount of housing benefit. From October 2013 the cap applies directly to all new claims to universal credit. For 2013/14 to 2015/16 the cap is £500 a week for couples and for single parents whose children live with them and £350 a week for single adults with no children or whose children do not live with them. Where the cap is applied directly to universal credit, the restriction is made on a monthly basis: £2,167 a month for couples and for single parents, and £1,517 a month for single adults without children. The Government has announced that the cap is to be reduced to an annual limit of £20,000 (£23,000 in Greater London).

Social security tax credits and universal credit

Tax Credits	2015/16	2014/15
Child tax credit per annum	£	£
Family element	545	545
Child element	2,780	2,750
Disabled child additional element	3,140	3,100
Enhanced disabled child additional element	1,275	1,255
Working tax credit per annum/weekly equivalents		
Basic element	1,960	1,940
Additional couple's and lone parent element	2,010	1,990
30 hour element	810	800
Disabled worker element	2,970	2,935
Enhanced disabled adult element	1,275	1,255
Childcare element (weekly)		
— maximum eligible cost	300	300
— maximum eligible cost for 1 child	175	175
— percent of eligible costs covered	70%	70%
Common features		
Income threshold	6,420	6,420
Withdrawal rate	41%	41%
Income threshold for those entitled to child tax credit only	16,105	16,010
Income rise disregard	5,000	5,000
Income fall disregard	2,500	2,500
Pension credit (weekly amounts)		
Standard minimum guarantee		
— claimant with partner	230.85	226.50
— other claimants	151.20	148.35
Additional amounts for severely disabled		
— single	61.85	61.10
— couple (one qualifies)	61.85	61.10
— couple (both qualify)	123.70	122.20
Additional amount for carers	34.60	34.20
Capital disregarded	10,000	10,000

Universal Credit	2015/16	2014/15
Monthly rates	£	£
Standard allowance		
Single under 25	251.77	249.28
Single 25 or over	317.82	314.67
Joint claimants both under 25	395.20	391.29
Joint claimants, one or both 25 or over	498.89	493.95
Child element		
First child	277.08	274.58
Second/subsequent child	231.67	229.17
Disabled child additions		
—higher rate	367.92	362.92
—lower rate	126.11	124.86
Childcare element		
— maximum for 1 child	532.29	532.29
— maximum for 2 or more children	912.50	912.50
Limited capability for work element	126.11	124.86
Limited capability for work and work-related activity element	315.60	311.86
Carer element	150.39	148.61
Non-dependants' housing cost contributions	69.37	68.68
Work allowances		
Higher (no housing element)		
— single, no dependent children	111.00	111.00
— single, one or more children	734.00	734.00
— single, limited capability for work	647.00	647.00
— joint, no dependent children	111.00	111.00
— joint, one or more children	536.00	536.00
— joint, limited capability for work	647.00	647.00
Lower		
— single, no dependent children	111.00	111.00
— single, one or more children	263.00	263.00
— single, limited capability for work	192.00	192.00
— joint, no dependent children	111.00	111.00
— joint, one or more children	222.00	222.00
— joint, limited capability for work	192.00	192.00

Stamp taxes

Stamp duty land tax

Land transactions (note (a))

Residential property (note (b))

Consideration (rates apply to the full consideration)			Rate	Consideration (rates apply to consideration in each slice)	Rate
1.1.10–5.4.11	6.4.11–21.3.12	22.3.12–3.12.14		4.12.14–	
Up to £125,000	Up to £125,000	Up to £125,000	Nil	Up to £125,000	Nil
£125,001–£250,000	£125,001–£250,000	£125,001–£250,000	1%	£125,001–£250,000	2%
£250,001–£500,000	£250,001–£500,000	£250,001–£500,000	3%	£250,001–£925,000	5%
£500,001 or more	£500,001–£1,000,000	£500,001–£1,000,000	4%	£925,001–£1,500,000	10%
—	£1,000,001 or more	£1,000,001–£2,000,000	5%	£1,500,001 or more	12%
—	—	£2,000,001 or more	7%		

Non-residential or mixed property

Consideration (rates apply to the full consideration)			Rate
1.1.10–5.4.11	6.4.11–21.3.12	22.3.12–	
Up to £150,000	Up to £150,000	Up to £150,000	Nil
£150,001–£250,000	£150,001–£250,000	£150,001–£250,000	1%
£250,001–£500,000	£250,001–£500,000	£250,001–£500,000	3%
£500,001 or more	£500,001 or more	£500,001 or more	4%

Premiums (note (c))

Lease rentals

On net present value of rent over term of lease (applying a discount rate of 3.5%) (rates apply to the amount of npv in the slice — but see note (c))			Rate
1.1.10–5.4.11	6.4.11–21.3.12	22.3.12–	

Residential property

Up to £125,000	Up to £125,000	Up to £125,000	Nil
£125,001 or more	£125,001 or more	£125,001 or more	1%

Non-residential or mixed property

Up to £150,000	Up to £150,000	Up to £150,000	Nil
£150,001 or more	£150,001 or more	£150,001 or more	1%

Notes

(a) Stamp duty land tax does not apply to transactions in land in Scotland with an effective date on or after 1 April 2015. Scottish land and buildings transaction tax applies instead to such transactions (see page 108).

(b) **Residential property acquired by non-natural person.** Where a residential property is purchased by a non-natural person (such as a company, collective investment scheme or a partnership of which a company or such a scheme is a member), a rate of stamp duty land tax of 15% applies if the consideration exceeds £500,000 (£2 million where the contract is entered into before 20 March 2014). The rate applies to the whole of the consideration despite the change to a 'slice' basis for residential property generally from 4 December 2014. Exclusions apply for certain corporate trustees, property developers and other businesses.

(c) The same tax is payable for a premium granted as for a land transaction. Special rules apply to a premium in respect of non-residential property where the rent exceeds £1,000 p.a.

(d) Interest on unpaid SDLT runs from 30 days after the effective date of the transaction, or the date of a disqualifying event, until the tax is paid. In the case of a deferred payment, interest runs from the date payment is due until the tax is paid. Interest is added to repayments of overpaid SDLT and runs from the date the tax was paid or an amount was lodged with HMRC to the date the order for repayment is issued. For rates of interest see page 77.

(e) **Disadvantaged areas.** For transactions with an effective date on or before 5 April 2013, no SDLT is charged on transfers of residential property if the consideration is £150,000 or less. This also applies to leases with an effective date on or before 5 April 2013; broadly, to rent where the net present value over the term of the lease does not exceed £150,000 and to premiums not exceeding £150,000. For areas designated as disadvantaged areas see *SI 2001 No 3747*. Claims must be made before 6 May 2014.

(f) **First-time buyers.** For purchases of residential property where the effective date is on or after 25 March 2010 and before 25 March 2012 and the purchaser is a first-time buyer intending to occupy the property as his only or main home, the 0% rate applies where the consideration does not exceed £250,000.

(g) **Other SDLT exemptions and reliefs.** No SDLT is chargeable on: (i) gifts inter vivos; (ii) transfers to beneficiaries under a will or an intestacy; (iii) certain transfers on divorce or dissolution of a civil partnership; (iv) transfers to charities for use for charitable purposes; (v) transfers to bodies established for national purposes or (where the effective date is on or after 17 July 2012) certain National Health Service bodies; (vi) land transfers within groups of companies; (vii) land transferred for shares on company reconstructions and acquisitions; (viii) transfers of intellectual property; (ix) certain transfers to registered providers of social housing; and (x) certain leases granted by registered providers of social housing.

With effect from 19 July 2011 a relief applies where more than one residential property is purchased from the same vendor. SDLT is charged on the mean consideration for each property, subject to a minimum rate of 1%.

Between 1 October 2007 and 30 September 2012 an exemption applied to the first sale of certificated zero-carbon homes and flats. No SDLT was chargeable where the consideration did not exceed £500,000. Where the consideration was more than £500,000, the SDLT liability was reduced by £15,000.

Stamp taxes

Land and buildings transaction tax (Scotland)

Land transactions

Residential property	Consideration (rates apply to consideration in each slice) 1.4.15–	Rate
	Up to £145,000	Nil
	£145,001–£250,000	2%
	£250,001–£325,000	5%
	£325,001–£750,000	10%
	£750,001 or more	12%

Non-residential or mixed property	Consideration (rates apply to the full consideration) 1.4.15–	Rate
	Up to £150,000	Nil
	£150,001–£350,000	3%
	£350,001 or more	4.5%

Stamp duty

Shares, etc.

Shares converted into depositary receipts or put into duty free clearance systems	1.5%
Purchase of own shares by company	0.5%
Transfers of stock or marketable securities	0.5%
Takeovers, mergers, demergers, schemes of reconstruction and amalgamation (except where no real change of ownership)	0.5%

Stamp duty reserve tax

Agreements to transfer chargeable securities for money or money's worth (e.g. renounceable letters of allotment)	0.5%
Chargeable securities converted into depository receipts or put into clearance services (note (g))	1.5%
Dealings before 30 March 2014 in units of unit trusts and shares in OEICs	0.5%

Notes

(a) Land and buildings transaction tax (LBTT) applies to transactions in land in Scotland with an effective date on or after 1 April 2015. Stamp duty land tax does not apply to such transactions.

(b) **Leases.** LBTT applies to non-residential leases but only to certain very long residential leases. Where a lease is chargeable the amount of tax payable in respect of the rent is 1% of the amount of net present value of the rent above £150,000. The same tax is payable for a premium in respect of a lease within the charge as for a land transaction. Special rules apply to a premium in respect of non-residential property where the rent exceeds £1,000 a year.

(c) There are various exemptions and reliefs from LBTT, all of which currently apply to SDLT. See page 107. Penalties apply for late returns, late payment and inaccuracies in documents. Interest is charged on late payments and is payable on overpayments.

(d) Stamp duty applies only to shares and marketable securities and to the transfer of an interest in a partnership holding stock or marketable securities.

(e) Stamp duty is not chargeable where the amount or value of the consideration is £1,000 or under.

(f) **Stamp duty exemptions and reliefs.** No stamp duty is chargeable on:
(i)   gifts inter vivos;
(ii)   transfers to charities for use for charitable purposes;
(iii) transfers to bodies established for national purposes;
An exemption from stamp duty and stamp duty reserve tax applies with effect, broadly, from 28 April 2014 for transfers of securities admitted to trading on recognised growth markets. From April 2014 transfers of units in exchange traded funds will similarly be exempt.

(g) Following the Tribunal decision in *HSBC Holdings plc and Bank of New York Mellon Corporation v HMRC* FTT, [2012] UKFTT 163 (TC), the 1.5% stamp duty reserve tax charge is no longer applicable to issues of UK shares and securities to clearance services or depositary receipt issuers anywhere in the world. The charge continues to apply to transfers of such shares or securities to clearance services or depositary receipt issuers. See HMRC Notice, 27 April 2012.

Time limits claims and elections

	Provision	Time limit
General		
TMA 1970, s 43(1)	Under self-assessment for individuals etc., unless otherwise prescribed	With effect from 1 April 2010 (2012 for taxpayers outside self-assessment), 4 years after end of tax year. Previously, on or before 5th anniversary of 31 January following tax year
FA 1998, Sch 18 para 55	For companies, unless otherwise prescribed	With effect from 1 April 2010, 4 years after end of accounting period. Previously, 6 years after end of accounting period
	Listed below are the more important *prescribed* time limits. Unless otherwise stated, time limits run from the end of the chargeable period	
Income tax		
ITTOIA 2005, s 239	**Barristers** — election for increased adjustment under transitional spreading provisions (repealed for 2013/14 onwards)	1 year after 31 January following tax year
ITA 2007, s 202	**Enterprise investment scheme relief**	5th anniversary of 31 January following tax year in which shares issued
ITEPA 2003, Sch 5 para 44	**Enterprise management incentives**—notification of grant of options to HMRC	92 days after grant of option
ITTOIA 2005, ss 222, 225	**Farming**—averaging of profits	1 year after 31 January following second tax year to which claim relates
ITA 2007, s 426	**Gift aid**—election to treat donations as made in the previous tax year	On or before date the donor delivers his tax return for the previous tax year but no later than 31 January following the end of that tax year
	Losses set off against other income	
ITA 2007, s 124	(a) Property business losses	1 year after 31 January following tax year of loss
ITA 2007, s 64	(b) Trading losses	1 year after 31 January following tax year of loss
ITA 2007, s 72	(c) Trading losses in any of the first 4 tax years	1 year after 31 January following tax year of loss
ITA 2007, s 132	(d) Losses on disposal of shares in unlisted trading companies	1 year after 31 January following tax year of loss
ITA 2007, s 96	**Post-cessation expenditure**—set off against income	1 year after 31 January following tax year of payment
ITTOIA 2005, s 257	**Post-cessation receipts** received within, broadly, 6 years of date of discontinuance to be treated as received on that date	1 year after 31 January following tax year of receipt
ITTOIA 2005, s 818	**Qualifying care receipts**—election to tax on the alternative method of calculating profits	1 year after 31 January following tax year
ITTOIA 2005, ss 799, 800	**Rent a room relief**—(a) relief not to apply; (b) relief to apply to gross income in excess of limit; or (c) withdrawal of claim under (a) or (b)	1 year after 31 January following tax year
ITA 2007, s 357EA	**Seed enterprise investment scheme relief**	5th anniversary of 31 January following tax year in which shares issued
ITA 2007, s 257P	**Social investment relief**	5th anniversary of 31 January following tax year in which investment made
ITTOIA 2005, s 185	**Trading stock**—work in progress on discontinuance valued at cost	1 year after 31 January following tax year of cessation;
Income tax and corporation tax		
CTA 2009, s 122 *ITTOIA 2005, s 124*	**Herd basis**	2 years after first accounting period in which herd kept (CT) or 1 year after 31 January following first year of assessment for which herd kept in basis year (IT)
CTA 2009, s 178(6) *ITTOIA 2005, s 194(6)*	**Know-how** used in trade—sale not to be treated as goodwill	2 years from date of disposal
CTA 2009, ss 914(5), 917(4); *ITTOIA 2005, ss 590(6), 591(3)*	**Patents**—capital sums to be treated (a) by UK residents as charged in period received, or (b) by non-residents as spread over 6 years	1 year after 31 January following tax year of receipt (IT); 2 years after accounting period of receipt (CT)
CTA 2009, s 268(6);	**Rents etc**	1 year after 31 January following tax year (IT)
ITTOIA 2005, s 326(6)	**Furnished holiday lettings**—averaging provisions	2 years after accounting period (CT)

Time limits claims and elections

	Provision	Time limit
CTA 2009, s 1275(5); ITTOIA 2005, s 842(5)	**Unremittable overseas income** to be excluded from liability to tax	1 year after 31 January following tax year in which income arises (IT); 2 years after accounting period in which income arises (CT)

Corporation tax

	Provision	Time limit
	Controlled foreign companies — old regime	
ICTA 1988, Sch 24 para 9	(a) Losses in pre-apportionment accounting periods to be taken into account in computing chargeable profit	20 months
ICTA 1988, s 751A	(b) Reduction in profits for activities of EEA business establishment	Filing date for the return
FA 2000, Sch 15 para 68	**Corporate venturing**—relief for losses on disposal of shares against income	2 years
TMA 1970, Sch 3ZB para 1	**Exit charge payment plans**—application for	9 months from end of accounting period of migration
FA 1998, Sch 18 para 83W	**Film, television, video games and theatre tax reliefs**—claims to be made, amended or withdrawn in the company tax return	1 year from filing date for the return
FA 1998, Sch 18 para 74	**Group relief**	The latest of: (i) 1 year from the filing date of the claimant company's return for the accounting period for which the claim is made; (ii) 30 days after the end of an enquiry into the return; (iii) if HMRC amend the return after an enquiry, 30 days after the issue of notice of assessment;(iv) if an appeal is made against the amendment, 30 days after the determination of the appeal; (or such later date as HMRC allow). (NB filing date is generally 1 year after end of accounting period)
	Intangible assets	
CTA 2009, s 730(3)	(a) Election to replace accounts depreciation with fixed WDA of 4%	2 years
CTA 2009, s 816(2)	(b) Election to exclude certain expenditure on computer software	2 years
FA 2013, s 60	(c) Disincorporation relief	2 years beginning with date of transfer
	Losses set off against other income	
CTA 2010, s 37(7)	(a) Trading losses	2 years
CTA 2010, s 70(4)	(b) Losses by an investment company on disposal of shares in unlisted trading companies	2 years
CTA 2009, s 458(2)	(c) Non-trading deficit on loan relationships	2 years
CTA 2010, s 357G(3)	**Patent box**	1 year from filing date for the return for the first accounting period for which the election is to apply
FA 1998, Sch 18 paras 83E, 83LE	**Research and development**—tax relief claims to be made, amended or withdrawn in the company tax return	1 year from filing date for the return

Capital allowances

	Provision	Time limit
	(NB: A 'chargeable period' for capital allowances purposes is an accounting period of a company or a period of account of an individual.)	
CAA 2001, s 3(2),(3)(b); FA 1998, Sch 18 para 82	**Companies**—claims for capital allowances (including variations and withdrawals)	1st anniversary of filing date for claimant company's tax return but deferred in cases of HMRC enquiry (NB: filing date is generally 1 year after accounting period)
	Connected persons	
CAA 2001, s 266	(a) Successions to trades between connected persons: machinery or plant treated as transferred at tax written down value	2 years from date of succession
CAA 2001, s 570(5)	(b) Sales between persons under common control treated as being at tax written down value	2 years from date of sale
CAA 2001, s 177(5)	**Equipment leasing**—fixtures treated as belonging to lessor	1 year after 31 January following tax year in which ends lessor's chargeable period in which expenditure incurred (IT); 2 years after that chargeable period (CT)

Time limits claims and elections

	Provision	Time limit
CAA 2001, s 260(6)	**Excess capital allowances**—set-off against other income of companies	2 years
	Plant and machinery	
CAA 2001, s 183(2)	Fixture on land subsequently let to be treated as belonging to lessee	2 years after lease takes effect
	Oilfields	
CAA 2001, s 164(2)	General decommissioning expenditure	2 years
	Ships	
CAA 2001, s 130(4)	(a) Postponement, disclaimer or reduction of first year allowances or writing down allowances	1 year after 31 January following tax year in which chargeable period ends (IT); 2 years after chargeable period (CT)
CAA 2001, s 129(2)	(b) 'Single ship pool' provisions not to apply	1 year after 31 January following tax year in which chargeable period ends (IT); 2 years after chargeable period (CT)
	Short life assets	
CAA 2001, s 85(2)	(a) Plant or machinery to be treated as short life asset	1 year after 31 January following tax year in which chargeable period ends (IT); 2 years after chargeable period (CT)
CAA 2001, s 89(6)	(b) Transfer of short life asset to connected person at tax wdv	2 years after chargeable period
Chargeable gains		
	Assets held on 6 April 1965	
TCGA 1992, Sch 2 para 4	(a) All disposals of quoted securities to be treated as acquired at market value on that date	2 years after end of accounting period in which first relevant disposal after 5 April 1985. CT only
TCGA 1992, Sch 2 para 17	(b) Disposals of other assets computed by reference to market value on that date	2 years after end of accounting period of disposal. CT only
	Assets held on 31 March 1982	
TCGA 1992, s 35(5)(6)	(a) Universal re-basing	2 years after end of accounting period in which first relevant disposal after 5 April 1988. CT only
TCGA 1992, Sch 4 para 9	(b) 50% reduction in taxing deferred gains arising from assets acquired before 31 March 1982	2 years after end of accounting period of disposal or in which gain treated as accruing. CT only
TCGA 1992, s 187(1)	**Companies ceasing to be UK resident**—postponement of charge on deemed disposal where 75% subsidiary of UK company	2 years after ceasing to be UK resident
FA 2013, s 60	**Disincorporation relief**	2 years beginning with date of transfer
TGCA 1992, ss 169H–169S	**Entrepreneurs' relief**	1 year after 31 January following tax year of qualifying business disposal
TCGA 1992, s 162A	**Incorporation relief**—election to disapply incorporation relief under *TCGA 1992, s 162* on a transfer of a business	2 years after 31 January following tax year in which transfer takes place (reduced by 1 year where transferor disposes of all shares received in exchange by end of the tax year following that in which transfer takes place
TCGA 1992, s 253(3)(3A)	**Loans to traders** becoming irrecoverable	2 years
TCGA 1992, s 24(2)	**Negligible value securities**	2 years after end of chargeable period of deemed sale and reacquisition
TCGA 1992, s 222	**Private residences**—determination of main residence	2 years after acquisition of second residence
TCGA 1992, s 261B	**Trading losses** to be relieved against gains	1 year after 31 January following tax year of loss
TCGA 1992, s 62(7)	**Variations and disclaimers** of dispositions made within two years of death	6 months after making the instrument

Time limits claims and elections

	Provision		Time limit
Inheritance tax			
	Death		
IHTA 1984, s 142	(a)	Variations and disclaimer of dispositions made within two years of death	6 months after making the instrument
IHTA 1984, s 125	(b)	Valuation of woodlands	2 years after death
IHTA 1984, ss 8A, 8B	(c)	Transfer of unused nil-rate band to spouse or civil partner	2 years after end of month of survivor's death or, if later, 3 months after personal representatives first act
IHTA 1984, s 57	**Termination of interest in possession**—notice to trustees of available exemptions on termination		6 months after termination
IHTA 1984, ss 30, 78	**National Heritage property**—property transferred to be designated as such, and thus exempt		2 years after transfer or other chargeable event after 16 March 1998

Value added tax
annual accounting scheme, capital goods scheme, cash accountancy scheme and deregistration

Annual accounting scheme

A business may, subject to conditions, complete one VAT return each year. It can join the scheme if taxable supplies in the next tax year are not expected to exceed

1.4.06 onwards	£1,350,000
1.4.04–31.3.06	£660,000

but must leave at the end of any accounting year in which yearly taxable supplies exceed

1.4.06 onwards	£1,600,000
1.4.04–31.3.06	£825,000

Before 1 April 2006, only businesses with taxable turnover up to £150,000 could join the scheme immediately; other qualifying businesses had to have been registered for 12 months. Quarterly or monthly payments on account may be required.

Capital goods scheme [SI 1995 No 2518, Regs 112-116]

The scheme applies to capital items within the list below which the owner (or person who holds an interest) uses in the course of, and for the purpose of, a business carried on by him. Input tax adjustments are required where, during the adjustment period, there is a change in the extent of the taxable use of the item.

Item	Minimum value	Adjustment period
Land	£250,000	10 years
Building (or part)	£250,000	10 years
Civil engineering work (or part of such a work)	£250,000	10 years
Computer or computer equipment	£50,000	5 years
Aircraft	£50,000	5 years
Ship, boat or other vessel	£50,000	5 years

Where the minimum value would otherwise be £250,000 it is reduced to £1 where the owner, or a person to whom the owner has granted an interest, uses the item to make a grant falling within *VATA 1994 Sch 9 Group1 Item 1(ka)* (self-storage facilities) and decides, before 1 April 2013, to treat the item as a capital item within the scheme. A written record of the decision must be kept.

Aircraft, ships, boats and other vessels are within the scheme only where the item is acquired on or after 1 January 2011. The adjustment period is shortened in certain cases where, at the time of the owner's first use of the item, the number of yearly intervals in the adjustment period exceeds the number of complete years that his interest in the item has to run or where the owner already owned the item prior to VAT registration. For land, buildings and civil engineering work where the adjustment period started before 1 January 2011, the period is five years if the owner's interest had less than ten years to run on acquisition. The adjustment formula is:

$$\frac{\text{Total VAT on item}}{\text{Length of adjustment period}} \times \text{adjustment percentage}$$

where the 'adjustment percentage' is the percentage change in the extent to which the item is used (or treated as used) in making taxable supplies between the time at which the original entitlement to deduction of the input tax was determined and the adjustment period interval in question. For goods acquired on or after 1 January 2011 total input tax includes any non-business VAT.

Cash accounting scheme

A business may, subject to conditions, account for and pay VAT on the basis of cash paid and received. It can join the scheme if taxable supplies in the next year are not expected to exceed

1.4.07 onwards	£1,350,000
1.4.04–31.3.07	£660,000

but must leave if taxable supplies in the previous year have exceeded

1.4.07 onwards	£1,600,000
1.4.04–31.3.07	£825,000

Deregistration

(i) UK taxable supplies

A registered taxable person ceases to be liable to be registered if, at any time, HMRC are satisfied that the value of his taxable supplies in the year then beginning will not exceed the following limits

Effective date	£	Effective date	£
1.4.15	80,000	1.4.12	75,000
1.4.14	79,000	1.4.11	71,000
1.4.13	77,000	1.4.10	68,000

unless the reason the value of taxable supplies will not exceed the limit is that in the period in question the person will cease making taxable supplies or will suspend making them for a period of 30 days or more

(ii) Supplies from other EC countries ('distance selling')

A person registered under these provisions ceases to be liable to be registered if, at any time

(a)   his relevant supplies in the year ended 31 December last before that time did not exceed the following limits; and

(b)   HMRC are satisfied that the value of his relevant supplies in the year immediately following that year will not exceed the following limits

Effective date	£
1.1.93	70,000

(iii) Acquisitions from other EC countries

A person registered under these provisions ceases to be liable to be registered if, at any time

(a)   his relevant acquisitions in the year ended 31 December last before that time did not exceed the following limits; and

(b)   HMRC are satisfied that the value of his relevant acquisitions in the year immediately following that year will not exceed the following limits

Effective date	£	Effective date	£
1.4.15	82,000	1.4.12	77,000
1.4.14	81,000	1.4.11	73,000
1.4.13	79,000	1.4.10	70,000

Value added tax
EU country codes, EU sales lists and exempt supplies

EU country codes

Any registration number contained in a VAT invoice provided to a registered person in another EU country must include the appropriate country code as listed below. Country codes are also needed for the completion of EU sales lists.

Country	Code	Country	Code
Austria	AT	Italy	IT
Belgium	BE	Latvia	LV
Bulgaria	BG	Lithuania	LT
Croatia	HR	Luxembourg	LU
Cyprus	CY	Malta	MT
Czech Republic	CZ	Netherlands	NL
Denmark	DK	Poland	PL
Estonia	EE	Portugal	PT
Finland	FI	Romania	RO
France	FR	Slovak Republic	SK
Germany	DE	Slovenia	SI
Greece	EL	Spain	ES
Hungary	HU	Sweden	SE
Ireland	IE	United Kingdom	GB

EU sales lists [SI 1995 No 2518, Regs 21-23]

A business registered for VAT in the UK which:

(a) makes supplies of goods to traders registered for VAT in other EU countries;
(b) transfers its own goods from the UK to another EU country;
(c) is the intermediary in triangular transactions between VAT-registered traders in other EU countries; or
(d) (with effect from 1 January 2010) makes supplies of services to a person in another EU country which are subject to the reverse charge in the customer's country,

must submit to HMRC statements ('EU sales lists') containing particulars of the transactions involved. Such lists may be submitted electronically or using Form VAT 101 as follows.

Type of supply		Frequency
Goods only	Where the value of supplies to registered traders in other EU countries exceeds £35,000 (£70,000 before 1 January 2012) in the current or four previous quarters	Calendar monthly
	Where the value of supplies to registered traders in other EU countries does not exceed £35,000 (£70,000 before 1 January 2012) in the current or four previous quarters	Quarterly (i.e. for each calendar quarter ending 31 March, 30 June, 30 September and 31 December)
Services subject to reverse charge		Quarterly (as above), but business may choose to submit lists monthly
Goods and services (where monthly lists required for goods)		Monthly for all supplies, or monthly for goods and quarterly for services

A business which makes annual VAT returns can apply to HMRC for approval to submit an ESL once a year only if total annual taxable turnover does not exceed £145,000; the annual value of supplies to other EU countries does not exceed £11,000 and sales do not include new means of transport (boats, aircraft and motorised land vehicles). A business can apply to HMRC for approval to submit a simplified annual ESL if total taxable annual turnover does not exceed the VAT registration threshold plus £25,500; supplies to customers in other EU countries do not exceed £11,000 per year and sales do not include new means of transport.

If an ESL is completed online it must be submitted within 21 days after the end of the reporting period. In other cases the list must be submitted within 14 days after the end of the reporting period.

Exempt supplies [VATA 1994, Sch 9]

A supply of goods or services is an exempt supply if falling within one of the Groups listed below. Where a supply falls within one of the Groups but is also covered by the zero-rating provisions, the latter takes priority.

Group 1	Land
Group 2	Insurance
Group 3	Postal services
Group 4	Betting, gaming, dutiable machine games and lotteries
Group 5	Finance
Group 6	Education
Group 7	Health and welfare
Group 8	Burial and cremation
Group 9	Subscriptions to trade unions, professional and other public interest bodies
Group 10	Sport, sports competitions and physical education
Group 11	Works of art, etc.
Group 12	Fund-raising events by charities and other qualifying bodies
Group 13	Cultural services, etc.
Group 14	Supplies of goods where input tax cannot be recovered
Group 15	Investment gold
Group 16	Supplies of services by groups involving cost sharing (from 17 July 2012)

Value added tax flat-rate scheme for small businesses

Flat-rate scheme for small businesses

A business which expects its taxable supplies (excluding VAT) in the next year to be no more than £150,000 and, before 1 April 2009, its total business income to be no more than £187,500 can opt to join a flat-rate scheme. It can then calculate net VAT due by applying the appropriate flat-rate percentage from the list below to total turnover generated, including exempt income.

Category of business	Appropriate %		
	1.12.08–31.12.09	1.1.10–3.1.11	4.1.11 onwards
Accountancy or book-keeping	11.5	13	14.5
Advertising	8.5	10	11
Agricultural services	7	10	11
Any other activity not listed elsewhere	9	10.5	12
Architects	11	13	14.5
Boarding or care of animals	9.5	10.5	12
Business services that are not listed elsewhere	9.5	10.5	12
Catering services, including restaurants and take-aways	10.5	11	12.5
Civil and structural engineers and surveyors	11	13	14.5
Computer and IT consultancy or data processing	11.5	13	14.5
Computer repair services	10	9.5	10.5
Dealing in waste or scrap	8.5	9.5	10.5
Entertainment (excluding film, radio, television or video production, see below) or journalism	9.5	11	12.5
Estate agency or property management services	9.5	10.5	12
Farming or agriculture that is not listed elsewhere	5.5	6	6.5
Film, radio, television or video production	9.5	11.5	13
Financial services	10.5	12	13.5
Forestry or fishing	8	9.5	10.5
General building or construction services (note (a))	7.5	8.5	9.5
Hairdressing or other beauty treatment services	10.5	11.5	13
Hiring or renting goods	7.5	8.5	9.5
Hotel or accommodation	8.5	9.5	10.5
Investigation or security	9	10.5	12
Labour-only building or construction services (note (a))	11.5	13	14.5
Laundry or dry-cleaning services	9.5	10.5	12

Category of business	Appropriate %		
	1.12.08–31.12.09	1.1.10–3.1.11	4.1.11 onwards
Lawyers or legal services	12	13	14.5
Library, archive, museum or other cultural activities	7.5	8.5	9.5
Management consultancy	11	12.5	14
Manufacturing fabricated metal products	8.5	9.5	10.5
Manufacturing food	7	8	9
Manufacturing that is not listed elsewhere	7.5	8.5	9.5
Manufacturing yarn, textiles or clothing	7.5	8	9
Membership organizations	5.5	7	8
Mining or quarrying	8	9	10
Packaging	7.5	8	9
Photography	8.5	10	11
Post offices	2	4.5	5
Printing	6.5	7.5	8.5
Publishing	8.5	10	11
Pubs	5.5	6	6.5
Real estate activities not listed elsewhere	11	12.5	14
Repairing personal or household goods	7.5	9	10
Repairing vehicles	6.5	7.5	8.5
Retailing food, confectionery, tobacco, newspapers or children's clothing	2	3.5	4
Retailing pharmaceuticals, medical goods, cosmetics or toiletries	6	7	8
Retailing that is not listed elsewhere	5.5	6.5	7.5
Retailing vehicles or fuel	5.5	6	6.5
Secretarial services	9.5	11.5	13
Social work	8	10	11
Sport or recreation	6	7.5	8.5
Transport or storage, including couriers, freight, removals and taxis (note (b))	8	9	10
Travel agency	8	9.5	10.5
Veterinary medicine	8	10	11
Wholesaling agricultural products	5.5	7	8
Wholesaling food	5	6.5	7.5
Wholesaling that is not listed elsewhere	6	7.5	8.5

Notes

(a) 'Labour-only building or construction services' means building or construction services where the value of materials supplied is less than 10% of relevant turnover from such services; any other building or construction services are 'general building or construction services'.

(b) Once in the scheme a business may continue to use it until its total business income exceeds £230,000, and if income does exceed this limit, the business can still remain in the scheme if the income in the following year is estimated not to exceed £191,500. The £230,000 threshold is normally compared to total income (including VAT but excluding sales of capital assets) in the year to the anniversary of the start date (of using the flat rate scheme). However it is also necessary to leave the scheme when there are reasonable grounds to believe the total value of income in the next 30 days will exceed £230,000.

Value added tax interest, partial exemption, rates and reduced rate supplies

Interest

Default Interest [VATA 1994, s 74]

Interest runs on the amount of any VAT assessed (or the amount of any VAT paid late by voluntary disclosure) from the reckonable date (normally the latest date on which a return is required for the period in question) until the date of payment (although in practice it runs to the date shown on the notice of assessment or notice of voluntary disclosure if paid within 30 days of that date). The period of interest cannot commence more than three years before the date of assessment or payment. The rates of interest are as follows

6.9.05–5.9.06	6.5%
6.9.06–5.8.07	7.5%
6.8.07–5.1.08	8.5%
6.1.08–5.11.08	7.5%
6.11.08–5.12.08	6.5%
6.12.08–5.1.09	5.5%
6.1.09–26.1.09	4.5%
27.1.09–23.3.09	3.5%
24.3.09–28.9.09	2.5%
29.9.09–	3%

Interest in cases of official error [VATA 1994, s 78]

Where VAT has been overpaid or underclaimed due to an error by HMRC, then on a claim HMRC must pay interest from the date they receive payment (or authorise a repayment) for the return period in question until the date on which they authorise payment of the amount on which interest is due. This provision does not require HMRC to pay interest on an amount on which repayment supplement is due. The rates of interest are as follows

6.9.05–5.9.06	3%
6.9.06–5.8.07	4%
6.8.07–5.1.08	5%
6.1.08–5.11.08	4%
6.11.08–5.12.08	3%
6.12.09–5.1.09	2%
6.1.09–26.1.09	1%
27.1.09–28.9.09	0%
29.9.09–	0.5%

Note

(a) *FA 2009, ss 101–104A, Schs 53–54A* create a harmonised interest regime for all taxes and duties administered by HMRC. The regime is being phased in over a number of years for different taxes.

Repayment supplement — VAT [VATA 1994, s 79]

Where a person is entitled to a repayment of VAT, the payment due is increased by a supplement of the greater of (i) 5% of that amount; or (ii) £50 provided

(a) the return or claim is received by HMRC not later than the last day on which it is required to be made;

(b) HMRC do not issue a written instruction making the refund within the relevant period; and

(c) the amount shown on the return or claim does not exceed the amount due by more than 5% of that amount or £250 whichever is the greater.

The '*relevant period*' is 30 days beginning with the receipt of the return or claim or, if later, the day after the last day of the VAT period to which the return or claim relates.

Partial exemption

A registered person who makes taxable and exempt supplies is partly exempt and may not be able to deduct (or reclaim) all his input tax. Where, however, the input tax attributable to exempt supplies in a prescribed accounting period or tax year is within certain de minimis limits, all such input tax is treated as attributable to taxable supplies and recoverable (subject to the normal rules). The de minimis limits are

Exempt input tax not exceeding	£625 per month on average: and 50% of all input tax for the period concerned

Rates

Standard rate	4.1.11 onwards	20%	VAT fraction 1/6
	1.1.10–3.1.11	17½%	7/47
	1.12.08–31.12.09	15%	3/23
	before 1.12.08	17½%	7/47
Reduced rate		5%	1/21
Flat-rate scheme for farmers		4% flat-rate addition to sale price	

Reduced rate supplies [VATA 1994, Sch 7A]

A supply of goods or services is charged at the reduced rate if falling within one of the following Groups.

Group 1	Domestic fuel and power
Group 2	Installation of energy-saving materials
Group 3	Grant-funded installation of heating equipment or security goods or connection of a gas supply
Group 4	Women's sanitary products
Group 5	Children's car seats (and, from 1 July 2009, car seat bases)
Group 6	Residential conversions
Group 7	Residential renovations and alterations
Group 8	Contraceptive products
Group 9	Welfare advice or information
Group 10	Installation of mobility aids for the elderly (from 1 July 2007)
Group 11	Smoking cessation products (from 1 July 2007)
Group 12	Caravans (from 6 April 2013)
Group 13	Cable-suspended transport systems (from 1 April 2013)

Value added tax registration, returns and payment of VAT

Registration

(i) UK taxable supplies

A person who makes taxable supplies is liable to be registered

(a)   at the end of any month if the value of taxable supplies in the year then ending has exceeded the limit in column A below; or

(b)   at any time, if there are reasonable grounds for believing that the value of taxable supplies in the next 30 days will exceed the limit in column A below

except that a person does not become liable to be registered under (a) above if HMRC are satisfied that the value of taxable supplies in the year beginning at the time he would be liable to be registered will not exceed the limit in column B below. With effect from 1 December 2012 a non-UK established business is required to register for VAT regardless of the value of taxable supplies in the UK.

Effective date	A (£)	B (£)
1.4.15	82,000	80,000
1.4.14	81,000	79,000
1.4.13	79,000	77,000
1.4.12	77,000	75,000
1.4.11	73,000	71,000
1.4.10	70,000	68,000

(ii) Supplies from other EC countries ('distance selling')

A business person in another EC country not registered or liable to be registered in the UK under (i) above is liable to be registered on any day if, in the period beginning with 1 January in that year, he has made, and is responsible for the delivery of, supplies to non-taxable persons in the UK exceeding the following limits

Effective date	£
1.1.93	70,000

(iii) Acquisitions from EC countries

A person not registered or liable to be registered under (i) or (ii) above is liable to be registered

(a)   at the end of any month if, in the period beginning with 1 January in that year, he has made acquisitions of taxable goods for business purposes (or for non-business purposes if a public body, charity, club, etc.) from suppliers in other EC countries whose value exceeds the following limits; or

(b)   at any time, if there are reasonable grounds for believing that the value of such acquisitions in the next 30 days will exceed the following limits

Effective date	£	Effective date	£
1.4.15	82,000	1.4.12	77,000
1.4.14	81,000	1.4.11	73,000
1.4.13	79,000	1.4.10	70,000

Returns and payment of VAT

Subject to below, a completed VAT return must be sent to HMRC, and any VAT due paid, not later than one month after the end of the return period. From 1 April 2012 all businesses (subject to limited exceptions in the case of insolvency or religious objection) must submit returns online using the eVAT service. Previously, from 1 April 2010, businesses with VAT-exclusive turnover of £100,000 or more had to submit returns online using the service as did businesses registering for VAT on or after that date. In other cases, returns could be submitted by post or online.

Where a return is not made online, the prescribed VAT returns are

Form VAT 100	All purposes except where Form VAT 193 applies
Form VAT 193	Final VAT return (unless registration allocated to the purchaser on the transfer of a business as a going concern)

Where returns are sent electronically via the eVAT service, any VAT due must also be paid electronically. Otherwise, payment can be made by post to VAT Central Unit at Southend-on-Sea, by debit card or, subject to a fee, by credit card, or electronically by Bank Giro Credit transfer, BACS or CHAPS.

Where payment is made electronically, a business automatically receives a 7-day extension for the submission of the return and payment of VAT. The concession cannot be used (i) by businesses required to make payments on account unless it makes monthly returns; (ii) by businesses using the annual accounting scheme; or (iii) to make VAT payments other than VAT return payments (e.g. assessments).

Businesses with an annual VAT liability of £2.3m or more (£2m or more before 1 June 2011 (1 December 2011 for annual reviews)) must make interim payments on account (POAs) at the end of the second and third months of each VAT quarter with a balancing payment for the quarter with the VAT return. All POAs and balancing payments must be made by electronic transfer.

Digital services — VAT mini one-stop shop (VAT MOSS). With effect from 1 January 2015, businesses which supply digital services to consumers in EU states may opt to use the VAT MOSS online service. The business can then submit a single calendar quarterly VAT MOSS return and payment covering all its EU digital service supplies. If the business registers for the VAT MOSS online service in the UK, HMRC will send an electronic copy of the appropriate part of the VAT MOSS return, and the related VAT payment, to each relevant member state's tax authority.

Zero-rated supplies   *[VATA 1994, Sch 8]*

A supply of goods or services is a zero-rated supply if falling within one of the following Groups.
Such a supply is a taxable supply with a nil rate of tax

Group 1	Food
Group 2	Sewerage services and water
Group 3	Books, etc.
Group 4	Talking books for the blind and handicapped and wireless sets for the blind
Group 5	Construction of buildings, etc.
Group 6	Protected buildings
Group 7	International services
Group 8	Transport
Group 9	Caravans and houseboats
Group 10	Gold
Group 11	Bank notes
Group 12	Drugs, medicines, aids for handicapped, etc.
Group 13	Imports, exports, etc.
Group 15	Charities, etc.
Group 16	Clothing and footwear
Group 18	European Research Infrastructure Consortia (from 1 January 2013)

Value added tax car fuel scale rates

Return periods beginning 1.5.13–30.4.14

CO_2 emissions g/km	Scale charge Yearly returns £	Scale charge Quarterly returns £	Scale charge Monthly returns £
120 or below	675	168	56
125	1,010	253	84
130	1,080	269	89
135	1,145	286	95
140	1,215	303	101
145	1,280	320	106
150	1,350	337	112
155	1,415	354	118
160	1,485	371	123
165	1,550	388	129
170	1,620	404	134
175	1,685	421	140
180	1,755	438	146
185	1,820	455	151
190	1,890	472	157
195	1,955	489	163
200	2,025	506	168
205	2,090	523	174
210	2,160	539	179
215	2,225	556	185
220	2,295	573	191
225 or more	2,360	590	196

Return periods beginning 1.5.14–30.4.15

CO_2 emissions g/km	Scale charge Yearly returns £	Scale charge Quarterly returns £	Scale charge Monthly returns £
120 or below	627	156	52
125	939	234	78
130	1,004	251	83
135	1,064	266	88
140	1,129	282	94
145	1,190	297	99
150	1,255	313	104
155	1,315	328	109
160	1,381	345	115
165	1,441	360	120
170	1,506	376	125
175	1,567	391	130
180	1,632	408	136
185	1,692	423	141
190	1,757	439	146
195	1,818	454	151
200	1,883	470	156
205	1,943	485	161
210	2,008	502	167
215	2,069	517	172
220	2,134	533	177
225 or more	2,194	548	182

Return periods beginning after 30.4.15

CO_2 emissions g/km	Scale charge Yearly returns £	Scale charge Quarterly returns £	Scale charge Monthly returns £
120 or below	536	133	44
125	802	200	66
130	857	213	70
135	909	227	75
140	965	240	80
145	1,016	254	84
150	1,072	267	88
155	1,123	281	93
160	1,179	294	97
165	1,231	308	102
170	1,286	320	106
175	1,338	334	111
180	1,393	347	115
185	1,445	361	119
190	1,501	374	124
195	1,552	388	129
200	1,608	401	133
205	1,660	415	138
210	1,715	428	142
215	1,767	441	146
220	1,822	455	151
225 or more	1,874	468	155

Notes

(a) Subject to (d) below, a taxable person is required to account for output tax where fuel is supplied for private motoring to either himself or his employees. The scale charges set out above can be used to represent the tax-inclusive value of the fuel supplied and apply separately to supplies to each individual in any prescribed accounting period in respect of any one vehicle. Where there is a choice between using the scale charge and another method of determining the value (broadly for periods beginning on or after 1 February 2014), if a taxable person opts to use the scale charge it must be used for all cars in which business fuel is made available for private use.

(b) The rules apply to all cars but not to other vehicles such as vans, motorcycles and invalid cars. They do not apply to pooled cars or cars used exclusively for business purposes. Travel between home and work is regarded as a private rather than business journey.

(c) Where the above scale rates are used, a taxable person can reclaim input tax on all fuel purchased, even if used for private motoring.

(d) For VAT periods beginning before 1 February 2014, a taxable person need not use the above scale charges where there is an element of private motoring provided he does not reclaim input tax on *any* fuel purchased, whether used for business or private purposes and whether in cars or commercial vehicles.

(e) Where the CO_2 emissions figure of a vehicle is not a multiple of five, the figure is rounded down to the next multiple of five to determine the level of charge. For bi-fuel vehicles, the lower CO_2 emissions figure is used. Vehicles which are too old to have a CO_2 emissions figure are treated as having an emissions figure of 140 g/km for vehicles with an engine capacity of 1,400 cc or less, 175 g/km for vehicles with an engine capacity between 1,401 cc and 2,000 cc and 225 or more g/km for vehicles with an engine capacity of more than 2,000 cc.

(f) Employers can use HMRC's advisory fuel rates to reclaim VAT on fuel costs reimbursed for business travel by employees in company cars. The employer must obtain and keep a valid VAT invoice. See page 79.

Value added tax civil penalties

	Nature of offence	Penalty
Default surcharge [VATA 1994, s 59]	Failure to furnish a return in time or pay the VAT shown on it as due. Where no VAT is due or the VAT due is paid on time but the return is submitted late, although HMRC record the default there is no *liability* to a surcharge	The greater of £30 or the following percentages of outstanding VAT
	The provisions also apply to the Payments on Account Scheme	1st default in surcharge period 2% 2nd default in surcharge period 5% 3rd default in surcharge period 10% 4th default in surcharge period 15% 5th default in surcharge period 15% Further defaults 15%
VAT evasion (note (a)) [VATA 1994, s 60]	Any act or omission for the purpose of evading VAT where conduct involves dishonesty Penalty does not apply to acts or omissions relating to an inaccuracy in a document or failure to notify HMRC of an under-assessment (where penalty under *FA 2007, Sch 24* applies — see page 94) or to offences within *FA 2008, Sch 41* (see page 94).	The amount of the VAT evaded (or sought to be evaded)
Incorrect zero-rating [VATA 1994, s 62]	Issuing an incorrect certificate stating that certain supplies fall to be zero-rated or taxed at the reduced rate	Difference between the VAT which should have been charged and the VAT actually charged
EU sales lists (ESL)	(a) Submission of an ESL containing a material inaccuracy. [VATA 1994, s 65]	£100 for each ESL submitted within two years following a penalty notice from HMRC identifying an earlier material inaccuracy
	(b) Failure to submit an ESL. [VATA 1994, s 66]	Greater of £50 or a daily penalty (maximum 100 days) of £5, £10 or £15 depending upon whether the ESL is the first, second, or third or subsequent ESL in a default period specified by HMRC
Import VAT [FA 2003, ss 24–41]	(a) Non-compliance in cases of 'occasional serious error' involving at least £10,000 duty and/or VAT; persistent failure to comply with regulatory obligations; and failure to correct deficiencies in systems, etc.	£2,500 maximum
	(b) Evasion penalty (as an alternative to criminal prosecution)	Up to the amount of duty and/or VAT sought to be evaded
Failure to notify [VATA 1994, s 67]	Failure to notify (a) liability for registration; or (b) Changes in the nature of supplies, etc. by a person exempt from registration (c) Acquisition of excise duty goods or new means of transport (Replaced, from 1 April 2010 by penalty under *FA 2008, Sch 41* – see page 94)	Greater of £50 and the following percentages of the VAT for which the person would have been liable *Period of failure* (a) and (b) (c) 9 months or less 3 months or less 5% 10–18 months 4–6 months 10% Over 18 months Over 6 months 15%

Value added tax civil penalties

	Nature of offence	Penalty
Unauthorised issue of invoices [*VATA 1994, s 67*]	Issue of invoice by any person not authorised to do so (Replaced, from 1 April 2010 by penalty under *FA 2008, Sch 41* – see page 94)	15% of the amount shown as or representing VAT or, if greater, £50
Electronic returns [*SI 1995 No 2518, Reg 25A*]	Failure to make return electronically by person required to do so	*Annual VAT exclusive turnover* *Penalty* £100,000 or less £100 £100,001–£5,600,000 £200 £5,600,001–£22,800,000 £300 £22,800,001 or more £400
Breach of walking possession agreement [*VATA 1994, s 68*]	Breach of agreement under which property distrained remains in possession of a person who has failed to pay VAT	One half of the VAT due or amount recoverable
Records [*VATA 1994, ss 69, 69B*]	Failure to preserve for six years or such lesser period as HMRC allow	£500
	Failure to preserve records specified in HMRC direction	£200 for each day of failure (maximum 30 days)
Breaches of regulatory provisions [*VATA 1994, s 69*]	Failure to notify end of liability or entitlement to be registered, failure to keep records or failure to comply with any regulations, order or rules made under *VATA 1994*	Greater of £50 or a daily penalty (maximum 100 days) of No of failures in previous two Daily rate years 0 £5* 1 £10* 2 £15* * or, where the failure consists of not paying VAT or not making a return in the required time, 1/6, 1/3 and 1/2 of 1% of the VAT due respectively, if greater
Investment gold [*VATA 1994, s 69A*]	Failure to comply with key requirements of the investment gold scheme	$17\frac{1}{2}$% of the value of the transaction concerned
Use of avoidance schemes [*VATA 1994, Sch 11A paras 10, 11*]	Businesses with supplies over £600,000 — failure to disclose the use of an avoidance scheme included in a statutory list published by HMRC	15% of the VAT avoided
	Businesses with supplies over £10 million — failure to disclose use of certain schemes within 30 days of the due date for the first VAT return affected (unless the promoter of the scheme has already registered it with HMRC)	£5,000

Index

Entries printed in bold type are main subject headings

Index

Index

Index